the

Regift

horse

Ocala Horse Girls

Book 3

Natalie Keller Reinert

Chapter One

"DIE, RADIO, DIE!"

Christmas carols have been chasing me around all month, and I am over it. Hiking up my jeans, I brace my boots against the side of the last stall in the barn and manage to hoist myself up to the dusty radio playing away on its shelf above the center-aisle doorway. The stall's resident bounces backwards in alarm, the whites of his eyes showing. He's just a weanling. He doesn't yet know the lengths humans will go in order to *not* hear a terrible song.

I manage to switch off the radio before another second of that godforsaken *I Saw Mommy Kissing Santa Claus* can bore its way into my brain. Then I glance down at the horse I startled, feeling guilty. He's retreated to the corner of his stall and is staring at me like I'm a giant bat coming to eat him.

"I'm sorry, Morrie," I tell the colt in a soothing tone. "But that song was literally going to deliver me to an early grave. And if I die, who will feed you dinner?"

Morrie sticks out his tongue and then slowly loosens his jaw. He makes a chewing motion, an equine sign of understanding.

Yeah, he gets it.

"See?" I hop down from my perch above the little horse, landing easily in the shavings. "Smart boy."

I dig into my pocket and find a horse cookie. Morrie steps forward with pricked ears, happily accepting the peace offering. *Crunch, crunch, crunch.*

"You eat too loud," I whisper. "Someone else is going to hear you."

Little horses have big ears, and the weanling barn is full of them.

In a couple of weeks, these babies will officially be yearlings. Gangly Thoroughbred horses with short tails and long legs, still too small to ride but plenty big enough to cause trouble. I've been working the weanling barn by myself most afternoons since November. All I have to do is clean stalls, bring the babies in from the pasture where they play all day, and get them their dinners. I get to head home before five. No boss breathing down my neck, no barn manager fussing at me about cobwebs or polishing the brass.

Hah, I've *played* that game. I'm not a kid anymore, though. I'm on the far side of twenty-five and freewheeling towards thirty, and I have simplified this equestrian life.

Get up in the morning, gallop racehorses in the training barn, have a nice lunch, drive down to the weanling barn, do the chores here, head home. Wash, rinse, repeat. It's a far cry from some of the tough jobs I've worked in the past, but over the last few years, my motivation to work seven days a week, fifteen hours a day, simply burned out. I still love working with horses, but I don't see myself making it as a top rider.

Not anymore.

So, I work these two half-day jobs at my friend Posey Malone's farm, and everything is just fine.

The only problem, as I see it, is that someone else feeds breakfast and turns the weanlings out, and whoever that person is keeps putting the radio station on the Christmas carol station.

Like, what kind of sicko does that? Don't I make it perfectly clear, when I change the station every single day, that I am not a Christmas person?

"Okay," I ask the barn of little horses. "Who wants to go outside first?"

Everyone has been inside since last night. One of those nasty Florida winter storms, the ones with cold wind and a whole hurricane's worth of rain, rolled in late and Posey was worried about these little sweeties getting too wet and cold. It was still raining this morning, so they just got extra hay and told to wait it out—Posey's orders.

Lucky them to have sweet and loving Aunt Posey in charge this morning, because mean old Uncle Adam was the one running ops at the training barn, and he wasn't worried about how wet and cold *we* got running a bunch of youngsters around the track. We groaned and moaned, but he sent us out, anyway. With that cold wind blowing and the rain coming in sideways, our horses were throwing themselves around like it was the bucking bronco finals.

December in Florida can be such a rodeo sometimes.

I went home after the last set and took a scalding-hot shower while Romeo, my black-and-white cat, meowed at me through the shower curtain, and then I ate ramen noodles under a fleece blanket while Romeo ate half a can of some expensive wild-caught salmon entrée. It is safe to say I spend more on Romeo's diet than my own. And today it paid off, because a full and happy Romeo curled up on my feet for my lunch-break nap, and they were warm and toasty when I woke up fifteen minutes before I had to be back at work.

Now he's probably still in my bed, the lucky feline, while I'm out in this drafty barn, about to turn out twelve pent-up weanlings with the wind up their tails.

I'm just slipping a halter over Morrie's fuzzy ears when Posey comes into the barn. Her dark, curly bob is caught up in a bandana and tucked securely under a baseball cap. Not for the first time, I think I should cut off my long chestnut braid and go for the tidy look the way Posey does.

But this skinny braid of mine gets me recognized all over Ocala. It would be a shame to give up what little notoriety I've got. Maybe I'll never make it as an eventing star, but at least this ten-million-horse town knows that *I* know everything going on behind closed tack room doors. People tell me things. They can't help themselves. And I love being the keeper of this town's worst-kept secrets.

Lose the signature braid and who will spot me in a crowd on Grand Prix night at Legends Equestrian Center, sneak up beside me, and whisper the latest dirt in my ear?

At least, that's what I tell myself. Could be that I'm just too lazy to make an appointment for a haircut.

"Hey, Pose, in Morrie's stall," I call as she looks around, missing me entirely. "I'm turning everyone out so I can clean stalls."

"Evie!" Posey exclaims, peeking through the stall bars. "Babe, I can't believe Adam made you guys ride this morning!"

"Me neither," I grunt, fastening Morrie's halter while he shoves impatiently at my shoulder. "We need you back in the training barn."

"Apparently," she sighs. "I thought I could catch a break during foaling season coming up. All those overnights…"

"No. Have your mom do it. She *loves* foaling mares."

"I know she does, but she also loves telling me she's retired now."

"Don't accept that kind of back-talk from your employees."

Posey snorts with laughter. "Anyway, I wanted to invite you to our Christmas—"

"No thanks," I interrupt. Morrie turns in an anxious circle around me, desperate to get outside. I rub his neck soothingly.

Posey persists. "But it's—"

"Not for me."

"Well, *Kayla's* coming," Posey says, sounding put out. "And Basil. All the way from the wilds of Alachua. And I think both the Whitehalls, Alex *and* Alexander. You know Alexander doesn't go to many parties. You'd be the only one who doesn't come."

"I'll leave the party for your Ocala royalty," I tell her firmly. "I know I did the Christmas gala thing with you guys last year, and it was fine, but I'm really not a holiday person and I would rather not subject myself to it this year. I just do not feel up to it. Maybe you didn't notice I am working two jobs."

"Two half-day jobs equals one job."

"Says the manager."

"It's not a big charity gala. It's *our* Christmas party," Posey reminds me. "The Malone-Salazar Farm party."

"But it's still going on your business expenses for the year," I say. Morrie is still pushing at me, anxious to leave. "Can you grab a colt by any chance? These monsters need turn-out."

Posey goes to the neighboring stall and halters the colt inside. Together, we walk them out to the pasture and turn the weanlings free. They take off like the racehorses we hope they'll be someday, launching themselves through the sand around the gate and flying across the fading green grass. Morrie kicks and bucks, a fart escaping his hind end like a shot, and both of us giggle like we're five years old.

"What a goober," Posey says fondly.

"He's going to be a pistol on the track someday." I'm looking forward to riding Morrie. Another year, and he'll be in the training barn. Going out to the training track every morning, learning to be a racehorse.

But for now, he's just another goober playing with his friends, the other goobers.

"Let's get the rest out," Posey says, and we turn back towards the barn. "It will give you time to think about how mean you're being by refusing to come to the party."

"How is it mean?" I demand, exasperated. "We're still friends. I just don't like Christmas."

"Come on, Evie. I'm going to feel bad if you don't come."

"Christmas is just not my thing," I repeat, picking up a halter. The colt inside turns in excited circles. "I appreciate the invite, I really do, but...I would rather work on Christmas. Put me down for feeding and whatever else needs done. I can give someone else the day off."

"Evie," Posey sighs, disappointed. "Really?"

"Really," I say, sliding open the stall door. "Trust me, I'd rather be working."

Christmas is when people get fuzzy and sentimental about their lives, and if there's one thing I'm not ready to do, it's pretend everything is perfect with friends and family.

"Hey, Buster Brown," I greet the bay colt, who is waiting for me with pricked ears and bright eyes. "Wake me up when December ends, right?"

I always take a break around three thirty. I'll bring the horses back in at four, and I'm done feeding and out the door by five, so this is a nice time to pause, drink a Coke, and flick through my phone apps, looking for something interesting to distract me from my own life. Since my own competition dreams were squashed by a double-whammy of anhidrosis—that's when a horse stops sweating—and a ligament injury that refuses to heal, I've been living vicariously through the Instagram accounts of people the eventing gods have favored.

Maybe it's not the healthiest hobby, but I enjoy flicking through their full-color lives, guessing at their woes, reminding myself that underneath the bespoke breeches and jackets, a heart that has been broken is still beating. To be equestrian is to be battered, inside and out. I might have recalibrated my hopes and dreams, but I won't give up the lifestyle.

That's my usual routine, the Instagram scroll.

Today, for some reason, I check my email.

And to my surprise, there's an actual email waiting in my inbox. Like, not just emails about saddle pads on sale or timeshare weekends for ninety-nine dollars, but an actual email from a real human. I thought these things were extinct.

"What's up, cousin Madison?" I mutter, tapping the email. I can feel a frown across my forehead. Madison and her Aunt Rachel are my only family in Florida, but I haven't seen either of them in several years. They live in Sarasota, over on the Gulf coast. And while Madison showed ponies when she was a kid, she hadn't been what you'd call a horse girl in her entire adult life. She's one of those people that did it as a hobby. I've never understood those people.

Her email is short.

Short and surprising.

I know you never come to our holiday parties, but I think you'll want to be at this one. My aunt met a guy named Malcolm Horsham at some charity thing not too long ago—

My eyebrows are at the top of my head. Malcolm Horsham, the handsome eventing terror of Ocala? Looks like a pirate and treats his staff like one, too? Talk about worlds colliding. There's virtually no reason my aunt would run into an eventing star like Malcolm. Just dumb, strange chance.

She's been really secretive ever since, but I've seen some emails and I think she might have bought a horse.

Unbelievable. Why don't I have "maybe I'll buy a horse" money? Why doesn't *my* mom?

Yes, I can walk out to the side of the road, put my hands to my mouth, and holler, "Hello Ocala, I have room for a horse!" and fifteen trailers will appear, some with actual, sound, show prospects in the back. But I know Aunt Rachel isn't picking up an ex-racehorse after a meeting with a big name like Malcolm.

Rachel does things *big*. Big house, big car, big boat. She's the opposite of her sister—my mom does things small. Small house, small car. No boat, obviously.

If she thinks I'm getting on some psycho event horse, she's out of her mind, Madison writes. *But if you show up, unexpected, who knows?*

Unexpected, hah. I haven't been invited to the holiday parties since the first year I was in Florida. I'm not festive, what can I say?

Also, I don't like Aunt Rachel. I hated family trips to Florida when I was a kid, seeing how much Madison had, the way Aunt Rachel threw money around...and going back to our tiny house in Maryland afterwards, wondering why she didn't throw any of that money at *us*.

I look at the email again.

Who knows? Madison wrote.

What is she suggesting here?

I chew on my tongue for a minute, wondering if she really thinks there's a chance here.

Madison was generous, unlike her mother. She gave me rides on her pony. She always kept cast-off breeches and boots for me, hiding them from her mother and the box for Goodwill.

What's the worst that could happen?

I'll be there, I type back to Madison. *Try not to eat all the deviled eggs this time.*

Inside joke.

Here is one thing I know: there won't be any deviled eggs on the overloaded buffet table at Aunt Rachel's expansive Sarasota house.

The truth is, Madison ate *thirteen* of them at a holiday party when we were both ten, and those bad boys escaped in a hurry about ten minutes later. Madison booked it up the stairs to the pink-and-white bathroom off her bedroom, taking the steps two at a time, clutching her stomach and moaning, while I hooted from the foyer, urging her on.

It was pretty hilarious (if you were me) but Aunt Rachel wasn't impressed with her daughter's gluttony *or* the results.

My laughter didn't go over great, either.

Standing outside the same candy-pink house, a solid seventeen years later, and I swear I can still feel the disdain emanating from the walls. I'm early for the party; I don't want to be in Sarasota all night, and it's a long drive back to Ocala. Madison lets me in. She's wearing a plush lavender robe, and smells freshly showered.

"Evie, you look exactly the same."

"I hope not," I say dubiously, stepping into the house's two-story foyer. "I was eighteen the last time I was here, and I still had braces."

"Yeah, you had those for a long time."

"Don't remind me." I glance at myself in the gold-framed mirror above the foyer console table. I do not look eighteen any more, thank goodness, *and* my teeth still look pretty great. If I cut my silly hair, I might even look, dare I say it, hot.

"Well, come have a glass of wine before you deal with my mom," Madison says, slipping off down the shiny tile hallway ahead of me. "She's upstairs getting primped."

The kitchen is a dazzle of late-day sunshine, light reflecting off the canal behind the house and pouring through the floor-to-ceiling windows. I wince and wish for sunglasses, but Madison doesn't seem to notice it. She takes a bottle of white wine from the wine fridge beneath a marble-topped counter and pours into two waiting glasses.

"I'm impressed you came, honestly," she says. "I know our family was never your cup of tea."

"You were fine," I assure her. "At least, until you quit riding."

Madison snorts. "I knew you'd say that. I have a design store online now, you know. I sell bespoke dresses and blouses."

"Very fancy, and thanks for the wine." I take a gulp. "Mmm, taste the oak. Or whatever."

"Heathen." Madison leans against the counter and smiles at me. "You know, I really think this could work out."

"You weren't clear about what *this* is supposed to be, though."

"It's exactly what you think it is. I found the paperwork. Wrapped up in a pretty box with a bow on top. I was right. She bought me a horse."

"But *why?*" I can't help an edge of anger in my voice.

"Easy, killer. I'll tell you why. Every so often, my mom meets a rich, eligible man and decides I should spend time in his presence, so that he naturally falls in love with me. I know, I know, it's very wicked stepmother of her. But that makes *you* Cinderella, so stop making that face."

"How am I Cindere—oh." I realize what she's implying.

"Yes. I am going upstairs to turn down her thoughtful Christmas present. She is going to insist I take it. And then I am going to inform her that my long-lost cousin is here, and I am going to regift that horse to her at the party, in front of everyone, and there's nothing she can do about it."

I put down my wine glass quickly, because my hands are shaking. "You don't mean it."

"Oh, I mean it," Madison replies, and I see the determined set of her jaw. *Her mother's daughter,* I think. And I have no choice but to believe her.

Chapter Two

SOMEHOW, I MANAGE to hold it together until the party is in full swing.

The holiday party takes place in the living room at the back of the house, and like the kitchen, it has floor-to-ceiling windows. These let in the golden-purple bruise of the fading sunset over the Gulf, the white lights tastefully decorating the boathouse perched above the deep canal, and the glimmering blue-green pool, surrounded by tiny Christmas palms (no relation to the holiday).

All that beauty, and yet Aunt Rachel's Christmas finery is the first thing anyone sees when they enter the room. She's dressed as a huge floral explosion of poinsettias and ribbons, her crimson and white dazzling the eyes. She might as well *be* the Christmas decorations for the party. For the house. Maybe for the whole tacky neighborhood.

I think the Christmas tree itself looks a little small, if we're nitpicking. Maybe she spent all her decorating funds on her ensemble.

All around the living room, the family and so-called friends are gathered. They're mostly strangers to me. My mom had this idea in her head that when I moved to Ocala I'd be "safe"—her word— because I had family in Florida. But once Madison stopped riding in high school, my only connection with this branch of the family was severed. I honestly never give these people any thought.

And my mom has never had anything to worry about. I melted right into Ocala, my horsey self melding with the other horsey people. I make it just fine on my own.

If you consider a single-wide trailer on a handful of acres with enough space to manage one slightly broken horse making it.

I do, thanks.

But I stick out here. The rest of the party-goers look me over with confusion, bordering on distaste. *Here is a woman,* their expressions clearly state, *who has no pride, no self-respect, and probably no prospects.*

They're not really far off, but I'd never give them the satisfaction of knowing it. I find a seat on an overstuffed chair in a corner of the room and sit on my hands so I won't play with my braid. Bad enough that I have that rope of hair halfway down my back. I'll look like a twelve-year-old if I start messing with it.

Madison waltzes over around seven o'clock with a champagne flute in one hand. She's had a few of those this evening, and I'm jealous. "Still dry?" she teases.

"Still have to drive home tonight," I remind her testily. "Think you can get to the main event soon?"

"I've been waiting for the right moment," Madison replies, looking around at her mother. "I need everyone's attention. It's the only way she can't refuse me."

This is insane, I think. *I drove all the way here so Madison can piss off her mother.*

A rich kid's catspaw, at the age of twenty-seven. You'd think I'd have figured that out sooner.

"Oh, here we go," Madison murmurs to me. "Listen!"

Aunt Rachel is launching into a new story, loud enough to let everyone know they are her captive audience. It's a tale of rich friends and weekends spent shopping in Boca Raton and, finally, the latest sensation to hit her attention-loving little brain. "So Annette says to me, you have to see what my daughter's been up to in Virginia, and she shows me these videos of the most beautiful horses you've ever seen in your life!"

I stiffen. Madison gives me a little elbow.

Rachel is holding up her phone and I see a horse galloping across the screen. At this distance, it's hard to tell what's going on. Just galloping, and then...

The horse flies over a ditch and wall.

I realize we're watching an immensely talented, impeccably trained event horse, and my breath stops short.

Is this the horse?

He gallops up to an Irish bank and hops up the embankment as if he's a jackrabbit.

"Adorable, isn't he?" Rachel coos. "I haven't thought about horses in years, but you know, Madison here was *quite* the little equestrian. And then that very evening, Annette and I are at the Wellington Village Dressage Against Alzheimer's—you know, an equestrian charity event, Princess Chantal was there—"

"Princess Chantal?" I whisper in Madison's ear.

She shrugs. "No idea."

Rachel is still describing the white tents, the six-course meal, the glorious prawns. It seems to me that all the money spent on the party could have just as easily gone to fighting Alzheimer's, but I am not rich. What do I know about money?

"And I meet the most *handsome* man!" Rachel shrieks.

"This will be the trainer," Madison hisses.

"Just a few years too young for me, sadly..."

Laughter from the audience. "Never!" someone says gallantly, a man with a comb-over that reaches from ear to ear.

"My darlings, when I tell you he was wearing *skin-tight* white riding pants—"

I sniff. "Did she already forget the word is *breeches*?"

Madison laughs silently, her face scrunching up.

"Five o'clock shadow like a pirate—"

"Didn't shave for a charity gala?" I whisper. "Bad form."

Madison puts her hands over her face.

"A jaw you could crack nuts on—"

"Oh, he's gay. Well, that makes sense."

Madison balls herself up, her face in her lap, her shoulders shaking. I'm really glad we're at the back of the room. But I realize I have to stop the commentary if she's going to force her way to her mother's side and make her move once the Christmas present to end all Christmas presents is announced.

"We got to talking and—well, one thing led to another, you know how it is." Aunt Rachel covered her mouth and tittered, implying any number of flirtations.

"You bought a horse, didn't you?" the comb-over man asks.

"Of course I did," she laughs. She looks at her phone screen with what seems like real fondness. "The perfect horse for us all to cheer on. When Madison trains on him and is ready to show him, we'll all go see them!"

Madison hears her cue and stands up. She faces her mother and Aunt Rachel squares her jaw, ready for the showdown.

"Mom, it was *really* generous of you to buy me a horse—"

"Hmm-hmm," Aunt Rachel hums, mysteriously.

"But I think you know I haven't ridden in ten years."

"There's *training,* dear," her mother says, smiling widely. It's so fake it might as well be one of the ficus trees in the corners of the living room. "Training with this lovely man, Malcolm Horsham. Just up in Ocala!"

"What a coincidence," Madison says, determination in her tone. "Because Evie's here, and we haven't seen her in years, and she *lives* in Ocala, and I think this horse would be perfect for her."

"Oh, I don't know about that," Aunt Rachel says, unperturbed.

Why isn't she mad? Suddenly, I'm suspicious. She should be hissing at her daughter not to do this now, to take the conversation somewhere private. Not smiling while the whole room looks on in avid wonder, enjoying the rare spectacle of a public family disagreement.

Madison is caught on the back foot as well. I can see her floundering for her next line. This isn't going the way she rehearsed in her head. Finally, she says, "It seems perfect to me. She actually does eventing, unlike me. I've never even *considered* eventing."

"This horse has experience," Aunt Rachel says blithely. "And he'll get even more with Malcolm. You can go up and take lessons with him, and by the time he's ready for you to show, you'll be fit. Ready for horse shows—"

"You mean *events*," I interrupt, fed up with this back-and-forth. Deny me, kick me out, just *get on with it*.

Aunt Rachel's gaze fastens on me. "Excuse me, dear?"

"You mean *events*," I repeat. "They aren't shows. He's an event horse. He goes to *events*."

She shrugs. "Well, if you say so. I just know it looks a bit more exciting than the old dog and pony shows we used to do with *you*, Madison!" She looks fondly at her daughter. Again, I get the feeling she's playing with us. She's having fun giving her daughter the opposite of what was expected.

Madison is annoyed. "I did those stupid horse shows because *you* wanted me to," she says, crossing her arms over her chest. "Don't go blaming me if everyone fell asleep."

"I'm hoping this will change things for you. Because I've bought this horse for *you*, Madison! To compete! After," she says archly, "you and he have had some training. It's all taken care of, darling. This is your Christmas present. The horse, training, and coaching through your first six months."

She must have the horse under contract with Malcolm Horsham. Which means that horse—that gorgeous bay horse in the video— must be in Ocala or on his way.

Just one more beautiful, athletic horse in a sea of beautiful, athletic horses all around my little farm, but the idea of him up there, owned by Rachel, ignored by Madison, makes my palms itch.

"So, he's mine?" Madison asks, in a little girl voice that makes her mother smile. "That lovely horse is really mine?"

"All yours, darling," Aunt Rachel says. "I've already transferred him to your name. Merry Christmas!" She claps her hands together and then opens her arms, ready to welcome her argumentative daughter in for a sweet embrace. The rest of the party lets out their breath and begins to clap.

I look at Madison: *now, please.* She takes a breath.

"Well, Mother," Madison says, "I hope you're happy he's staying in the family. Because we don't have a gift for Evie."

Rachel's lips purse.

"So I'm giving him to her. Merry *Christmas*, Evie!"

She did it. The crazy girl did it. For whatever her announcement is worth, anyway.

But the party is decidedly weird after that. Lots of staring at me from the rest of the party, and Aunt Rachel is drinking with a heavy hand and plenty of hooded glaring at me. I will not be invited to the Easter Sunday brunch, and I can forget about ever coming back to one of her Christmas parties.

Well, I don't like the way this vibe is going. Evie is not the center of attention; that's not how this has ever worked. I like to *know* what's going on...not *be* what's going on.

Madison sees me heading for the front door and is one step jump ahead of me, barring the way with her hands. "We did it," she announces. "Aren't you going to thank me?"

I shrug. "Not to sound too ungrateful, Mads, but do you really think it's going to happen?"

"The horse is in my name, she said. It's going to happen. He's mine...until he's yours."

"Well, let me know, I guess." I'm tired and the interstate home will be crowded with holiday traffic.

"Oh, I'll let you know," Madison says with a smirk, and I know the devious note in her tone isn't meant for me. It's meant for her mother. Maybe I'm just a means to an end for Madison, helping her pull one over on her manipulating mother.

Or maybe she genuinely believes this horse will make my life better.

Well, why not both?

I hesitate a moment, then step forward and surprise Madison with a hug. We aren't close, but we might have been, when we were kids— if we hadn't lived in different states and been raised in different worlds. We might have been those cousins who hung out and shared each other's clothes and who knows, maybe we might have done some zany cousin adventure together that we copied off a Disney Channel movie.

Suddenly, I'm wishing we had that kind of history, that kind of friendship.

The truth is, my two best friends are paired off with the men they'll marry and busy making their dreams come true, and my heart horse is permanently lame, and I've been living on fumes for the past six months, just going through the motions because I feel like I've been left behind by everything and everyone.

I need a win, but maybe more than that, I need to know someone else is looking out for me.

Madison rubs my back for a moment, and then we step back and look at each other.

"I wish you lived closer," she says.

"Me, too," I agree, even though the truth is I'd never live anywhere near this fancy-pants city.

"But it's better you don't," she continues, "because you're about to have a horse at Malcolm Horsham's farm, and that would be a long commute from here!"

Oh, god. I forgot that Malcolm Horsham is involved in all this.

Here's hoping if that horse actually materializes in my life, training with the eventing terror of Ocala is no longer part of the deal.

Chapter Three

FERN GROVE BUCKEYE, affectionately known as Bucky, comes off the trailer with a hop, a twist, and a high-pitched neigh that makes me laugh despite my nerves. Three weeks ago, I didn't think this day was coming. But Madison came through for me. And now he's here.

My new horse.

He's cute, I think, and I almost have to pinch myself as the tall horse does a quick, nervous spin around the groom who just unloaded him. Is this a dream? Seriously, one long, involved dream that's absolutely going to wreck me when I have to wake up from it?

A Fern Grove horse is a big deal in the eventing world—bred in Virginia at Fern Grove Farm by the old money Williamsons, who have been breeding horses in the United States since 1835 but only discovered by my grubby Aunt Rachel back in autumn. This horse only has one year of eventing competition behind him, but his name alone would make him a prize to any amateur in the eventing game, and a pretty decent get for a professional trainer, too.

Seasoned on the hunting field and prepared for his first Florida winter, the horse is already sleekly muscled, his mahogany bay coat gleaming with good health. He has two white hind stockings, a big white blaze that narrows to a stripe between his flared nostrils, and a black mane that falls over his curving neck like a wave. His withers are high, his croup is long, and his legs go for days. We're standing on the service driveway of Malcolm Horsham's Fine Day Farm, and with the elegant gray-and-white stucco barn as a distant backdrop, Fern Grove Buckeye looks like he's here for his photoshoot.

This is a really, really nice horse. I find myself wondering how much Aunt Rachel paid for him, and decide I don't want to know. I'm now indebted to Madison and Rachel for the rest of my life. Let's just leave it at that.

I can't resist sharing him immediately; I pull out my phone and dial up Posey and Kayla on a quick video call.

"*This* is the gift horse?" Posey shrieks when she sees him, nearly blowing out my phone speaker.

The groom leading the horse swivels his head and grins, then walks the horse up and down the driveway for my friends' benefit. He knows all about horse girls in Ocala. We only want one thing. And that's more horses.

"This is the *regift* horse," Kayla corrects Posey, laughing. "First he was a gift for the cousin, then she gave the horse to you—right Evie?"

I've explained it all too many times to count, so I just snort in reply. The girls get it. They know this horse is my lucky day, probably better than I do, because they don't see any issue with taking him.

And they aren't facing six months of dealing with Malcolm Horsham, like I am.

I'm still extremely nervous about that. I've never met the man, but I've heard so much about him.

All of it nerve-wracking.

Sallyann, my favorite single-woman feed store gossip mill, smiled like a Cheshire Cat when I told her I was going to have a horse in training with Horsham. "Watch how he treats his staff," she advised me, chortling. "If he *has* any staff."

The man's a monster, from all accounts. Which is a shame, because I've seen him ride and he's an elegant, sensitive horseman. Riding with him is an opportunity that should send me swooning with delight. Especially since I'm a client, not a member of his staff. He's not going to shout at *me*.

But I'm used to being the employee. Before I gave up the working student life in favor of getting paid enough to eat and feed my horse, I was kicked around by plenty of angelic riders with demonic tempers. No one ever openly shouted at me, but I was still put upon enough to feel like a drudge.

I'm not in a hurry to see my horse's trainer do that to other people.

Still, Aunt Rachel paid for six months of training, and Madison insisted I take advantage of it.

"What does his farm look like?" Posey is asking. "Is it as nice as Salazar?"

I think it's funny that we still call Malone-Salazar Farm just plain "Salazar" for short, even though renaming it for Posey Malone's father was a very big deal to the racing community at the time. "It's pretty nice," I tell her, which is the understatement of the year.

"Describe it!"

"Can't I just hold up the phone?"

"I can't see everything. What's that in front of the barn up there?"

The groom is waving for me to follow, my regift horse's hindquarters swaying with a cheeky sashay as he leads him up the service driveway. "We're between hedges, with palm trees lining the driveway," I narrate, holding the phone up to give the girls a view. "In front of the barn up there, the main driveway meets this one and there's a fountain. Looks like the barn is Spanish-style, with a big arch dividing two wings of stalls. There's a covered arena at the far end, I think, and I guess the outdoor arenas are behind the barn."

"Oh, he has a fountain," Posey purrs. "I think I'd like one of those."

"You've gotten *so* bougie," Kayla tells her, laughing. "A fountain. Wait until I tell Adam."

"Guys, focus," I interrupt. We're getting so close to the barn I can hear the fountain out front splashing, and I want to be the one to take my horse into the barn. "I have to go. I'm grabbing the horse from the groom."

"Okay, Evie, you've got this," Posey says immediately, reverting to loyal friend mode. "You're an excellent horsewoman and nothing bad or crazy is going to happen."

I've never met Fern Grove Buckeye—or Bucky, as I'm calling him in my head—so the idea of walking him into that elegant barn when it's the first time I've ever held his lead-shank? With who knows who waiting and watching from inside? It definitely feels a little worrisome.

Posey instantly going there in her speech makes it more so.

I don't know what to say. Suddenly, my mouth feels dry and sticky.

Kayla takes my silence for encouragement to continue rallying the troops. "Just let him go out to the end of the shank and look around. He won't do anything stupid if he feels like he has room to move."

"Anything stupid, like *what?*" I squeak.

"Oh, you know," Posey says vaguely. "Horse things."

I do know.

I'm just really hopeful Bucky will be a nice, quiet old pasture pony, and mosey up to that beautiful stable without a care in the world. I just need conditions to be perfect. I glance back over my shoulder to make sure there aren't any cars creeping up the service driveway behind us.

"Whoa!" the groom demands, which in horse-speech comes out like a bullet: *Ho!*

I whirl around, just in time to see Bucky dancing at the end of his leather lead-shank, his front end dangerously light. If the groom keeps yanking at him like that, the horse is going to rear and someone might just get hurt. "I better go," I stammer into the phone.

"Leave us in your pocket!" Kayla cries, so I drop the phone into the thigh pocket of my black riding breeches without ending the call.

The groom is walking Bucky in tight circles with his right hand close to the halter, basically doing the opposite of what Kayla suggested, and the tall horse is fussing anxiously.

"I'll take him," I say, and slip into the groom's place.

Bucky barely glances at me; he's too busy snorting at his surroundings—black-board fences, green fields studded with cross-country fences, the palm trees overhead. The palm fronds are rustling noisily in the chilly January breeze, and Bucky is clearly convinced they're full of horse-eating tigers.

When will landscapers stop doing this to horse-people? Put up some nice quiet trees, oaks or something!

"You got 'im?" the groom asks me, already at a safe distance. "He's a silly one."

"Yeah," I say, digging my fingers into the leather shank. "I got 'im."

Bucky sniffs at my shoulder and flutters his nostrils gently.

"Please do not snort on my good riding jacket," I plead. "This is the nicest thing I own."

And if I show up with horse snot all over my jacket, someone will carry the tale to the local tack and feed shops. Fine Day Farm does not produce a lot of gossip—probably because there's never enough staff to create any—but I do have to accept that every time I come here to ride Bucky, I'll be part of what little chatter there is.

Talk about turning the tables.

"I got dressed specially to come here and settle you in," I tell Bucky, who rolls his left eye and snorts. "And I think I look really nice."

Early this morning, after I fed my horse and cat, I stuck a piece of toast in my mouth and surveyed my dresser drawers while I chewed.

What did I have that was nice enough for an arrival as an owner at Fine Day Farm?

I ended up in black breeches with purple piping at the waist and pockets, a matching purple riding top, and a black shell jacket with the Ariat logo embroidered on the chest. I wiped off my black jodhpurs boots and was happy with the result. I even rolled up my braid into a fairly tidy knot at the nape of my neck. Let no equestrian say that Evie Ballenger doesn't know how to dress for her sport.

And the purple's a good choice for stable colors, I think now, looking at Bucky's dark coloring as he runs his nose down my leg, giving me a close inspection. Much of his coat is brown, slowly deepening to black, like the grain of a fine piece of furniture. He'll look really cute with a purple saddle pad and matching polo wraps.

Bucky decides he is done inspecting me. He tugs hard on the lead, gesturing with his elegant head towards the barn. *That's where the food is,* he's thinking.

"Alright, man," I agree. "Let's do it."

But almost as soon as we start, the trouble begins. There's the small matter of the fountain splash-splashing merrily in front of the archway.

Bucky doesn't like it.

As we get closer to the scary fountain, Bucky's head gets higher. Problem: I'm not a tall girl, but he's a very tall horse. By the time we are within six feet of the fountain, Bucky's at giraffe status.

And now he's putting on the brakes, as well.

"Oh, no, you don't. Let's move." I push on his shoulder to shift his front hooves. She who controls the feet, controls the horse. It's a well known fact.

But facts can't save me this morning. Bucky doesn't step politely to the right, as requested.

He *explodes* to the right.

24

The big horse shoots sideways, snorting loudly at the fountain as he goes, and takes me with him. I'm stumbling after him, the lead-shank taut in my hand, when I first notice we're not alone. People are coming out of the barn's elegant front archway, drawn by the sound of shoes on pavement and my own inelegant shouting.

"No, no, no, no, no," I'm saying, barely in control of my own words, when Bucky shoves me forward with his head and neck. I lose my balance and barely manage to hang onto the lead-shank. But I won't let go of that leather strap, not for anything. I will *not* have a loose horse on my first day here.

We're both teetering alongside the tinkling fountain, close enough to see the pennies some silly rich person has flicked into the water, when that cold January wind suddenly picks up again with a vengeance.

A palm frond shoots through the air like a laser-guided missile, landing right on Bucky's gleaming hindquarters.

He squeals and leaps forward, yanking my arm and wrenching my shoulder, and as the splash hits my face, I realize what's happening a split-second before I'm dragged into the fountain, too.

Suddenly I'm shin-deep in freezing cold water, while Bucky's already staggering out of the pool from the other side. "Oh god," I gasp.

Grasping hands move to take charge of the marauding horse. "Let go," someone commands, and I finally give up the lead-shank, closing my eyes against the indignity of it all.

Because this is the reality of the matter:

I'm standing in a fountain, water streaming down my black breeches, while Malcolm Horsham holds the lead of my now-immobile and very contrite new horse.

His expression is dark as a thunderstorm, but at this moment, I couldn't care less what Mr. Hotshot Five-Star Trainer thinks of me.

All I can think is, *The feed store girls are going to love this.*

And from my pocket, a tinny voice says, "Hello? Evie? What happened?"

Chapter Four

As I STAND there, dripping wet and embarrassed beyond belief, my mind clues in on one pointless, irrelevant fact.

Malcolm Horsham is the best-dressed man in eventing. Possibly in Ocala. Maybe the entire equestrian world.

"The style professor"—that's what some of the girls at Dress to Win Riding Apparel call him. Apparently, his roguish English-teacher-on-an-adventure looks, coupled with his money-to-burn shopping habits, earned him a reputation around here even before he started winning big events and snagging syndicate investors.

And his expensive taste in riding clothes certainly shows this morning. Although my horse is systematically destroying it, while I stand knee-deep in his farm's beautiful fountain. Bucky is shaking himself like a dog, spattering water droplets all over Horsham's gorgeous countryman ensemble. The outfit is certainly built to take a few spills, but I can't help wincing as my horse's run-off dances across his olive-green sweater, tan twill breeches, and high brown riding boots.

Oh, and a bit splashes on his face, too. A few drops of water sparkle in his short, dark beard. He rubs one tanned hand over his face, wiping the water away, then extends that hand towards me.

"Would you like to step out of the fountain, madam?" he asks, without a hint of tease or humor in his deep voice.

I'd love to, but first I have to gather my wits about me. And right now, I don't know where they've gone. He's not helping any, gazing at me with those emerald green eyes. He looks away as Bucky tugs on the lead, which should be helpful, but just gives me a view of the rugged cliff that is his strong profile.

Jeez, I knew he was handsome, but close up, Malcolm Horsham is a straight-up ten.

"Evie," a tiny voice shrieks. "Get out of the fountain!"

Horsham looks back at me. His eyebrows go up. "Did your pants just say something?"

There are a lot of bawdy jokes to be made here, but I don't dare say any of them. I just slowly draw my phone from my pocket. Kayla and Posey wave at me wildly. "Not now, guys," I say, and hit the red button. Their faces disappear.

Horsham is holding out his hand to me. "Let's get you out of there," he murmurs, something funny happening around the corners of his mouth. Is he trying not to laugh at me?

I feel my cheeks turn red and snatch at his hand, gripping him so quickly that he nearly tumbles into the fountain as well. And wouldn't *that* have been a moment for the ages? But luckily, he recovers himself, stepping backwards as I hop out of the water and land hard on the brick pavers around the fountain.

Bucky snorts at me in alarm.

"We've met," I inform him, snatching his lead-shank from Horsham. "Quit acting like I'm a space alien."

"I suppose this is Fern Grove Buckeye," Horsham says from behind me. "Or maybe just another random horse has landed in my fountain. Again. I hate when that happens."

I walk the horse in a quick circle, watching his legs to make sure I haven't broken him in the first five minutes of ownership, then I reply, "Yes, this is Bucky. And I'm Evie Ballenger."

Horsham looks at me carefully. "Oh, *you're* the niece."

"Uh..." His expression is closely guarded, so I can only assume he's being insulting. Why? What did I do? Besides splash my way onto the farm like a misguided whooping crane? "Yes?"

"I was given an exhaustive update on the horse's new ownership," Horsham assures me. His tone implies he's already had enough of Aunt Rachel.

Join the club.

"Hopefully we won't be hearing from her a lot," I say, to let him know we're on the same page there.

"Heh." I suppose that was a chuckle. Horsham glances at the barn. "Well, let's get you inside."

Suddenly, a young woman appears in the archway. She's a textbook horse girl, about my age, which I like to call just south of thirty. Blonde and slim and pretty, wearing skinny jeans and a big Joules jumper in a muted olive green.

She's dressed in the same color as Horsham, I think, glancing down at my hyacinth-purple riding top. Clearly, it was the wrong choice.

I feel like a bright helium birthday balloon let loose in a cool, sophisticated lounge.

"Alison, this is Evie Ballenger," Horsham says.

She nods. "Your horse is ready."

Horsham nods and heads into the barn. The dazzling sunlight makes the barn interior a dark shadow; he disappears instantly.

Alison extends a cool hand to me, then looks over Bucky. "Let's get this guy into his house, okay?"

Bucky seems to stretch even taller as we walk beneath the arch. Inside, I find a beautifully appointed stable. In American equestrian culture, we nearly always call equine facilities "barns", even though in other countries the term "stable" is more common. This is one of the facilities that is so nice, the word "barn" doesn't even seem fair. It's a true stable, with all the poshness that word implies here.

Warmly stained wood lines the stable aisle, forming the bottom half of the stall fronts, while curving black bars form the top halves and give each horse enough space to put their heads into the aisle and look up and down at their surroundings. The interior walls are lined with wood to head-height but above that, the stable walls have a creamy stucco finish, giving the place a sturdy, home-like feel. The windows at the back of each stall have a little arch to them, mimicking the front archway where we entered. And as he walks down the aisle, Bucky's hooves land softly on equine-friendly cushioned pavers, their herringbone pattern stretching away from us towards the stable doors at the far end. They open into a covered arena, and I can see wash-stalls and grooming stalls clustered there as well. Horses are in cross-ties, in various states of tacking-up and untacking.

"Right here," Alison says, stopping before an open stall door near the center of the barn. I lead Bucky into a spacious stall with a thick pile of shavings swept into the center, a window overlooking a white-sand dressage arena, and two new water buckets filled to the brim. He takes a quick spin after I unhook the lead shank, snorting at everything, then sinks into the fluffy pile of shavings with a low groan, like he's been waiting for this roll all day long.

"Very nice," Alison observes as he thrashes around in the bedding. "Spread that out, buddy. That's exactly why I don't do it for you. They love flinging their own shavings around," she adds to me as I step out of the stall and join her in the aisle. "So I just pour the bags into the middle and let them go to town."

"Works for me," I agree, sliding the stall door closed. Bucky looks at me as he hears the latch click into place, then he stands up and shakes. Curls of wood shavings cling to his wet legs and tail, and hang cartoonishly in his forelock. The big, scary horse of five minutes ago has been reduced to a cute, blinking foal.

Suddenly, I realize I like him. Bucky and I might have just met, but I have the distinct feeling that I have a lot of future with this horse.

I'm still marveling at him when Alison takes the lead-shank from my hand and hangs it neatly on the hook. "We have a halter for him," she says. "I'll find it while you're putting your things away."

"The halter he came with is fine," I say, but Alison gives me an apologetic little head-shake.

"All our horses wear the same halters," she explains. "Malcolm likes the way it looks. Same with blankets. We have a Baker blanket and a black turnout rug here—" Alison gestures to the horse blankets on the rail attached to the sliding stall door.

"Right." Well, I already knew Malcolm Horsham was a tyrant who is obsessed with style, so I guess matching halters and rugs shouldn't come as a huge surprise. "And my things..." I look around and realize the groom with the shipping company has brought a tack trunk and several rubber storage containers into the stable. Alison waves him past us and towards a tack room a few stalls away. "They're really Bucky's things," I confide. "I don't even know what's in there. Whatever my aunt paid for."

Alison smiles, like she's used to having this conversation. "Let's go find out."

In a golden-hued tack room, we unpack new blankets, sheets, polo wraps, galloping boots, and a complete grooming kit from the storage containers. They all go into a floor-to-ceiling tack locker. Alison pulls an old label off the locker door and disappears; a few minutes later she comes back with a new one. "Ballenger," she says, holding up the label. "Spelled right?"

"That's right," I say, pleased, and watch as she sticks my last name on the tack locker. "I guess the only thing she didn't buy this horse was a saddle. Which is fine. I have my own."

"We'll have our saddle-fitter take a look when you come for your first lesson," Alison says. "Malcolm does the assessments on his own saddles, but he knows them pretty well. He'll pick the right one for your horse, don't worry."

"Sure," I agree, pretending I was worried sick about saddle-fitting. The truth is, I don't think about it much. I mostly ride racehorses, who go in half-tree saddles. And I've been riding Breezy in the same saddle for years. Suddenly, I wonder if it actually fits him. Not that it matters anymore, of course.

Alison is already pushing the storage containers into a closet with a lot of other bins. She glances over her shoulder at me. "All done? Then you should go see Malcolm. He'll be in his office for another fifteen minutes, then he's on horses back-to-back until one."

Great, time to face the man himself, and figure out just what the program here will be. And maybe this time I can stay dry and not look like an idiot in front of him.

I try to smile as I head out of the tack room and walk down to the door marked *OFFICE,* right next to the covered arena. I pause outside the doorway, taking a few deep breaths to compose myself. Then I hear his deep voice rumbling from inside.

"Well, dammit, Lillian, the answer is no. I don't have a full *staff.* Because the last working student didn't work out. I said she didn't work out! Don't worry about it!"

Every gossip-loving tentacle in my brain is waving at high alert right now. Everyone knows Malcolm can't keep working students for more than a few months; he's too harsh and too exacting for even the most dedicated of hopeful equestrians. And we put up with a *lot* for the privilege of working in this world, being paid with riding lessons and a tiny stipend, if we're lucky.

I'm glad I'm past the point in my life where I'd take that kind of gig. I did it enough. Riding racehorses pays me actual money, the kind that I can invest in riding lessons and clinics and my own little farm.

Of course, that hasn't gotten me very far towards reaching any of my competition goals. I competed Breezy through Preliminary Level eventing before anhidrosis ended his cross-country galloping, and put in a few decent dressage performances before he injured a suspensory that chose not to heal.

Everything I've done was pretty decent for an amateur. But it wasn't the extent of what I set out to do when I moved to Ocala. Not even close. I'd be lying to myself if I didn't admit that Malcolm Horsham has what I want: the career, the horses, the farm.

I'll never get it now, but that doesn't snuff out the desire.

"Fine," Horsham is announcing, having let whoever Lillian is have her say on the other end of the line. "No, it's fine. I'll have Alison run an ad and we'll get someone else in. But the timing is terrible. We're coming into the busiest part of the season—yes, I *know*. Yes, I'll be sure to blame myself. Thanks, Lillian. Goodbye."

There is a moment of silence. I can hear Horsham breathing heavily, as if the phone call has put him under serious stress. The sound is oddly intimate, and I'm grateful when a horse neighs somewhere down the stable aisle, setting off a whole conversation that drowns out whatever else is happening inside that office.

Then Horsham is in the doorway, his hands gripping the frame. "Alison!" he shouts, before seeing me standing right next to him. He starts slightly, his green eyes widening. "Good grief, you're a small one, aren't you—"

"She's here to go over the training plan," Alison interrupts quickly, appearing out of nowhere. "If you can take ten minutes to do that, please? And then get on this horse. He's been waiting." She gestures at the tacked horse waiting for him in the grooming stall.

Horsham glances at the horse as well, then down at the heavy watch on his left wrist. It's a Longines watch, the first one I've ever seen on someone's arm. He must have won it; Longines sponsors the biggest equestrian events in the country. "Ten minutes," he tells Alison. Then he turns to me and says, "Come in and have a seat."

The command makes me feel like I'm stepping into a doctor's office, with all the fear and stress that implies. But once I am in his beautiful office, the comparison ends. Horsham's wood-paneled office could have been lifted from an English manor, from the stuffed leather chairs to the embroidered hunt scenes on the cushions lining a bench overlooking the covered arena. All it lacks is a fire licking hungrily at seasoned wood, but of course, this is Florida. That would be massive overkill, even on a chilly day like this one.

Horsham settles behind his desk and leans back in his chair. Sunlight filters through the openings along the top of the covered arena, and it catches his green eyes, making them glitter. It's a bright January day out there, and suddenly I'm wondering how I'm going to fill it after I leave. No horse to ride, the day off from work...I wish I could stay here, and get to know Bucky better. It's weird to think that horse down the aisle is mine when I've barely touched him.

But that's ridiculous. No way Horsham wants owners hanging around all day. That's not how these trainers operate. He'll want me out of his hair so he can work.

Still, I think, maybe if I ask—"I was wondering if I could stay—"

"The boarding contract stipulates—" Horsham begins at the same moment.

We look at each other, each daring the other to go on. I give in to the force of his gaze and nod at him.

"The boarding contract stipulates," he repeats, his words clipped, "that I'll work the horse for four weeks, then bring you in weekly for riding lessons. We have some wiggle-room for horse shows, events, as we see fit. Coaching and additional lessons will be extra, but if you're prepping for an event, I'll work your rides into the schedule so that you can school him yourself. If you'd like me to show him, I have a fee schedule with your rates marked in Row B." He pushes a paper towards me with rows of figures marked out for different levels of training agreements. The numbers are all astronomical to my eyes. There's no way I can afford to let a pro like Malcolm Horsham show my horse.

He seems to sense my shock; I see a faint smile play on his lips. He knows I'm in over my head. *Come on*, I think, *no need to be a jerk about it.*

But Horsham's already heading down a new tangent. "You should know that if I'm the one in the saddle at events, the horse's value has the potential to grow exponentially. Especially with his breeding, if he does as well as we hope, we're talking about the high five figures after one successful season. I doubt you'll get the same results so quickly, so if you want to sell him, it's worth thinking about."

"Oh," I say blankly. "Okay."

"Do you want to sell him on?" Horsham asks.

I stare at him and instantly lose track of the conversation. He has indecently high cheekbones, I think. And his lips are thin, but curved, and I don't usually like beards but with his country-rugged style, the look suits him.

"Ma'am," Horsham prompts.

I realize I haven't answered and I'm probably looking at him like a crazy person. "I, uh, hadn't worked it all out yet," I admit.

Horsham runs a hand through his dark hair. "Right," he says, sighing. "Well, give it a little thought, if you don't mind. It will affect my spring calendar and we're already sending entries out for late February. Now through April is the busiest part of the season. I have students arriving from all over and my calendar will be full very quickly."

"Of course," I blunder. "Yes. Um."

Horsham's phone vibrates on his desk, and he picks it up. Suddenly, his brows come together. It's like a thunderstorm has broken over a quiet harbor. He looks fierce, dangerous even. "Dammit," he whispers, and I know he's holding back a world of rage with that quiet curse. The stories of his legendary temper flood through my mind, giving me a shiver.

"Is everything okay?" I venture, feeling a weird need to placate him.

His gaze flicks back to me. "Yes," he says tersely. "Sorry about that. My—uh—associate is giving me a hard time today. Let's just say I need a new working student by, oh, one o'clock, or my entire schedule is going to hell in a hand basket."

"I hope that works out," I say politely. In truth, I'm tired of this interview and I need an excuse to leave. Malcolm Horsham is too volatile for me. Maybe having nothing to do but pet my cat and stare out the window at my broken horse is the best thing for me right now. There's too much potential for upheaval in this place, for all the pretty polished brass and honey-colored wood on the surface.

"It won't," he sighs, staring down at his phone. "It never does."

I'm too surprised by his candor to answer. Is everything okay with this guy? I glance around for Alison, hoping she'll come save me— but she's across the aisle, soothing the horse still waiting in the cross-ties.

"Sorry," I say softly, feeling like *something* has to be said.

Malcolm Horsham glances up at me, and something in his green eyes seems to flicker with amusement. "Unless *you* want to be my new working student."

Chapter Five

IT'S MY TURN to look amused. "Oh, I don't think so," I answer quickly.

"That was fast." He raises his eyebrows. "Why not? Some people in Ocala would think that's the job offer of a lifetime."

He has no problem patting himself on the back, does he? "Because I have a job," I reply smoothly. "I gallop at Malone-Salazar, and I handle their weanling barn, too. Well, they're technically yearlings now. Anyway, it's full-time."

"But you came here to event, didn't you?" Horsham says. "Unless —oh, is this just a hobby? I didn't realize. Sorry about that."

"It's *not* just a hobby," I retort. He knows exactly how to get under my skin, doesn't he?

But then I realize that eventing must be my hobby—one I'm not even practicing at the moment. Because I'm sure as hell not the professional I thought I'd be by now.

I shift in my seat, uncomfortable with the turn the conversation has taken. Wasn't this supposed to be a quick rundown on what was included with the training contract my aunt so foolishly signed with this man? "I'm just between horses right now," I mutter, feeling mutinous. "My guy had a soft-tissue injury. He's a pasture pet now."

"Oh, I'm very sorry about that," Horsham says, and I get the feeling he really is. "But if you don't mind my saying so, you're not between horses. You have a horse in this barn."

"Right." Bucky. My horse. "That's going to take some getting used to," I admit, smiling sheepishly.

"Well, I have to start or I'll be off my schedule for the rest of the day, and that kind of thing doesn't fly around here. Listen, if you know anyone interested in the working student job, I don't skimp on the riding time. It's a lot of hard work, but if a person sticks around, they'll reach their full potential. That's a promise."

And he gives me a meaningful look that keeps my butt rooted in the chair.

Neither of us are getting up, I realize after a moment of silence. He's staring me down. He's daring me to ask for the job.

But why? He doesn't even *know* me.

"You don't know that I could even do it," I challenge him.

Horsham shrugs. "I'd put you on a horse first to see what you're made of. But you handled that horse like you know what you're doing. And I'm just looking for someone to help my barn manager get me through the day, not an Olympic-level rider. Anyway, it would be good for you. If you want to make things work with that horse. He's going to be special, I think. Don't you want to see how far the two of you can go?"

He has me there. I can't help but glance past him, at the covered arena waiting for his next ride. Mirrors line the long side opposite us, and the footing looks cushioned and manicured. Watered to the perfect consistency. No dust, no holes, no hard spots, I was sure of it. The sight of that footing seemed to hit me like a punch in the gut.

If I'd had footing like that to school Breezy on, would he still be competing in dressage today? It was my choice to take him home from my last working student gig and ride him in the sand and grass paddock. My choice not to find a job that would have paid for board at a farm with a good arena. My choice to take him out on uneven ground that wet day.

It was cool out, the first time all year. I thought he'd enjoy working in the rain.

He took a bad step. That's what they always say, when a fracture or a bow or a strain ends a horse's career. *He took a bad step.*

My fault.

Breezy suffered from my choices. I know I can't make the same mistake with Bucky. Leave out the fact that this new horse is worth a small fortune; financial stuff doesn't really matter to me, but a horse's health and happiness means everything.

"Are you okay?" Horsham is looking at me closely, one eyebrow cocked curiously.

"Fine," I say faintly. "Just...thinking it over."

I'm considering this. I must be insane.

Horsham picks up a pen and flips it in his hand. "Stick around if you want," he says, and pushes back from the desk. "Why not watch this ride? Artsy is a good example of a horse I took from round pen to four-star."

"Artsy?" The name makes me stand and spin around. I look at the dark bay across the aisle, realizing the little white star and over-large ears on the horse do look familiar. "That's Artsy Ballad," I stammer.

"The one and only," Horsham says fondly. The tone in his voice catches my attention, and my gaze shifts to Horsham's face. He's looking at that horse like Artsy is his large bay son, and suddenly he's a *lot* more human to me. "We're prepping for a huge season for him and my other Advanced horse, Oceanus," Horsham adds. "In addition to students, sales horses...it's going to be a really busy spring around here. That's why we need help so badly. It's not a stall-cleaning job. Did I mention that? We have stall-cleaners. It's grooming, tacking, cooling out, assisting with lessons. Sure you don't want to groom a couple of five-star horses?" His tone has turned wheedling.

Five-star competition is the toughest of the tough. My breath catches in my throat. It's not that I didn't know Malcolm Horsham was one of the top riders in the sport; obviously I came in fully aware of he was. But to be suddenly *confronted* with the fact, in plain English, in casual speech, while looking at the horse who has taken Malcolm around the biggest three-day events in North America, is a lot to take. Especially after the morning I've had around here. My wet socks won't let me forget that I met the man while standing in his fountain.

"Are you coming?" Alison calls. "Today?"

Horsham gives me a final grin. The familiarity of his smile is the cherry on top of this unexpectedly tantalizing sundae. I feel my mouth run dry as he leaves me standing in the office and crosses the aisle to take his horse from Alison.

"Show Evie to the lounge," he tells her, scooping up the reins in one hand and dropping a helmet onto his thick head of hair with the other. "She wants to watch Artsy go before she leaves."

Alison smiles at me as her boss takes his big horse into the covered arena. "Shall we?"

I can't believe any of this is happening. Can't believe I'm upstairs above Malcom Horsham's office in his plush and climate-controlled viewing lounge, while Alison makes a fresh pot of coffee and offers me a granola bar from the little plate laid out along the bar at the back of the room. This is a space made for owners to watch their horses go in comfort, to invite friends and feel good about their foolish investments. The sofas are deep, the chairs are cozy, and the windows overlooking the covered arena are clean. Below us,

Horsham walks Artsy on a long rein through a freshly dragged arena, his feet hanging loose from the stirrups.

"The coffee will be done in a minute. Anything else I can get you? I just have to go down and groom Rap, because our working student —well, she—"

"Quit," I finish for her. "I heard."

Alison grins and shakes her head. "We go through them, don't we?"

"You really do! Everyone talks about it," I add. "Have you thought about...I don't know, calming him down somehow?"

"The thing is, it's *not* all Malcolm's fault, despite what you've probably heard," Alison confides, and then an alarm on her phone chimes, cutting off what was probably some pretty choice gossip. "Sorry! I really do have to go. So listen, if you aren't going to take the job—yes, I heard everything—then it's no problem. I'll send you a text later tonight with the time Bucky falls onto tomorrow's schedule, and you can feel free to come out and watch him go. Just come right up here, okay? Don't worry about looking for us; we'll be too busy to do much meeting and greeting for a while."

And with that, Alison dashes out of the lounge.

Left alone in the comfortable confines of the owner's lounge, I try to get excited about the posh turn my day has taken...but it quickly turns to discomfort. I don't like being left up here in silence while the real work of running a top stable is being done downstairs. I guess I'm not cut out for Madison or Aunt Rachel's lifestyle, paying for other people to do the heavy lifting. I like to get the job done by myself.

Sighing, I make up my mind to concentrate on the rider below. Maybe I can learn something from watching Horsham's ride.

In the arena, Artsy is trotting on a loose rein, stretching his neck while Horsham gives him all the space he wants. It's a pretty view, but from up here I can't hear his hooves connecting with the groomed footing, and I can't tell if Horsham is crooning to him, telling him what a good boy he is. Even just losing the jingle of bit and buckle makes watching the ride feel empty.

I was never meant to be an observer in the lounge, I remind myself. I'm supposed to be out there, doing the things. A part of it.

I can't help but think enviously of Alison, who is clearly the manager and then some. She's running the show under Horsham's lead, keeping him on schedule and managing the clients. People like me, who have to be watched and escorted and kept out of trouble. Told when we can visit to see our horses work, and asked politely to leave when they're done.

I think of Bucky down there, this new dark horse in my life. Maybe I should just leave him here for six months, then sell him. I can take that money and...

Do what?

Buy another horse, I guess.

But it seems so futile. I think of Breezy grazing on the thin grass outside my trailer. We worked so hard, accomplished so little.

Five years in Ocala, five years of working every day to afford the lessons and clinics and competitions, and yet here I am, back at the beginning. A better rider, sure, but no pro.

No Malcolm Horsham, that's for sure.

Horsham is picking up contact now, and Artsy slides into a beautiful frame, his hind legs working beneath him and his black tail fluttering behind like a banner. His neck arches and he mouths the bit gently, trotting with all the precision of a ballet dancer, playing with all the finicky precociousness of a royal child. He was born for this life, I think.

And then I wonder if I was thinking of the horse or his rider.

I was born for this life, too, but somehow Malcolm Horsham got it and I did not.

The scent of coffee is what finally tears me away from the window. Like a good little racing girl, I never turn down a hit of caffeine. I pour myself a mug and doctor it up with some fancy flavored syrups and milk from the glass-fronted fridge, then return to the view. Artsy is cantering now, while Horsham sits tight in the saddle, his body barely moving despite the rocking-horse motion of his mount.

I'm jealous as hell. I can't sit the canter like that. Despite all my experience, despite all my lessons, I haven't mastered the sitting canter—not properly, like I should have by now. Somehow my lower leg always slips forward, and I end up in what's called a "chair seat," which means my upper body is behind the motion of the horse. I break up the horse's balance, and the horse hollows its back in response, coming out of the collection we're trying to achieve.

Every. Single. Time.

Malcolm Horsham sits the canter like he was chiseled in place by a master sculptor.

Suddenly I want it, so badly I can barely hold the coffee mug still. A little sloshes over the brim and onto my damp boots, but I don't care. I just want to find a way to fix my seat, to fix my riding, to fix my *life* so that it's me down there in the covered arena, riding my upper-level horse, knowing that all day today I will ride good horses and tomorrow will be another day just like today.

And I've been offered an open door to reach that goal, if I am brave enough to take it.

I bite my lip, wondering if this is the day that everything changes in my life...or if I missed the transition, and it was really three weeks ago in Aunt Rachel's living room, when my cousin regifted me the horse that she hadn't asked for.

* * *

44

I'm standing in front of the office when Horsham leads Artsy in, the horse's nostrils flaring and his mouth wet with drool. Alison races past me with Artsy's halter, but it's Horsham I want to talk to. He hands off the horse and growls, "Liniment bath for him."

"I *know*," Alison snaps back.

"I don't see a bucket!"

"The hot water heater is refilling," she hisses. "I'll do it in a minute."

"He hasn't even had a carrot yet." Horsham looks around him and snatches at a bag of carrots left on a folding chair by the wash-rack. "Come on, woman, move faster!"

"I'll move as fast as I want," Alison informs him. "Stop waving that carrot around and deal with your client."

Horsham looks over his shoulder and sees me. His taut expression slackens. "Oh, you're still here," he says.

"She saw everything," Alison sings out, leading Artsy into the wash-rack. His saddle is already on a stand. Wow, she can untack fast.

"Sorry about that," Horsham says. "We can get snippy with each other when we're crunched for time."

Alison snorts.

"It's fine," I say uncertainly, second guessing everything I planned to say. He really does have a mean streak. Or just a very short temper. Either way, it's not something I want to deal with every day. Maybe I should just go. "Sorry, Mr. Horsham, I'm actually heading out."

"Call me Malcolm, please," he says, and with one hand he unclips his helmet, sweeping it away from his head. He's damp and sweaty underneath, and suddenly, he doesn't look so scary. "Question for me, ma'am?" he asks, slinging the helmet onto a rack and turning for the office.

I follow him, watching as he pulls a bottle of water from a fridge. Now I don't know what to say. Everything I rehearsed in the lounge as I watched him school Artsy has vanished from my brain. He drinks deep and sighs, then caps the bottle again, his eyes on me.

I can't do this, I think. I'm afraid of him, and with good reason. This is the infamous Malcolm Horsham, destroyer of working students.

"Out with it," he says, dropping the client-friendly persona. "I have horses to ride."

I want horses to ride, I think. *Event horses, not racehorses.*

I want my own success. I want my riding to matter.

"Interview," I blurt.

"What?"

I take a breath. "I'd like to interview," I say carefully. "For the working student job. You said you'd put me on a horse to see what I had."

Amusement creases his lips. "All it took was one go on Artsy to make you change your mind, huh?"

Embarrassed, I nod and push through. "I want to be an upper-level eventer," I tell him. "I feel like it would be crazy not to try for this. If you'll give me a shot," I add. "And it doesn't affect Bucky's training in any way."

"No," he said. "*That* is paid for, up-front. This would be something different." He nods slowly. "Tell Alison to get Diamond out for you," he says. "And you can ride for me while I'm on Oceanus."

"Diamond," I repeat. "Okay." That's all I can say for a while, but it's fine, because Alison understands.

Chapter Six

EVERYTHING IN MALCOLM'S tack room is neatly labeled. I suspect the work is done by Alison's own hand, but she's not around to ask. She points out Diamond, a chestnut gelding eating hay in the stall next to Bucky's, and tells me to put him in the brown dressage saddle and use the grooming kit in the cross-ties. Those are all the instructions I'm given.

My helmet is in my Jeep, so before I get started, I walk out to the service parking lot where I left it earlier this morning. That was only an hour ago, but it already feels like a lifetime since I walked Bucky up this driveway. I skirt the fountain like a nervous dog, as if I'll somehow fall into it again if I get too close. The water tinkles cheerfully at me as I return, my helmet swinging by the harness. "Nice try, fountain," I tell it, before nearly running into Alison just inside the barn.

She's leading a chocolate-brown horse who towers over both of us, and her eyes widen as the horse skitters sideways to get away from me. "Come on now, Oceanus," she scolds. "Stop acting like everything is going to eat you. Typical big horse," she adds to me as she gets the horse moving forward again. "No idea that he's bigger than everything else in the world."

Alison already has Oceanus clipped into cross-ties when I walk Diamond down the aisle to join her. The chestnut horse was clearly named for his big diamond, so geometrically perfect it makes him look like a child's drawing of a horse, and I'm happy that he's a more normal size than Oceanus. Closer to sixteen hands than seventeen, he's built like a Thoroughbred and I have a feeling riding him will be a pretty comfortable experience.

If I can get over the fact that I'll be watched by Malcolm Horsham the entire time.

"Go quick," Alison warns as I linger a little over Diamond's grooming. "He'll want to see what you can do on a schedule. Time is money around here."

"Gotcha," I agree, and put on my racetrack face. I can get a horse tacked in less than five minutes. Of course, there's less tack and less expectation about a horse's turnout in the training barn. I pluck a few shavings from Diamond's tail, pick out his hooves, and knock the dust off his back with a horsehair brush so he'll gleam underneath the covered arena's big lights. Then I settle a white saddle pad over his back and get the brown dressage saddle Alison assigned to me.

It's ancient. Any padding this saddle once had has long since gone to wool heaven, and it was clearly designed before the modern era of knee rolls and thigh blocks.

"Practically a polo saddle," I mutter as I fasten the girth.

With Diamond bridled and my helmet on my head, I present myself to Alison for inspection. But she just waves me into the arena, where Malcolm is already on Oceanus. "Stay out of his way," she says.

Apparently, that's all the instruction I'm going to get.

I wait at the entrance to the covered arena until I'm sure Malcolm and Oceanus are safely at the other end, then walk him out and find the mounting block in the closest corner. Diamond wiggles as I mount and walks away before my feet are in the stirrups. I find them with difficulty. I'd set the stirrup leathers to a length that should have worked for me, but they're much longer than exercise length, and I haven't ridden in a dressage saddle for months.

I must look ridiculous, I think, panicking a little. Diamond feels my heartbeat quicken and his steps come a little faster. With a doomed sensation, I tighten the reins. I'm still searching for a grip on the stirrups; even though my boots are in them, the connection just isn't there. I'm grasping for a position that feels secure when Diamond decides that there is a scary ghost in the arena.

Diamond is a narrow horse, did I mention that? When he tucks his tail and scooches forward, running away from whatever spirit he thinks resides in the corner behind him, I feel like I'm hanging onto a broomstick. My legs go forward, my stirrups are lost to me, and only the high cantle of the old brown dressage saddle holds me astride. Well, the cantle and poor Diamond's mouth, because I have a death-grip on the reins. He throws his head up in protest and he grows light in the front, which feels suspiciously like a rear waiting to happen.

Oh no, no, no. I can't get tossed now. Not when everyone's eyes are on me—and by everyone, of course, I mean Alison and the all-important Malcolm. Even if I decide here and now that I don't want this stupid job, the story of the exercise rider who tried and failed to ride one of Malcolm's kindly old Thoroughbreds will go down in Ocala gossip history. It'll be all over town by Saturday night. Although I don't know how, because the only people here are me, Malcolm, and Alison.

So I ball up whatever energy and strength I still possess, tighten my core like I'm doing sit-ups in front of an angry gym teacher, and *hurl* myself forward despite the momentum pressing me towards Diamond's tail. I get a grip of his mane in my hands and I cling for dear life, while swinging my legs up and back into a position which feels more natural.

Diamond doesn't know what's going on, but he's pretty sure he doesn't like it. The Thoroughbred bolts forward. Luckily, that's exactly the kind of behavior I'm accustomed to—and now I'm in the right position to deal with it. Despite the change in saddle, I'm able to stay forward, hands on his withers and knees pressed close to his sides, and I ride his quick, frightened canter right back down to a nervous trot, and finally a head-tossing walk. When he *whoas* to a halt at last, I give him a pat on the neck, then turn him towards Malcolm.

The trainer has halted Oceanus in the center of the ring and is watching my performance with a blend of astonishment and amusement I really can't blame him for. I must have looked like a complete idiot out there.

But as my horse nears Oceanus, his ears pricked with the hope of being safe with a friend, Malcolm surprises me. "Nice riding," he tells me.

All I can do is stare at him, assuming it's an awful joke. He's going to be mean to me literally while I'm riding? Maybe this isn't just a bad idea. Maybe it's the worst idea of all time.

Or maybe he's...not kidding around?

"Seriously?" I ask after a moment's silence.

His thin lips curve into a grin. "Yes, seriously," he laughs. "You were like a fish out of water in that dressage saddle, but you found your place when you had to. I like a rider with instincts. Sometimes on cross-country, that's all you'll have to go on. How high did you say you competed at?"

I let Diamond halt next to Oceanus. He reaches out and nips at the older horse, who squeals in reply. "Preliminary," I reply, reining my horse back before he can start a war. "That was last year, before my horse went lame. He's retired now."

"Where'd you finish?" Malcolm asks.

"Sixth," I answer, remembering the rainy sky as I picked up our green sixth-place ribbon. A muddy spring day, the last event before we realized Breezy wasn't sweating anymore. The first nail in the coffin of our career together.

Malcolm is turning Oceanus in a circle around Diamond now, looking me over like I'm a piece of merchandise. I know he's observing the way I sit a horse, which is abundantly clear since my feet are free of the stirrups and I've found my own position in the featureless dressage saddle, but there's something oddly stimulating about his gaze. As if he's considering more about me than just my equitation.

Don't be ridiculous, I tell myself. *Just because he's hot and dresses well doesn't mean you have to turn this into something it's not.*

"I'll take you on," Malcolm says.

"What?" I'm shocked out of my weird mental ramblings. "Based on *that?*"

He's grinning again. "You really should work on the way you sell yourself, Evie."

My name sounds different coming from his lips. Mischievous, somehow.

"You showed me you can ride by staying on Diamond just now," Malcolm continues. "And how hard you worked to get off his mouth —that shows empathy for the horse, which I appreciate. More than anything, though, I need *someone* right now, and you're the one sitting in front of me."

"How flattering," I joke.

Malcolm chuckles. "I hope you don't mind blunt truth. Because that's what you're going to get around here. I don't sugar-coat anything with my staff. If you'd rather stay an owner and a client, and get the nice version of me, just say so. I'll understand completely. But if you're interested in moving up the levels, and you're willing to work, this job will get you there. This job—and that horse in there."

Bucky.

I bite my lip. He's still circling us, making me feel as if Diamond and I are being hunted by some sleek, handsome shark. Oceanus enjoys the game, tossing his head and nipping at poor Diamond whenever he gets the chance. *Like owner, like horse,* I think confusedly.

"Are you asking me for a decision right now?" I ask.

"It would be nice," Malcolm admits. "I'm sure Alison can put you to work right away. We have a lot of horses to get through today, and she's the only one here at the moment."

"Today's my day off, but tomorrow I work," I tell him. "I already have a full-time job, remember?"

He just shrugs. "Do you want to work here or not?"

There are a million variables to consider. I don't know what the job pays, or where he expects me to sleep at night—plenty of working student positions are live-in only, with the student expected to do night-check every night. I'd have to find a place for my horse to live. Pack and bring over my things. Quit my job at Posey's farm. I'd be easily replaced, of course. Exercise riders and stall muckers are a dime a dozen in this town.

None of these tasks are insurmountable. It all just seems a little... crazy. I wasn't even thinking of working here when I arrived this morning. I just needed to get Bucky settled in, go over the contract, and leave.

You should have left, I scold myself. *Why are you on this horse?*

"Suppose we finish up with Diamond," Malcolm suggests. "Shorten your stirrups two holes, find a comfortable position, and let's do a nice thirty-minute lesson while I'm riding Oceanus. Go ahead and warm him up with some twenty-meter circles and serpentines at the trot."

Well, I can't turn down a free riding lesson from the man himself. "Okay," I agree. "Thanks."

"I talked to your aunt," he adds as I start to ride away.

I turn Diamond around again. "Yeah? How was that?"

"Insufferable," Malcolm says. "She bought that horse for her daughter, who doesn't ride anymore? Pretty strange."

Not really, I think, looking at his rugged good looks. Rachel saw a rich horseman who'd make a hell of a son-in-law. She went for it. I'm not sure I blame her.

"Anyway," Malcolm continues, "I'm supposed to make that horse into an eventing machine. But something tells me you'd rather be the one who does it. Am I right?"

He has me there. I nod mutely; Malcolm has my gaze locked on his now, and I'm waiting for him to finish his speech like my whole world depends on it.

"She doesn't think you're a good enough rider to do it," he says, shaking his head sorrowfully.

"She *said* that?" I gasp. The *nerve* of that woman—

"I think you should stay," Malcolm says. "And I think you should prove her wrong."

And just like that, he has me.

Chapter Seven

MALCOLM TEARS ME apart in my riding lesson, ripping my position, my hands, even the set of my jaw when I ask Diamond for transitions. When the half-hour is over, I feel like I've been skewered, then raked over the coals; meanwhile, Malcolm just dismounts from Oceanus, hands the horse off to Alison, and goes into his office to rehydrate. Before I can get Diamond back into the grooming stall to untack, he's already leading his next horse into the covered arena.

Alison is hosing off Oceanus, using some kind of herbal liniment in a sprayer that smells deliciously of peppermint. She has the heat lamps on overhead to ward off the January chill, bathing Oceanus's dark coat and her blonde ponytail in a yellow-red light. "You can use the wash-rack as soon as we're done," she promises. "I'll leave the lamps on."

"Thanks," I say gratefully. I'm already feeling the cool air licking at my sweaty body. I pull Diamond's tack off quickly and find a light cooler hanging next to the grooming stall; I fling it over his body to keep him from getting a chill. The day seems to be turning colder, and I'm not really dressed for it.

"Here you go," Alison says, unclipping the cross-ties from Oceanus's halter. "As soon as you have him cleaned up, put him away with that cooler on, then come find me and I'll tell you who to tack up next." She leads Oceanus off down the stable aisle, leaving me gaping after her.

Oh god, does she think I am starting work *right now?*

Didn't I just say I was going home after this?

I said it to Malcolm, but I have a sneaking suspicion Alison is the real boss...and there's no time to question the situation. Diamond is waiting for his bath; Malcolm is already cantering the horse in the arena, so I'm guessing he'll be back in fairly quickly. I'll let him deal with it.

I move Diamond into the wash-rack, thankful for the heat from the lamps overhead, and give him a bath with the same sprayer attachment Alison used on Oceanus. The peppermint liniment smells like Christmas, and I can't help but think about Aunt Rachel in her poinsettia dress, overseeing her party like the duchess of nowhere. Unable to stop her daughter from foiling her plans. What a family.

And now I have a regift horse, I think, smiling to myself. And now here I am, caught up in the clutches of one of eventing's top trainers. Who could ever have predicted I'd go from her living room to this wash-rack in three short weeks?

As for taking the job with him—something I've apparently decided to do, to my eternal confusion—she'll probably be upset with me, although she won't say anything to my face. But she'll tell the rest of the family I took one look at Malcolm Horsham and decided to get a little of that classy trainer action for myself. And she'll tell poor Madison it should have been *her.*

Because that's all this ever was for her, I'm sure of it. A ploy to get Madison in with Malcolm. A desperate shot at finding some American landed gentry for her spinster daughter.

She must be furious Madison wasn't willing to play along.

Alison appears next to Diamond's head, scattering my thoughts like dandelion fluff. "Good grief, are you still hosing him off? Get him scraped and under a cooler, then put him away and take out the horse in the stall across from him. His name is Mozart—it's on the halter and the stall door, so you can't get that wrong. Bring him down here and get him groomed and tacked in the brown Stubben jumping saddle in the tack room. I'm going to pick up lunch."

She turns on her heel and stalks off down the stable aisle.

I look at Diamond, and he flutters his nostrils back at me.

"I guess I'm working," I tell him. "So much for my day off."

What to do? Put Diamond away and get out the next horse. Easy-peasy. I slide the sweat scraper across Diamond's wet body, pulling away as much water as I can, and then get the cooler buckled across his chest. With a warning that he isn't to roll and mess up his nice cooler, I shut his stall door and look across the aisle. *Mozart* gleams on a brass nameplate, and above it, a small gray horse with black-tipped ears watches me. He huffs a sigh.

"Your turn, buddy," I tell him. "Let's go."

Mozart chooses not to leave his stall.

"Uh, what's up?" I look him over. He's a compact little horse with dark points and a short black tail which only reaches his hocks. Something about him says Quarter Horse blood to me, which is interesting in an upper-level eventing barn. It's not that Quarter Horses can't do the job, it's just that they're not very fashionable for the job. And, I think, can't they be just the slightest bit stubborn?

"There's nothing wrong with you that I can see, Mister," I tell Mozart.

He looks away.

He actually looks away from me, like I'm boring him.

"No, uh-uh," I say, giving the lead-rope a healthy tug. "I'm a racehorse girl, and I know all about silly barn tricks. You're not standing in this stall all day. Now, come *on!*" I punctuate the last word with a swing of the cotton lead-rope, flicking the end of it against his hindquarters.

Mozart doesn't move. Instead, he glances at me with one large dark eye, blinks very slowly, and sighs. As if he's seen this show before and he knows how it ends.

With the working student in tears, I can only assume.

This is ridiculous. I work with *racehorses,* I remind myself. Of all ages. The naughtiest horses on the planet. I will not be bested by a stubborn Quarter Horse. I try moving his feet instead, giving his shoulder a good shove to the right.

But he doesn't budge.

Okay. This is fine. I'll just get a little sharper with the lead-rope. Taking a careful hold with my left hand, I use my right hand to pop him sharply on the hindquarter with the end of the rope.

He shifts a little, but doesn't hop into the aisle with a burst of angry energy, which was the desired result.

I take a breath, thinking hard. Clearly, Mozart is a test. This is the horse they use to break in new employees. Once he has reduced me to tears, someone will come along and show me the magic trick that makes this horse go. And then I will be humbled, put in my place and ready to learn everything they have to say about horses, with no back-talk allowed or even considered. Hazing. I'm being hazed.

But that's not fair. I'm no eighteen-year-old greenie with stars in her eyes. I'm a twenty-seven-year-old horsewoman with experience moving all kinds of horses. And I can move this one.

"Mozart, my man, I'm going to pop you so hard in a minute," I warn him.

Mozart flicks his ears back and forth, listening to me, then something down the aisle. I think Alison must be back already and I panic, bringing the lead-rope down on his rear end like I'm trying to kill a giant spider with one blow.

Whack!

Oh, now he's in the aisle alright. He's galloping away, lead-rope trailing, while I stand in the stall and wonder what the hell just happened.

That's the thing about Quarter Horses, I remember. They can go from zero to sixty in one stride. It's kind of what they were originally bred for. And I just witnessed that breeding in action.

"What the *hell?*"

And that's Malcolm.

I dart into the stable aisle and run towards the covered arena, where Mozart is already cavorting, running full-steam up the long side while throwing bucks that would make a rodeo rider salivate. There's a bang, the sound of a hoof hitting the wooden planks along the arena's side, and then Malcolm appears in the entrance. He's trying to straighten out his horse, who is wiggling and prancing, desperate to get in on the action with Mozart. He turns to face me as his horse whips around in a circle, and for a moment I see his furious eyes blazing, his chin clenched like granite, and my heart sinks.

But there's no time to wallow in misery. I have to fix this mess. I splash through a puddle of water pooling in the aisle and into the covered arena, running for Mozart as fast as I can.

Yeah, he doesn't want to be caught.

I'm trailing after him, feeling like I've been outwitted by a horse much, much smarter than me, when I hear a shriek behind me. Spinning around, I see Alison in the aisle, two paper bags in her hands. "What did you *do?*" she cries. "The *water!*"

Mozart chooses that second to launch himself past me, heading for the arena entrance as if he's certain Alison is here to save him from the mean working student. Malcolm has dismounted by now and is leading his horse around in circles, looking like he's going to dismember me the moment he gets his hands around my neck. But he'll have to wait, because Mozart shoves me to the ground with his shoulder as he plunges past, and I'm choking on a mouthful of arena dirt before I even know what's happening.

I'll just stay here, I think, once my brain catches up with my body. *It's better here in the dirt. Maybe no one can see me.*

Maybe I can dig myself a little hole and just cover myself up with the rich red-brown footing and vanish forever.

Yeah, that would be good.

"Evie?"

It's Alison.

I spit out some dirt and look up at her.

"Hi," I say.

"We have a problem," she replies.

It turns out Mozart isn't the main concern, although Malcolm's pretty furious the horse interrupted his training session. The real issue is that I somehow didn't shut the water off, and I've flooded all the grooming stalls and part of Malcolm's office.

I stare at the vast lake covering the end of the aisle. Water is seeping into the arena, turning the footing a darker shade of brown. Mud, I think miserably. I have created mud in the perfectly controlled footing.

"How could I have missed this?" I mutter, then I remember running through a puddle as I went after Mozart. My brain skipped over the part where I was splashing through a growing lake, because I was too busy freaking out about the horse I'd accidentally-on-purpose sent galloping down the stable aisle.

"Here's the squeegee," Alison says darkly, picking her way around the edges of the puddle closest to the office wall. She passes me a rubber squeegee on a long pole. "Start shoving it into the wash-rack drain."

"I think it might be clogged." I can see water sitting heavy and still over the center of the wash-rack. That's what started this whole drama, of course; I didn't get the water in that special sprayer to shut off properly, and once the wash-rack drain was overwhelmed, things got soggy very quickly.

"There are rubber gloves on the rack by the hose," Alison says, her voice heavy with meaning, and then she turns away to take Malcolm's horse. "I'll untack him in his stall," she tells the boss.

Malcolm nods and goes into the office. He shuts the door behind him, sending a little ripple of water through Lake Stable Aisle.

A cold wind whips through the half-walls of the covered arena, making me shiver as I start to splash my way over the clogged drain.

After this is cleaned up, I think miserably, I'll just be on my way.

Chapter Eight

A QUARTER OF an hour and several horrifying handfuls of soggy, manure-laden horse hair later, I've got the puddle drained and am pushing the remaining water into the wash-rack to swirl away forever. I feel alone in the barn. Malcolm hasn't come out of his office yet; Alison stalked past a few minutes ago with the last horse's tack and put it back in the tack room, but after that I don't know where she went. That's probably for the best, I think. I don't need to say goodbye on my way out; no one will be expecting me to stay after all that.

All I want to do is salvage what is left of my day off. I'll go home, shower, put on some fuzzy clothes, and make some hot chocolate. Really get some value out of this cold-and-turning-colder afternoon. Maybe I'll make chili for dinner. I'm sure I have some beans in the pantry.

I'm happily imagining a huge bowl of chili, topped with sour cream and shredded cheese and a blood-red swirl of hot sauce, when Malcolm appears in the aisle.

I brace myself for the shouting.

He looks at my work and nods. "Good," he says.

That's it? Just *good?*

"Thanks," I reply, leaning the squeegee against the wall. "Um, yeah. Think it's done."

I don't know how to say I'm heading out. Not with him staring at me with those stern green eyes.

"There's lunch for you in the office," he says. "Go tell Alison to get down here and eat something. She can take five minutes out of her bloody schedule."

"Alison. Right. Uh...I don't know where she is." *Tell him you're leaving!*

"Well, go *find* her," Malcolm retorts, shaking his head at me. "Hurry up. We have the Chandlers coming in half an hour to see their horse go, and everyone needs to eat something first. I can't have my barn staff fainting on the job."

I'm very used to professionals who expect their staff to operate on a breakfast-dinner-only basis, lest they lose a single hour of precious daylight, so I'm surprised enough by Malcolm's insistence we eat lunch that I actually forget to tell him I'm quitting. Instead, I march off down the damp aisle in search of Alison, my boot soles squeaking on the pavers.

Alison is in a stall, pulling overgrown strands of hair from a chestnut gelding's mane with quick, efficient snaps of her wrist. She doesn't turn around when I call her name, so I slip inside. "Hey," I say, "Malcolm wants you to eat lunch before the Chandlers come."

"I'll be there in a second," she replies, still not looking at me. She plucks another long strand and lets it drop to the stall floor. The horse is munching hay and doesn't pay her any mind. "I just wanted to even out this mane before they come," she adds.

"Oh, is this the Chandler horse?" I look him over. Well-muscled and gleaming, the chestnut stands about sixteen two or sixteen three hands high. He's a warmblood, but one of those warmbloods who are mostly Thoroughbred, with a swan-like neck and a narrow chest. I like the look of him.

"This is Mr. Toad," she says, stepping back. "Does that mane look even to you?"

"Looks good to me."

Alison sighs and runs her hand along Mr. Toad's neck. "You're ready, big boy," she says softly.

"You like him, huh?"

She shrugs and turns for the stall door. "I like all of them," she says, but I think she's downplaying her affection for this particular horse.

And hey—I get it. There's a heartbreaker in every barn. I glance at Bucky as we walk past his stall. The dark bay horse still has shavings in his mane from rolling in his fresh bedding. I want to go in and clean him up, but of course, there's no time for that now.

Bucky ignores us as we pass, too busy with his hay to be bothered by saying hello. I wonder if we'll ever be close, or if he'll always be one of those aloof horses who doesn't really care who messes with him, as long as his meals come on time.

It would be nice if we could be friends. Staying here would probably make that process a lot easier—*if* I ever find time to work with him, in between dealing with Malcolm's horses and cleaning up my messes. Speaking of which...

"I'm really sorry about the disaster you came back to," I say to Alison. "I promise destroying an entire barn while the manager's out to lunch is not my usual M.O."

Her lips twitch into an unwilling smile. "It was pretty incredible," she admits. "The loose horse, the lake in the aisle...with the Chandlers coming today? Perfect storm."

"Are they particular?"

"Oh, my god," Alison answers, and that's enough.

"I don't have to stay," I offer. "I mean, if it's not going to work out, I understand."

Alison stops outside Malcolm's office door. I can hear him mumbling inside, on the phone with some client. She speaks low, so she won't be overheard. "No, please don't just leave," she says, and my heart lifts despite my previous determination to get in my Jeep and get the hell out of here. "We threw you right into the deep end, and that's just the way it's going to be. But you handled it. The horse is in his stall, the lake is gone, no one got hurt. Well—you got some dirt on your face, and I think a bruise on your cheek." She smiles and brushes my cheek with her fingers. "No, it's just more dirt."

"I'm not *physically* hurt," I assure her, grinning despite myself. "So, you think I should stay?"

"I do," Alison says. "Maybe it's not the rah-rah speech Malcolm gave you, but we need the help and I think you know what you're doing. That's rare around here."

"Wait, how do you know about the speech Malcolm gave me?"

Alison grins. "He gave you the line about proving someone wrong, didn't he?"

I blink at her, too shocked to respond. Those things he said, about making it happen with my own horse, about proving Aunt Rachel wrong—that was just a line?

It felt real. He *convinced* me. How powerful is this guy, anyway?

Alison shakes her head. "That's his go-to speech. It's how he hooks all the working students—and half the paying ones."

I feel myself blushing and I look away, inadvertently catching Malcolm's eye as he finishes his phone call. We look at each other for a long moment—or maybe it's just a second—and I feel the intensity of his gaze like a physical touch. My heart is suddenly thudding in my ears.

Then he blinks and looks away. "Get in here and eat, girls," he says brusquely. "We're on a tight schedule today."

"What else is new?" Alison grouses, and she leads me into the office.

Somehow, the next five hours pass in a daze, a whirlwind of tacking up horses, putting wet horses away, laundry and scrubbing bridles and sweeping endless acres of stable aisle. The Chandlers come and see their horse go, although I'm kept in the tack room where I can't destroy too much while they're on the property, taking apart bridles and scrubbing bits. They leave and Malcolm rides two more, then gives Alison a riding lesson, while I tack and untack and bathe, removing coolers from the dry horses, throwing the damp laundry into the washing machine. I do not break anything, do not flood anything, do not lose any more horses.

Alison sets up the evening feed around five thirty and the three of us get the horses fed. Then, they're blanketed and turned out for the night. Even though the day has been cold, the weather forecast swears the temperature won't fall below forty overnight, Alison's threshold for keeping the thin-coated show horses inside.

"If we turn them out during the day, it makes getting them groomed and ridden that much more difficult," she explains, when I ask why they don't just flip the schedule to daytime turnout during the winter like most Florida farms. "We're always behind and there are always ten more things to get done. It's you, me, Malcolm, and Patti and Ed to clean the stalls and do some of the maintenance. We do everything for twenty-some horses, depending on how many are in training at any given moment. It's tough, believe me."

She says this around an armful of laundry, dumping a pile of hot and fragrant saddle pads, fresh from the dryer, on the tack room bench. I immediately start folding the saddle pads and stacking them on their shelves alongside the rows of gleaming saddles. It's past six o'clock, but I know from experience that folding the laundry is the last job of the evening.

"Who are Patti and Ed?" I ask after a moment's thought.

"Oh, right, you didn't meet them. They were already finished this morning when you got here, and they're not back yet. Patti and Ed do stalls. So they come late in the evening and clean the stalls, and then they come back in the morning and feed breakfast and bring the horses in. They're really cool; you'll like them. Patti's a teacher and Ed's on disability from some government job. He can handle power tools and stuff, but he isn't supposed to lift hay-bales or bags of shavings—don't ever let him do that, okay? Sometimes you have to physically take them out of his arms."

"Got it," I say, pleased to learn there won't be any stall-cleaning. Or feeding breakfast at six a.m. If I'm going to take a break from racehorses, I can actually enjoy sleeping in for a few months. Or however long this job lasts me.

"And your apartment," Alison says, cleaning out the lint trap, "is just upstairs. So I'll show you that after we finish."

"Oh, I can't live here," I say, and suddenly I'm reminded of all the things that *haven't* been ironed out yet. Payment, hours, days off, contracts and releases and everything else that comes with working in the horse business. It's the first time I've ever started a job without extensive paperwork and conversations about compensation. I wonder if I've made a huge mistake, and just worked all day for free, in a job I won't be returning to tomorrow.

Tomorrow, when I'm supposed to be working at Posey's barn in my *real* job.

I bite back a groan.

Alison wouldn't have noticed, though. She's too busy shaking out polo wraps that have gotten knotted in the dryer. "You're going to have to live here at least part-time," she says, not looking up from her work. "I need you here to do night-check half the week. I'll take the other half, but I'm not driving back over here every night if we have a working student. That's your job."

"My horse, though—I have a little farm about fifteen minutes away. I have a cat and a horse. I can't just leave them there half the week while I stay here."

"They can move here," Alison says, shrugging. "Remember, Bucky is on a paid training contract...so you technically still get a stall as part of your job. And the apartment is really nice. You'll like it. Just wait and see before you make any decisions, okay?"

Yeah, that would have been smart, I think wryly. If I'd just waited before I'd made any decisions.

Before I can say anything else, Malcolm pokes his head into the tack room. "Alison, mind if I steal your working student?"

"She's all yours," Alison sings, waving me away.

"I thought I was *your* working student," I joke weakly as I follow Malcolm into the stable aisle. His presence feels larger than before; maybe I'm just exhausted from spending the day running back and forth between the stalls and the wash-racks, and from keeping my mouth shut and my face clean while the clients were here to see their horse go, but I feel overwhelmed by him.

"You are," he agrees, "but you'll do most of your work for Alison. She's my right hand. She makes this place work."

I feel a sudden stab of jealousy somewhere in my gut, and think wonderingly, *Well, that doesn't go here.*

Malcolm's walking ahead of me, turning a corner at the far end of the stable aisle. Suddenly we're outside, the dark night sky studded with stars. These early sunsets of winter are depressing in terms of finishing up barn work well after dark, but the trade-off tends to be stunningly clear skies at night. In summer, this view is usually choked with the remnants of afternoon storm clouds.

He doesn't stop to look at the heavens, just races up a staircase built along the stable wall, and I follow, one hand on the bannister. By the time I catch up, he's already opened the door at the top and is disappearing inside. Lights flick on and the stars disappear, but I'm so dazzled by the apartment in front of me that I don't register the loss.

Tucked under the barn eaves like a Swiss cottage, the apartment is almost just one large room with a kitchen to the left and a sofa and table in the center. A half-wall to the right must hide a small bedroom, and there's a little bathroom directly ahead against the back wall.

Everything is paneled in honey-colored wood like the stalls downstairs, and the floor is tiled with beige ceramic squares. A fluffy green rug is waiting for bare feet in front of the deep, squashy-looking brown sofa, and there is another carpet flung on the tiles beneath the kitchen table, perfect for chilly mornings eating toast and drinking coffee before heading down to the stable for the day. I look at the curtains over the windows and imagine pulling them back to look at the horses in their paddocks, and suddenly I realize I'm already picturing myself living here. It's a hundred times more pleasant than my run-down mobile home.

"I can't," I say.

Malcolm is checking the water pressure in the kitchen sink. "Can't what?"

"I can't just move here. I haven't—we haven't talked out anything. I don't know if I can even afford to take this job."

Malcolm turns off the water and shakes off his hands before he turns around. He gestures to the table and I see a folder there, waiting for me. When did he bring that up? "So," he says, "let's sit down and talk. I've got all the paperwork and contracts right there. You can make up your mind and we'll take it from there. But, Evie," he adds, his eyes smoldering on mine like a saint with a message from Heaven, "believe me when I say you can't afford to *not* take this job."

Chapter Nine

"I WAS BEWITCHED into it," I tell Posey. "There's no other explanation."

"Hmm." Posey puts a glass of wine on the table in front of me. "Is that what the kids are calling it these days?"

We're sitting on Posey's very comfortable couch in Posey's very comfortable apartment above the broodmare barn at Malone-Salazar Farm. Her boyfriend, Adam Salazar, is in the bedroom watching a basketball game. Posey sent him in there the moment I arrived on her doorstep, having called ahead to tell her that my news couldn't wait and had to be given in person. I stopped at home to feed the animals, then raced right over and explained my sudden defection from the racehorse business.

Posey heard me out, then got up and poured the wine. That catches us up to right now, and the skeptical look she's giving me.

"I'm *really* sorry," I tell her for the sixth or seventh time. "I know it's awful, just saying I won't come to work tomorrow—"

"It's fine, honestly," she says, rubbing her forehead. "I mean, we'll have to send out the morning sets a little differently, but someone's always absent, so that's nothing new. And I can call the staffing company and get someone to do the weanling barn in the afternoon. Or ask one of the other riders. Dandy might do it. She's always asking for extra horses to ride, so clearly she needs the money.

Anyway, that part is fixable. You do you. I'm just really confused about everything *else*. You're really okay with being a working student? At your age?"

I'm a couple of years younger than Posey, so I guess it's okay for her to call me out as too old for this kind of thing. Working students are usually young, tender, and easily duped. That's how they end up working full-time for no benefits and hardly any pay. I know, because I've played that game before.

But they can also turn into professional riders, I remind myself, before I can second-guess the decision I came to about two hours ago, when I signed on the dotted line and indentured myself to Malcolm Horsham for the next six months. Just because my first two working student gigs ended without a major breakthrough doesn't mean this one will. After all, I've never worked for anyone like Malcolm before.

"I'm okay with it," I say. "I mean, the worst-case scenario is I come crawling back to you in six months, begging for my old job back, right? And I'd be a better rider, anyway."

"I'd give it to you," Posey assures me. "Obviously. I just don't want you to get abused by this guy. He's got a hell of a reputation, as you well know. I mean, you're the one who loves to bring home all the crazy gossip."

It's true. I fill my mouth with wine while I consider how to answer. I *have* always been the source of gossip in our friend group. I'm not a gossiper, I just like to know what's going on. And in Ocala, in the horse business, there is always a *lot* going on. What can I say, knowledge is power. Keeping my ear to the ground has helped Posey out in the past, whether it was figuring out if she should trust Adam Salazar when they were on the outs, or finding out a horse she particularly wanted for the breeding program was for sale before anyone else knew about it.

71

But here's one thing I don't want to reach any gossiping ears at the feed store: Malcolm Horsham has a hold on my imagination that goes beyond what I think he can do for me in the dressage ring or the cross-country course. That much became clear to me this afternoon. When he looks at me, I'm riveted by his gaze. When he speaks, I hang on his words. There is something about that man which fascinates me—and frightens me. So when I told Posey it was like some kind of witchcraft made me sign on as his employee, I really wasn't exaggerating.

But no one needs to know that part. Not yet, anyway. Not until I figure out what it's all about.

So I just smile at Posey and say thanks, I appreciate her support more than she'll ever know. And Posey rubs my shoulder affectionately and tells me not to mention it, of course she always has my back. And then Adam roars like a wounded bull about some BS call on the basketball game he's watching in the bedroom, and the moment is kinda over. But that's okay. It's almost nine o'clock, and we both have early mornings in the barns.

Posey at her barn, and me at my new one.

That's going to be weird.

My horse, Breezy, waits for me at the paddock gate every morning. He rumbles a hello deep in his chest and watches as I go into the little lean-to I call a barn to get his breakfast ready—usually in the darkness before dawn. This morning, the sun is already up and Breezy has a perturbed expression on his face.

"I know, I'm late," I call. "But won't it be nice if we can both sleep in for a few months?"

Breezy whinnies in reply, and his plaintive tone lets me know he does *not* think it is great. The earlier the better, that's how Breezy feels about his breakfast.

Breezy urges me on with frequent whinnies while I scoop out his breakfast grain and add the toppings of supplements and medications he needs to stay comfortable on his compromised foreleg. He's a good eater, but even he was suspicious of all the added powders when they first started going into his grain. Fortunately, he's gotten over it. I add a little apple juice to the mix just to make things more palatable, and walk through the misty morning to the bucket attached to a fence post in his paddock. Breezy never comes inside unless the weather is atrocious.

But today's going to be a pretty day, I think, listening as he digs into his grain with the eagerness of a lion at the kill. The mist is already lifting, giving way to a purple and pink sunrise in a clear sky. Venus hangs like a diamond above the western horizon, one last shimmer before she sinks below the earth for another day. Birds are rustling in the oaks and palms scattered around my little farm, making sleepy peeps as they think about finding some breakfast for themselves. Breezy always spills a little, which makes the fawn-colored mourning doves happy. They'll come pecking around his bucket later, after he's gone off to graze on the stubby winter grass.

In the distance, I can hear more horses whinnying, and some cattle bawling. A rooster crows from the farm down the road where they have birds of every description marching around the property—guinea fowl and peacocks and chickens so large they look like Muppets. Ocala is full of serious horse-breeders and old-school cattle farmers and eccentric rural converts, a big old melting pot of the sort of people who want a lot of land and not a lot of winter. Or maybe it's not a melting pot—we tend to stick to our own kind. I don't know anyone here who isn't in the horse business.

Speaking of which, I need to feed myself and get rolling. The late hour makes me feel like I have another day off, but of course it's just that the workday starts later—and ends later—at an eventing farm.

The kitty gets breakfast and a quick pat while I devour a slice of peanut-butter toast and tug on a pair of riding breeches. We didn't discuss work attire last night when we were hammering out the details of my job, but Alison was in breeches and I assume Malcolm wants a uniform look. I choose a more conservative pair this time, without the bright piping or contrasting knee patches. The purple definitely got me some looks from both Malcolm and Alison. "You can't complain about navy blue with plain stitching," I mutter, tugging on the riding pants.

It's funny, though. I have a drawer full of colorful riding breeches, and I find myself working for the first eventing trainer I've ever come across who doesn't like to splash bright colors across all their horses.

The one thing I don't have is anything in that cool sage-green color Malcolm was wearing yesterday, and I think that might be his signature color. Hopefully, if he wants me in lockstep at events, he'll give me a clothing allowance. Horse clothes are not cheap, and he's not paying me much for this gig. It might be a good wage if I didn't already have a mortgage to cover.

I take one more look around my bedroom as I tug a black sweater over my head. My house is a crumbling single-wide trailer from the 1980s; the bedroom is hardly big enough for a double bed and an old dresser to hold all those breeches and boot socks. It's a room that resists cleaning; no matter how tidy I get it, the drab old walls and gray carpet refuse to look nice. But it's still my room, and I'll miss it.

I cannot believe I agreed to move over to Malcolm's place for the duration of the contract. Romeo isn't going to believe it, either. He comes into the bedroom and meows at me. It's a pretty obvious complaint: *Why are you still here?*

"I don't know, Romeo," I tell him. "I'm going to be late." And I stop dithering, wave goodbye to my cat and my horse, and head off to work at Malcolm Horsham's beautiful, perfect farm.

* * *

Alison is already in the office, furiously typing onto a small keyboard. At first, I can't figure out where the words are going; then I realize she has an iPad propped up against a stack of training books. She glances up at me, and I see her eyes rake up and down my outfit as if she was worried about what I'd show up in this morning. Her jaw relaxes. "You look nice," she says. "Our stable colors are sage and navy, so the blue breeches work."

"I'll have to work on the sage," I joke. "Maybe after that first big paycheck."

Alison snorts. "Sure. Let me know when *that* happens." She types a few more words, then pushes away the keyboard. "Okay, today's schedule is ready to go. What's your email?"

I hesitate long enough for her to explain, "I'm going to send you this schedule and that way, you have it in your pocket at all times. No running to the office to check what's next, get it?"

"Yeah, of course." At Posey and Adam's farm, we operate on the giant white-board system—get off a horse, check the white-board, find your next horse. But things here are slightly more twenty-first century. I rattle off my email and Alison clatters it into the keyboard.

"There," she says, looking satisfied. "You're on the distribution list."

Malcolm suddenly appears in the doorway, making me jump. He looks me up and down with the same appraising glance that Alison used, and then he nods, as well. "Looking good. Ready for day one?"

I *was* ready, until he came in. Now I just feel flushed, and nervous, and there are butterflies in my stomach which weren't there before. "Um, yeah," I stammer, hating my voice for coming out so thin and tremulous. "I'm all set," I continue, trying to pitch it a little deeper. I end up sounding like I'm imitating his deep voice, and his smile quirks.

Does he have a *dimple*? Oh, good god, this man was blessed with good looks.

Alison is immune to whatever he's sending out, though. She stands up and takes a gigantic sip from the coffee mug on the desk, her throat working like she's shotgunning a beer. "Okay," she announces when the coffee is gone. "Let's do this."

She leaves the office with a powerful stride, and I look after her in confusion. Am I supposed to know what happens next? Malcolm has pulled out his phone and is flicking through it casually. I watch him guardedly, hoping he'll realize I need directions. It's my first day, for heaven's sake.

Alison's voice powers down the stable aisle. "Evie! The *schedule!*"

Oh, right. Flustered, I pull out my phone and immediately drop it on the tile floor. It falls face down.

Malcolm stops scrolling through his phone and looks at my poor fallen soldier on the ground at our feet. "Uh-oh," he says.

"Oh my god, oh my god," I mutter, dropping to my knees. I pick up the phone and hear a *crack*. Sure enough, when I flip it over, a few shards of glass drop to the tile. The screen is so shattered, it's completely opaque. This is the deadest phone screen I've ever seen in my life.

"Yikes," Malcolm says. "Poor old phone."

Alison appears in the doorway as I look at my dead phone. "Oh my god," she says. "Are you kidding me?"

Frankly, I could do with a little more sympathy in my time of need. "This is a nightmare," I mutter, plucking at the little slivers of glass that have fallen on the floor. One of them cuts my finger and I can't help a little hiss of pain.

"Stop that," Malcolm commands, suddenly taking control of the situation. "I'll get the broom. Don't touch any more glass."

"You're going to have to get that fixed," Alison says while Malcolm opens a closet door and takes out a surprisingly clean broom—it must only see indoor use. "Unless you have another one for backup."

I probably have an ancient iPhone the size of a postage stamp somewhere in my closet at home, but that won't help me today. "I'll get it fixed tonight," I say, hoping I have the spare hundred dollars in checking. It would suck to dive into my paltry savings for something like a phone screen. "But for today, uh..."

Alison groans. "I'll print the schedule," she says, like I've just demanded she return to the Stone Age. "You can put it in your pocket. And then I need you to go get the first horse out! You're going to put us behind for the entire day."

As Alison leans over the desk, muttering to herself about butterfinger working students, Malcolm gives me a humorous glance. His green eyes catch the buttery office light and something inside of me seems to flutter and flip. *Nerves,* I think, *because this morning is starting off just super.*

"Don't worry about it," Malcolm says, like he heard my self-deprecating inner voice. "Everything is going to be just fine."

Next to him, Alison snorts.

Chapter Ten

MY PRIMARY ROLE in the barn seems to be tacking up horses and cooling them out. Alison busies herself in the tack room for the first hour of the day, dragging around tack trunks and pulling down expensive therapy equipment from storage containers stored on high shelves. Then she gets out a set of clippers and starts trimming fetlocks and bridle paths on each horse I bring into the cross-ties. I get the impression that she's catching up on work she missed while she was playing groom for Malcolm. I wonder how long they were without a working student, and why the last person quit.

That's always a question that demands an answer. I should try to make it to the feed store tonight before they close and see if anyone has the dirt on Malcolm's former employees.

I should have done that before I signed that contract, but of course, everything happened so fast.

By ten o'clock, Malcolm has ridden three horses and I'm absolutely starving. No wonder—this is a full hour past when we'd usually take a lunch break at the training barn. The Taco Lady would drive up the farm lane in her old van, open up the back hatch, and start selling whatever goodies she'd made the night before. I've gotten so used to a mid-morning taco or torta, I hardly know how I'm going to make it until lunchtime without one. I wonder if there are any snacks hidden away in the tack room or office. I'm trying to get up the courage to ask Alison when she looks at her phone, squeaks, and stares at me with wild eyes.

"Uh...is everything okay?"

Alison begins packing up the clippers in their plastic box. "No," she mutters. "Brady Nelson is coming to try a horse. He *never* makes appointments. He just texts and says when he'll be over."

"Brady *Nelson* Brady Nelson?" I repeat, halfway between aghast and amazed. Brady Nelson is a two-time Olympian, has finished in the top five at Badminton *and* Burghley, won Pau last year, and is currently favored to win Kentucky Three-Day Event in May. That is, if he bothers sticking around the U.S. this spring, and doesn't just go back to Europe to compete.

"Yes, the only one," Alison replies impatiently. "He wants to buy Oceanus. He's been threatening to come ride him for two weeks, but we can never pin him down."

"Oceanus? But isn't he one of Malcolm's best horses?"

Alison gives me a pitying look. "Yes, but Lillian's number one motto is, *everything has a price.*"

Lillian...where have I heard that name lately? I turn back to the horse I've been grooming as Alison stalks off with the clipper box, trying to recall anyone named Lillian from my most recent feed store conversations. Nothing comes to mind. But I've definitely heard it.

"Weird," I mutter, and the horse, a leggy mare named Adventure, shifts to look at me. "Not you, baby. You're just fine."

Malcolm comes into the barn as I finish bridling Adventure, looking around for someone to take the reins of Diamond. The horse I rode yesterday in my lesson looks done in after his work with Malcolm; he probably needed extra schooling after I made such a mess of things on his back. I slip Adventure's halter back over her bridle, cross-tie her, and run to scoop up Diamond's reins. Just as I take them, my stomach lets out a long, incriminating rumble.

"Good grief, Diamond," Malcolm says, and then he realizes whose stomach made the racket. A smile stretches across his face. "Oh dear, did we miss breakfast?" he teases.

"We missed lunch," I reply, and he's about to ask me what I'm talking about when Alison comes up the stable aisle with Oceanus haltered and looking bewildered—probably because he was Malcolm's first ride this morning.

"Brady's coming," she says, turning Oceanus into the second grooming stall.

"Oh, *shit*," Malcolm mutters, his expression darkening. "Right now?"

"Yes, he finally texted. He's on his way." Alison's voice is muffled as she cross-ties Oceanus. The horse sighs extravagantly. "Consider it a show day, Ocean," Alison tells him. "You're just going out for your second round."

"That man is a—"

"Careful," Alison warns. "Do you really want to say all that in front of the new girl?"

Malcolm gives me a once-over, like he just noticed I'm in his space. "Isn't she a racetracker?" he asks whimsically. "I think she knows more curses than I do."

"Still," Alison insists. "I thought you were going to watch your step with this one."

My cheeks are burning. "You can say whatever you need to," I venture, but Malcolm's already moving on.

"We'll have to take him outside," Malcolm grumbles. "He'll want to jump. Poor fella. I'm sorry, Oceanus."

"The arena's dragged, but the fences need set." Alison looks at me. "Go adjust everything on the outside course to three-foot-three," she commands. "Malcolm will tie up Diamond and I'll get him untacked in a few minutes."

I look at the reins in my hand, but Malcolm is already taking them back. "Hurry, now," he says, any trace of amusement gone from his voice. "Then hustle back in here and hack Adventure. Twenty minutes, long rein, walk and trot only."

I glance back at the mare, haltered and patiently waiting for someone to ride her. I didn't expect that someone to be me, not so soon into this apprenticeship. But Malcolm is already moving on with his morning, turning Diamond into the wash-rack to get him untacked. I take off down the aisle, anxious to get the course set.

I turn left at the archway in the center of the stable aisle and head out to the arenas. They're both blinding white in the mid-morning sunlight, their footing a blend of sand and something fibrous I can't identify, probably recycled fabric. The dressage arena is first, and then the jumping arena awaits, circled with a white PVC railing like what I'm used to seeing encircling a training track. I cut across the perfect grooves of the dressage arena's groomed footing and duck under the railing.

The fences out here are bright and colorful, the opposite of the smooth, traditional honey and walnut colors of the stable interior. Several fences are sponsored by local businesses, including an equine insurance company and a local feed store. There's a jump of planks painted with tropical fish swimming in a coral reef, and a jump set up to look like two orange trees with brown poles between them.

Jumper fences can be downright silly, especially when a horse is unlikely to realize the splotches of contrasting colors in front of him are actually angelfish. But they make up for their cartoonish appearance with sheer height and breadth. The big-time Grand Prix jumpers are almost casual-looking as they approach jumps larger and wider than the average pickup truck. In eventing, the show-jumping phase—still called "stadium jumping" by traditionalists and those who like to be professionally correct in all things—has much lower fences, even at Advanced Level, than the upper echelons of straight show jumping. But they can still look pretty imposing, especially when you've been an exercise rider galloping on the flat for a while, like me.

Three-foot-three isn't *that* high a fence, though. I do a quick count of the unmarked holes on each jump standard, wishing I hadn't killed my phone. The measurement app would have come in handy right about now.

I'm only guessing when I decide the holes start at eighteen inches and increase by three inches after that. And it's possible I miscount some of the jumps on my way up to the three-three holes. But by the end of my course reset, all the fences *look* like they're the same height. I dust off my hands and hustle back into the stable, waving hello to Bucky as I scamper past his stall. Once again, the horse is too busy eating hay to look up at me.

"Oh, thank goodness," Alison snaps as I race up to the grooming stalls. "Take Adventure and go." She's wiping Oceanus's nose with a tissue dipped in baby oil, giving a high sheen to the black skin around his mouth and nostrils. Malcolm is rubbing a spot off his breeches with a baby wipe. Both of them look impossibly fastidious.

For a moment I think of life with racehorses, where looks aren't as important as turn of foot and conditioning. I've seen horses go off to the races with a cursory grooming and their manes cut unevenly, the shavings plucked out of their tails but not much else out of the ordinary. Adam has told me that some trainers refuse to do anything special on race-days out of a worry they'll upset their horse's delicate little brains...even brushing out a tail or polishing hooves could be the game-changer in a race of inches.

But horses going into the show-ring, even in a discipline as famously rough-and-ready as eventing, don't warrant the same worries at all.

Malcolm sighs at the spot on his breeches and gives up scrubbing. His eyes rove around the stable before fixing on me. They're hard and bright, and suddenly I realize this is the Malcolm everyone talks about. The tough, scary one who makes working students cry.

"Are those fences set?" he barks at me.

I stiffen. I'm not a girl who cries easily, and I don't appreciate being shouted at on the job. "They're set," I say evenly. "Is that jelly on your breeches?"

Malcolm narrows his eyes at me. His mouth opens, but before he can snap back, Alison is on his case. "Oceanus is ready. Get him out there and warmed up. Brady will be here any minute. And come right back to me! I'll wipe off your boots after you mount."

Malcolm takes Oceanus's reins, but he nods at me. "She'll wipe my boots," he says to Alison. "You go wait for Brady. You can walk him in slowly and give me a few extra minutes alone."

Alison nods and tosses me a polishing cloth. Then she turns and strides off down the aisle, her blonde ponytail wagging behind her.

I look back at Malcolm, but he's already leading Oceanus to the arena, his shoulders high and stiff.

He doesn't want to sell him, I think. *So why the race for perfection?*

If I didn't want to sell a horse, I wouldn't turn him out perfectly, I wouldn't worry about having him warmed up before the buyer arrived, and I certainly wouldn't fuss about a jelly spot on my breeches or dust on my boots.

Whoever Lillian is, she must have a serious hold on Malcolm's finances. Is he being bankrolled by someone in the shadows? I'd always believed Malcolm Horsham got his start with family money and ran this farm on excessively high training fees and pricey sales horses. But now I have to wonder if there's someone in the mix that even I don't know about.

And believe me, if I haven't heard it from Sallyann down at the feed store, *no one* has heard about it.

"Evie!" Malcolm shouts, and I scamper after him, boot cloth at the ready.

He's already in the saddle by the time I reach the arena, flicking Oceanus's short mane into place with irritated little gestures. Cloth in hand, I start to knock off the dust on his black dress boots. It's odd to stand at eye-level with his knees and touch his legs through the soft leather. They're custom boots, fitting his calves and feet with silken precision, while settled into soft folds around his ankles. I spot a smudge on the toe-cap and take hold of his ankle to hold his foot still while I scrub at it.

There's something shockingly intimate about the feel of his ankle in my hand. I pause for a moment, the cloth hovering over the smudge, and try to let the sudden tremor taking over my fingers work itself out.

"We don't have all day," Malcolm growls from above me.

"Sorry," I mutter, pushing through the strange sensation, and I buff the boot clean.

I've just slipped around to do the right boot when Oceanus lifts his head, ears pricked. A truck is arriving out front. I glance up and see Malcolm working his jaw. He looks furious, and I can see his temper translating itself into Oceanus's muscles and attitude. The horse shifts and flicks his tail, ears tipping back and forth while he feels out the change in his rider.

He's looking for a reason to escape, and I wonder if Malcolm knows what he's doing. "You're making Oceanus tense," I blurt, and then I take a step back as Malcolm turns furious eyes on me.

"Did I ask you for your opinion?" he demands, his voice dangerously soft.

"No...*sir*," I add, something in his face tipping me off that right now is the right time to add a little honorific. "I'm just trying to help," I add, unable to stop myself.

"Well, don't," Malcolm snaps, picking up the reins and nudging his horse forward. "Go and get on Adventure. She's your problem, not me."

But I have to wonder if that's true. Adventure waits in the cross-ties, her nostrils fluttering in a silent greeting as I approach to rescue her from boredom. "You're no problem," I whisper to her, running a hand down her neck. She nudges at me with her muzzle, a big softie with anxious, doe-soft eyes. *"He's* my problem."

Chapter Eleven

WHEN WE HEAR the clank of poles bouncing in their cups and falling to the ground, both Adventure and I tense at the same time. I guess we both know what that sound means. I pick up the reins a little in case she bolts forward; our view of the jumping arena is obscured by the side of the barn and an oak tree next to the covered arena, but she's definitely aware of the impromptu one-horse-show going on over there. Oceanus's hooves have been hammering over the ground for the past twenty minutes, and occasionally I hear the horse snort loudly to clear his nasal passage. The day is chilly again, and I suppose the cold air probably stings his nose as much as it does mine.

Adventure, on the other hand, has been trotting around with her nose near the ground for most of our allotted hack time. She's an awfully nice mare. I keep waiting for her to show me some attitude, but she seems to think that as long as I keep my hands and my heels to myself, I'm not worth arguing with.

The hack is a nice chance for me to practice riding in a dressage saddle. After yesterday's messy ride on Diamond, I know I have a lot of work to do before I am sitting properly with my shoulders back and my spine straight. Any opportunity to just bop around the arena with a horse who doesn't want or need much guidance is an opportunity for me to focus solely on myself, and in my world of youngsters and novice rides, that's a rare treat.

Clunk! Another rail hits the ground, and Adventure's head is up now. Relaxation time is officially over. I gather up the reins, trying to be discreet about it so she doesn't decide that if *I'm* panicking, *she* should panic.

All the same, I bring her down to a walk. It's been twenty minutes, after all. Time is up.

"Good girl," I croon, walking her down the long side of the arena and away from the sound of a good horse botching a jumping effort. "What a nice baby..."

She plays up a little as another rail comes down with a heavy thud. Playing it safe, I dismount a few strides short of the arena entrance and hand-walk the rest of the way to the stable aisle.

It's not that I can't ride a silly horse. It's that I don't want to get a single hair out of line with Malcolm, and he told me to walk and trot on a loose rein for twenty minutes. Not get into an argument with a spooky mare and bounce around the covered arena for another five minutes after that.

I'm unsaddling the mare and looking for another carrot to reward her with when I hear hoofbeats and voices coming down the aisle. Adventure stands up straight and cranes her neck to see down the aisle. "It's just Oceanus," I say, and then pause with my hands still on the saddle. There is a tense discussion going on down there. A stranger's voice says, "I understand the fences were crooked, but I don't believe he should have touched *any* of them."

The fences were crooked?

My heart stops beating.

Adventure takes a step forward, testing the space she's granted by the cross-ties, and her hind hoof clips the toe of my paddock boot. I snap it backwards without a sound, desperate to hear what Malcolm says back.

His voice is a husky growl. "If you give us a few days' warning, we can have him sharp and ready to jump. He just had a jumping school two days ago, and dressage yesterday and this morning. You're asking for perfection from a living creature who is probably tired."

Three cheers for Malcolm! Standing up for his horse!

I lift Adventure's saddle from her back and settle it onto a folding rack in the corner of the grooming stall, just as Alison appears, gripping the reins of a very sweaty Oceanus.

Our gazes meet and she gives me a narrow-eyed glare that actually makes me take a step backward. My foot finds a coil of hose and I stumble backwards, falling onto the saddle rack. It collapses with a clatter, dropping the saddle onto the ground, and Adventure throws up her head, squeals, then darts forward to get away from me.

The cross-ties *break*.

I watch the black cross-ties fling upwards in the air like the entire scene is in slow-motion—the flying straps, the lurching horse, the alarmed faces on two of the most powerful men in three-day eventing as a giant mare comes lurching out of the grooming stall towards them like they've accidentally wandered in front of a starting gate at the races.

Malcolm goes one way, his hand connecting with Oceanus's tail, but fortunately Oceanus is too busy skedaddling forward to escape Miss Marauding Adventure to bother kicking out at the man grabbing his hind end.

The tall string-bean fellow that must be Brady Nelson goes the other way, skidding into the grooming stall just before Adventure's shoulder would have taken him out. Then she's off down the stable aisle, neighing frantically, while I'm stumbling to my feet, wondering how this could possibly be happening to me *again*.

I mean, yes, horses get loose at the training barn from time to time, but losing two in two days? This is a world record for clumsy horsemanship.

But there's no time to stop and consider how very bad I am at my job. I have to race down the aisle after Adventure before she ends up in that stupid fountain, like Bucky did yesterday.

Fortunately, the mare has a better head on her shoulders than my silly gelding. She stops at her open stall door, looks at it for a moment, then trots right in. By the time I reach her, she's already eating a mouthful of hay, gazing at me with wide, dark eyes that ask, *Are we through here?*

"Yes," I say, shutting the door. "We're done. No bath for you, miss."

She didn't get sweaty, anyway. It was just a hack.

Back at the grooming stalls, Malcolm and Brady have picked themselves up and dusted off their breeches, while Alison is untacking Oceanus for the second time today. He really does look tired this time, with his head drooping against the cross-ties and the hollows above his eyes looking deeper than usual.

Dehydrated, I think, wondering if they have any electrolyte paste in the fridge. Sometimes horses don't drink enough for two workouts in a day.

Alison gives me a look that is more glare than a welcome back, so I wander into the tack room and open the fridge. Amongst the bottles of water and various equine potions, I find a tube of electrolytes and bring it back to the cross-ties. Malcolm is rubbing his face while Brady continues to tell him all the ways in which Oceanus has come up short, but he nods at me when I hold up the syringe, and for the first time since we started work this morning, I get the impression I have done something right.

It's a nice feeling.

"Here you go, big guy," I tell Oceanus, slipping the syringe into the side of his mouth. It's a crapshoot, since I don't know how he takes medicines, but Oceanus is happy to slurp up the sweet electrolyte paste and actually licks his lips when it's all gone, giving me a careful eyeball in case I've got more up my sleeve.

I hold up my hands. "That's all!" It's a neat trick I taught Breezy, who is a real treat-hound. When I hold up my hands and tell him "That's all!" in a bright, cheerful voice, he knows I don't have anything else for him and goes about his business.

But Oceanus doesn't know what I mean, so he just lips at my fingers until I hide them behind my back. Then he turns his head as far as he can in the cross-ties and gives Alison a begging look.

She snorts and hands him a carrot.

"Dork," she tells him.

"Well, I have to get going," Brady announces.

"Oh, too bad," Malcolm says cheerfully.

It's so obviously chipper that we all turn and stare at him for a moment.

Then Brady laughs. "You're a jerk, Malcolm, and we all love you for it. Condition that horse and get his hind hooves up in the air, and I'll be back. We aren't done here."

"Oh, yes we are," Alison mutters as soon as Brady has walked away. "Because I am blocking your number, good sir. Lillian can get over trying to sell our horses."

Malcolm runs a hand through his hair. "I need you to do a lunch run," he says to her.

"We don't have time today," Alison complains, turning on the hose. She tests the heat of the water with her hand. "He threw everything off. We'll be here until seven if we stop now."

"Then we'll be here until seven and I'll get us pizza for dinner," Malcolm shoots back, as if he's weary of being talked back to today. "God, Alison, it's not as if any of us have anywhere *else* to be."

"You might not," Alison mutters darkly as Malcolm goes into the office. "But some of us *could,* if we ever got out of here on time."

"Do you want me to hose him?" I ask, feeling at loose ends with no horse in my hands.

"Yes," she says, handing over the hose. "And I want you to be more careful with jumps. Those heights were all over the place, and so were the back rails. Once he was tired, he pulled everything that was crooked."

"I'm really sorry," I gasp, aghast at myself. "I had no idea it would be such a trap for him."

"Don't worry about it," Alison says, pulling out her phone. "What do you want for lunch? I'm thinking subs."

We finish the last horse around six o'clock, earlier than Alison predicted, but still an hour later than she'd planned. Bucky was not on today's calendar, and I hover by his stall as Alison leads another horse out to turn-out for the night, blanketed against the chilly air. I don't know when Malcolm is planning on starting him, but it would be nice to groom the horse and get to know him. I've had Breezy since I was a kid, and I feel like we've been best friends most of my life. But Bucky is a stranger.

It's weird to look at him as I pass his stall and know he's going to be my new partner, but not know anything about him. Where are his ticklish spots? Where are the places he loves to have scratched? What are his favorite treats? What will he spit out, every time?

These personal quirks are just as important to know as anything we'll do together under saddle. They're the underpinnings of our relationship, the cornerstone of whatever competitive future we might have. They're questions I rarely get solid answers to when I'm riding racehorses, who come and go from the training barn with startling frequency, and who might be assigned to another rider every day depending on schedules. With Bucky, on the other hand, I could be on his back an hour or more every day for the next who knows how many years. We have to know each other inside and out.

Malcolm idles along the aisle, glancing into the stalls of horses who are still inside. He stops alongside me and looks over Bucky for a moment.

I want to ask him what the plan is, but I'm wary of him now. While he hasn't actually lost his temper with me yet, I still feel Malcolm's moods are as changeable as a Florida winter—first warm and sunny, then suddenly cold and brisk. And it's not always evident what turns him one way or the other.

It's going to make for a tough working relationship; I'm used to working for Posey, who, besides being one of my best friends, is as stable as they come.

One more thing, I think, that I should have considered before I took this job.

"I'm sorry we didn't get you on a horse besides Adventure today," Malcolm says, surprising me. "You should have gotten at least a short lesson. Tomorrow I'll make sure it's on the schedule. And I'll add Bucky, too."

I wonder how we're going to fit two more rides into the day, but I don't bring it up. No use looking for trouble now, when everyone's exhausted.

"I'll have you getting on at least three a day by the end of the week," Malcolm continues, poking Bucky's inquiring nose through the stall bars. "Students are arriving for the winter circuit. We'll be filling those end stalls with their horses and I'll be teaching in the afternoons. You and Alison will be riding everyone I can't get to."

"Oh," I say blankly. I'd had no idea. I thought every day would be like today: grooming, running, panicking. But no, there will be more people here, adding their own chaos. "Great," I add, in case he thinks I don't want to ride. "I'm used to getting on six or seven a day, anyway."

Malcolm's grin flashes. "I'll bet you are, racetrack girl. But remember, we sit up *straight* here. Alison!" he snaps, as she tries to pass us.

She turns, annoyed. "What?"

"What do you want on your pizza?"

"You haven't *ordered* yet?"

I let them bicker about pizza toppings and timing while I give myself a few minutes to worry about Breezy and Romeo, waiting for me at home. I'm planning on moving them over here next Monday, on my day off. But until then, they're going to have to get through some long days without me, and dinner *much* later than what they're used to. Poor guys. This job is really causing upheaval for all of us, and it's only just getting started.

Bucky nickers at me suddenly, and my heart lifts. "Hey, buddy," I whisper. "Can we be friends?"

He kicks at the door in response, and I realize it's all a ruse to get me back to work. "Got it," I say, opening the stall door and picking up the matched leather halter that Alison provided, the one which comes with the farm and probably stays here when and if we leave in six months. "One turnout, coming right up."

At the end of the day, all horses really want is to go outside and eat some grass. I'm happy to provide them with their heart's desire.

Chapter Twelve

THE MORNING IS fresh and clear, and I think today is going more smoothly than yesterday.

For one thing, there is some actual warmth in the sunlight, and Malcolm is jumping several horses in the outdoor arena. Alison gets him started, then tacks up her own horse. She hands me the schedule —since we stayed so late last night, there was no time to get my phone screen fixed. After lunch, Bucky's name is next to Malcolm's... and my name is next to Diamond's.

I can't help a little grimace. Alison catches it.

"Problem?" she asks, in a cool voice which tells me she really doesn't care.

"No," I say, folding up the schedule and shoving it into a pocket. I'm wearing tan breeches today, which will show every smudge of dirt and green hay slobber the horses choose to bestow on me, but at least they're comfortable for riding. I just wish I could ride Bucky.

Silly, I know. I set up tack for the second horse of the morning at the grooming stall, already moving a little mechanically after having done this work for nearly twelve hours yesterday. My mind has plenty of time to brood on the idea of Malcolm and Bucky, best friends forever. It's silly, I tell myself, again and again. Bucky is only here—*you're* only here—because Malcolm is putting the first six months of polish on what little the horse already knows. He's the trainer. You're the student. Get used to it.

But, my mind cries, as I take down Adventure's bridle from its hook in the tack room, *but I want to ride Bucky.*

Well, of course I do. I haven't had my own horse to ride in months. I had options, of course. I could have found a racetrack reject to retrain as a jumper or an event horse.

I just didn't feel like it. I always ride green horses. Working as a gallop girl, I get up in the morning and go to work riding six or seven young Thoroughbreds before lunch.

I hadn't been eager to bring my work home, so to speak, by starting yet another project horse. I'd appreciated Breezy's foundation of knowledge. We worked on advanced movements together, not the basics. It made riding Breezy a treat, not a job.

Now, Bucky is no project horse. He already has a show record. He already knows what he's doing out there. And with the right training program, he could go all the way to the top. Higher than even Breezy could aspire to.

That's not the kind of horse I usually get to ride.

So yeah, I'm a little impatient—and a lot jealous of the man who gets to ride him before me.

As I tack up Adventure for Malcolm, Alison sets up in the neighboring grooming stall with an iron-gray horse I don't remember from yesterday. His halter-plate reads *Heavensent*. Always a dangerous name for a horse, I think wryly. I rode a Heavensent at Posey's last year that had a reputation for bucking off every exercise rider that climbed on her back. And I was no exception. That filly left me spitting out sand for the rest of the morning.

This Heavensent seems more cool, though, snoozing against the cross-ties while Alison gives him a quick grooming. His coat is very dark, which marks him as fairly young, so I'd expect a little more playfulness in the grooming stall, but he's definitely sleepy. In fact, his eyes actually flutter closed while Alison is knocking off the dust with a horsehair finishing brush.

She sees me watching and grins. "Like him?"

"He looks nice," I say. "Quiet."

"He's a sleepy boy," Alison says, so affectionately that I have to ask, "Is he yours?"

"Yup." Alison runs a hand along his dappled neck, her pride in the horse evident. "Bought him back in November from his breeder. He's only four in March. We're aiming for the young horse championships next year."

I have a million questions, all of them inappropriate and one of them actually starting with "How much did you pay for him?", but luckily Malcolm comes in before I can show my mercenary side, handing me his horse's reins with barely a nod before he's taking the cross-ties off Adventure and slipping the mare's halter from over her bridle. He turns around and stalks away, Adventure clip-clopping after him.

I glance at Alison. "Is he—uh—tense today?"

Alison shrugs. "His normal self, I think. Oh, did you think he was extra-chipper yesterday? Yeah, that's his first-day attitude. He was being nice to you because you just started. But he can only hang onto that kind of front for about ten hours. Be prepared to be ignored and/or shouted out today." And with that exciting piece of advice, Alison puts on her helmet, ready to take her horse out.

Forgotten, I go back to work. Malcolm brought back Artsy in a sweaty state, and this horse is dying for a warm shower and a cool bucket of water. "I got you, buddy," I tell him, pulling the bridle from over his ears. "Bath-time, okay?"

And so the morning passes. It's a little lonely, working on my own, with just passing comments from Alison and little more than snorts from Malcolm, who seems determined to ride every horse he can without pausing. We stop for lunch at twelve thirty, and I'm so hungry that I practically fall on the sandwiches Alison brings back from the nearby gas station/deli.

Malcolm eats in a deep, dark silence, with his brows scrunched into a frown. His mood permeates the room. Alison chews quietly, her eyes on her phone. After the first few voracious bites, I feel my appetite leaving me. The atmosphere is just too thick and silent for me. I can't help but remember the good times at the training barn, the way we tease and mess with each other all morning long. I'm usually just as tired from how hard we laugh and go at one another as I am from the work of riding itself. It made the afternoons alone in the weanling barn feel like a welcome break to work in silence.

But all day quiet?

This sucks.

Suddenly, Malcolm puts down his sandwich and looks at me. I feel like two lasers are pointed at my face. "You need a lesson this afternoon," he says, as if it has just occurred to him.

"Uh, yeah," I agree. "It's on the schedule for two o'clock."

He glances at Alison, and she nods slightly. Her eyes never leave her phone. It's like they have a telepathic connection, or maybe she's just used to semi-ignoring him and can manage his moods in her sleep.

I wonder how long they've worked together.

A slow, leisurely feeling of jealousy unfurls itself from my stomach and takes a wander up my throat.

Defiant, I take a bite of my sandwich and force it down, smothering that ridiculous sensation of jealousy, and at the same time, denying that this new job is leaving me terribly lonely.

* * *

"Our heels are down, our eyes are up, our hands are still, our core is tight..." Malcolm's voice drones through the essentials of basic riding with a metronomic quality, somehow matching the steady footfalls of the horse below me. Diamond seems up for the challenge of dealing with my terrible riding for a second day; he didn't complain when I mounted up instead of Malcolm, anyway.

Alison gave me a quick spiel on the horse's back-story while I was grooming him—Diamond is what is known in the show-horse world as a "packer," meaning any amateur with a grain of common sense and the ability to sit a few silly moments from time to time can take him out and win a ribbon. His most recent gig was chauffeuring a high school student through the ups and downs of eventing through Preliminary, taking her to the American Eventing Championships last year. Then the girl got into college in London and the horse went through a few sets of new hands before he came back to Malcolm for a tune-up and a new sale. He has been back with Malcolm since October.

"Perfect school horse for you," Alison suggested casually, running her hands down his legs to check for any heat I might have missed. "He'll need some competition this spring before he goes back on the market. Maybe that can be your project."

I think of Bucky in his stall down the aisle. As nice as it is to be handed a packer who took third at last year's championships, I still don't want to be consigned to a school horse. I'm twenty-seven years old, for god's sake. I competed Breezy at Preliminary. I'm ready for so much more.

Malcolm apparently doesn't agree. He's still drilling me on the basics as he asks me to pick up the reins and get a nice working trot out of Diamond. "And I don't mean a collected trot, so don't go scooting his nose in towards his chest and pretending you've got a horse on the bit. I want his head in front of the vertical, I want his hindquarters swinging, I want him to reach around the corners with his outside foreleg. Can you get all of that?"

Of course I can, I want to snort. *Easy.* But it has been a while since I rode in anything but an exercise saddle or on anything older than three years old, and Diamond is a grown-ass horse with his own opinions about the way his body should be handled. When I ask for movement with the same questions that I would have used on Breezy, Diamond either doesn't respond, or gives me a half-hearted reply. I shift my seat-bones as we go around the turn from long side to short side, and for a moment I catch sight of my face in the mirrors lining the lower half of the covered arena walls.

I look scared and struggling.

Malcolm sees it, too. He sees *everything.* "Your weight went all over the place in that corner! Drop your right seat bone into the horse. Give him something to balance with. He needs to know where you're blocking and where you're opening. And open your inside rein —but lift—not that much, no. Again. Cut across the middle and change direction. Shift your seatbone—too much—keep him going, now!"

It batters me like hailstones, an endless barrage of commentary, and I can't decide what to follow and what to ignore. Because of course I can't listen to all of it. I realize in the silence of a walk on a loose rein that Malcolm is giving me a million directions to see which ones I'm actually capable of following. And the answer, I think, probably isn't very many. My muscles are in the wrong places, my balance is being carried in the wrong way. I'm an upside-down rider in a dressage saddle.

"Galloping has been hard on your position," Malcolm says, echoing what I've been thinking. We're walking in a circle around him now. I'm breathing hard, exhausted after twenty minutes of his taskmaster-teaching style. Diamond seems pretty chipper, most likely because he has just spent the same amount of time trotting with his nose in the air and his hindquarters all over the place, instead of tucking them underneath his body and actually working. "It's okay to gallop in addition to working on your flatwork every day —in fact, it's great, because it really builds strength and stamina, and that's two things that a lot of riders are lacking. But you haven't been doing that flatwork and it has really affected the way you sit a horse."

"I know," I say, "it's just that my horse has been lame and I haven't had anything else to ride."

"Well, now you do," Malcolm replies, not giving me any quarter. "I want you on three horses a day to start, with a lesson on Diamond every other day. It'll be good for him to remember how to carry weaker riders. He's had it good with me for too long."

I'm a little too lost in my own exhaustion to file a complaint about that statement, but it does hit home. I close my eyes for a moment. I'll store it up, a whole mental filing cabinet of Malcolm's understated insults, and bring it up for conversation at a later date.

When we know each other a little better.

"I'll have Alison fit your horses into the schedule every day," Malcolm continues, "but sometimes you'll have to ride after we're done for the day. It's just going to be so busy with the winter riders coming in."

"Sure," I say, not really paying attention. "Whatever works."

"Good. Cool him out and head inside. I need the arena in ten minutes for my three o'clock lesson."

Malcolm walks across the arena with his phone in his hand, reminding me that mine is still broken. I have to get that fixed tonight.

I sigh, knowing I'll feel this ride by the end of the workday. After at least two more hours of work, taking care of Breezy and Romeo, and heading into Ocala to find a repair shop, maybe I'll find the energy to take a hot, soothing bath. "Maybe if we're done by five thirty," I tell Diamond, who flicks his ears back to listen to me. "Say a little prayer to the eventing gods for me, okay?"

Chapter Thirteen

AT SEVEN O'CLOCK, I finally flag down Alison. She's rushing past with an armful of polo wraps, a fiercely held smile on her lips. It disappears as soon as I call her name.

"What?" she hisses. "If this is about finishing, we'll be done as soon as we can cool out the Brewer horse."

"He's just mounting," I point out, feeling desperate enough to complain. "He was supposed to be done an hour ago!"

The three o'clock lesson, a lithe forty-two-year-old named Abigail Henson, ran for nearly ninety minutes. The four o'clock started promptly at four-thirty, but Virgil Meade liked lengthy explanations of everything Malcolm asked him to do and Malcolm went along with it, albeit with a sardonic smile on his face as he lectured the middle-aged man on the mechanics of flying lead changes.

And that meant the five o'clock lesson didn't begin until five forty-five, when a teenager with Olympic dreams and a Wall Street daddy to finance them showed up to ride her dangerous and beautiful Thoroughbred Archer's Bow at ninety miles an hour around Malcolm, while Malcolm made ignored comments about her seat and hands until he finally made her pull up, get on the longe line, and trot for another half hour with no stirrups and no reins.

And now it is seven o'clock and the final lesson of the day, a last-minute add-on who would have pushed our ending time from five-thirty to six-thirty *if* things had gone on target, is waiting for Alison to bring her a fresh set of polo wraps from her trailer.

She scuttles down the aisle to present the waiting student with the polo wraps while I look desperately up and down the stable aisle, wishing some good fairy would pop out of the shadows and rescue me from this hell. Alison had informed me before lessons began that Malcolm's number-one rule with paying clients was *Be Accommodating,* and she recommended that I follow that rule to the letter if I wanted to last around here.

"Good students like to take care of the staff," she explained. "In a decent winter circuit, you might get surprise dinners, the occasional bottle of wine, a tip for taking care of their horse after a lesson or at an event..."

"What about bad students?" I'd asked.

Alison shrugged. "Then we just do our jobs to make Malcolm look good," she said. "That's our main job, right? To keep Malcolm looking good. Remember that, too."

All fine and dandy, kissing ass and making the boss look good, but now I've been here twelve hours, all chance of getting my phone fixed is now lost, and I still have a hungry horse and cat waiting for me at home.

It's hard not to think longingly of my job at Malone-Salazar Farm, and wonder who fed the little horses at four o'clock and got home fifteen minutes later in my place. Lucky bastard, they don't even know how good they have it. You don't know what you've got till it's gone.

The teenager turns her horse out of the wash-rack just as the last student of the night leads her horse towards the arena. I hear Malcolm calling her out, his voice cheerful but hoarse, and suddenly I wonder how *he's* dealing with this forced extension of a workday.

After all, he rode six horses today before teaching five riding lessons. He must be wiped out.

I'm still feeling just the slightest bit bad for my boss when the teenager, a shrill-voiced girl named—somewhat improbably—Wesley, thrusts her horse's lead-rope into my hands. I blink at her, not sure how she got up the aisle to me, and then I wonder if I actually fell asleep on my feet for a few seconds.

"Walk him, okay?" Wesley says, pulling out her phone. "Like, ten minutes. No grass."

And she wanders back down the aisle, where her tack has been flung on the floor. Alison is eyeing the piles of equipment. Trying to decide if she should cart it back to the girl's trailer herself or simply put it up on the saddle rack, I think.

The horse nudges me with his wet nose. He's a pretty boy, and his dangerous temperament seems to have been worked out of him with that longe line session, but I still don't trust him. I saw him snap his teeth at Alison while Wesley was tacking up, and he waved his hind legs around warningly anytime she got too close to his hindquarters. I'm not sure the girl even picked out his hooves.

"Hopefully you have a nice groom at home," I tell Archer, walking him through the archway. "Someone who handles all that boring stuff like keeping your hooves from rotting off."

We wander out of the stable and into the cool night—cutting a wide berth around the tinkling fountain. It's pretty after sunset, the lights beneath the water casting dancing reflections on the barn, but Archer snorts at the charming patterns and tries to drag me into the grass lawn in front of the stable.

"Your mother said no grass," I remind him. He tugs longingly on the lead-rope, but I keep him moving, walking him along the equine pavers laid in front of the stable. Out in the paddocks, the shapes of our horses move through the shadows, enjoying their turnout. No blankets tonight; the weather has turned mild again. I think everyone is happy to be naked after three nights of nylon and straps. I'm certainly glad to be out of a coat.

Beside me, Archer shakes a few times, as if there are flies on him, and I run a hand along his shorn coat to soothe him. He was clearly just clipped a few days ago; the hairs are still short and stiff. "You must feel so weird still," I say. "I hope you got a nice conditioning bath afterwards, to keep your skin from getting itchy."

As if in reply, the horse rubs his head hard along my arm and shoulder—so hard I stumble to one side. He spooks, dancing to the end of the lead-rope. But I brace my weight against him and gather my feet beneath me, thinking suspiciously that the whole move was orchestrated. Some horses are devilish like that. He definitely fits the naughty bill in a number of ways. "Nice try, smart-ass," I say witheringly.

"Calling my horse names?" Wesley appears in the archway, noticeably unburdened with all the tack she still needs to get back to her trailer. "Seems kind of rude, I don't know."

Is this kid for real? "No," I lie blandly. "I was talking to my phone. Some jerk was trying to get me to answer his junk call."

Wesley shrugs. "Whatever. He *is* a smart-ass. And a jackass, too."

"Well, he's a nice mover," I say, feeling a weird need to defend her horse, who seems to be all of these things.

"Oh, he can move," Wesley says darkly. "And if he keeps giving me attitude, he's going to move straight to the meat market."

"Hey, don't kid about that."

Another shrug. Teenagers have no idea what the horse world is really like, the levels of cruelty people are capable of, so they make stupid jokes and get annoyed when adults who have been out there in the trenches try to make them stop. But—in Wesley's words, *whatever*. She's a once-a-week-student for Malcolm, hardly a problem

I need to waste any time on. "You want your horse back?" I ask, holding out the lead-rope.

But Wesley's back on her phone. "Nah," she says, turning to leave. "You hang on to him. I'll get my driver to bring the trailer around in fifteen."

And I'm left there with her horse, while she wanders back into the barn, tapping away at her phone.

I look at the horse. He is still gazing longingly at the grass. "You know what?" I tell him. "Fine. Eat up."

After a while, my resentment begins to fall away. The horse seems happy. Wesley isn't bothering me. Malcolm and Alison aren't on top of me to work harder, faster, more. The sound of a horse grazing has a lot of soothing uses; one of them is making a person feel better about the sheer amount of time and energy horses take. Everything feels a little better after you've listened to a horse graze for five minutes.

We're both so at peace that I hardly notice when Malcolm appears in the archway. The horse startles, and I jump a little to keep up with him. "What are you doing out here?" Malcolm demands. "We need that horse wrapped and loaded for the trip home. Or did you want to stay here all night?"

The harshness of his tone wipes away all the progress I've made listening to this horse seek out the best blades of grass for the past ten minutes. I lift my head to snarl at him in return. "Yes, Malcolm, that's what I want. To stay here even *longer.* While my horse and cat sit at home wondering where the hell I am. Thank you for recognizing that."

Even in the half-light spilling from the stable aisle, I can see a muscle in Malcolm's jaw twitch.

He's furious, I think, wondering if my career as an eventing working student has stuttered to a sudden end. The idea is surprisingly unpleasant. As unhappy as I am with this day, apparently I'm not ready to give up this chance. Not yet.

"Just get him inside," Malcolm growls at once, turning on his heel. As he spins to leave, his boot catches on a loose patch of sod— probably left there by *my* horse running around like a banshee yesterday—and he skids a little. The sound brings Archer to attention, and he snorts loudly.

"It's fine," I say, offering him the last horse cookie in my pocket. He snorts and snuffles for more, so I hold up my hands in the "all done" gesture that Breezy knows so well.

Wesley's horse does *not* know the sign language for "all done." He sees my hands go wide, pins his ears, and *snaps.*

"It's still bleeding," I mew, feeling faint and hating myself for it.

"Press harder," Malcolm says, turning on the truck. "Push down with everything you've got. I promise it'll stop bleeding."

"I can't." I know I'm crying, and some part of me, far away and slowly slipping away, is deeply embarrassed. But a much larger part of me, right here on the surface, is simply shocked and in pain. My thumb is throbbing where Wesley's horse caught it with his teeth, and there is blood seeping all over my beige breeches, working its way through the cotton sheeting that Alison wrapped my hand in while Malcolm shouted for everyone to *just calm down.*

The pain makes me woozy, and the way Malcolm is taking these country roads is not helping. I'm not sure how he ended up driving me to the hospital—seems like the job should have fallen to Alison, while he hustled Wesley and the other students out of the stable, but it was his hands on my back, shepherding me to the truck, and it was his voice murmuring in my ear encouragingly, "Just keep walking, that's it, sit here, I'm going to fasten the seatbelt, okay, closing the door now. You're fine, you're fine, you're fine."

Now he's speaking again, but I can't focus on the words, so I just listen to his voice. When he pitches it low like this, the husky growl that sounds so demanding when he's in a bad mood becomes a throaty whisper that has quite the opposite effect. I feel like I'm being sung to sleep by a previously dangerous wild bear. A bear who has taken me into his den, wrapped me in a nice bear quilt, and is going to protect me from other predators all night long.

The truck screeches to a halt and my eyes snap open. Was I asleep? Something about a bear...

"In we go," Malcolm says, flinging my door wide. He reaches across my lap to unbuckle my seat belt, his fingers fumbling alongside my thigh. A little flood of heat follows his touch, and I bite back a gasp. Suddenly, I'm wide awake again.

And my thumb is still throbbing, throbbing, throbbing.

"Oh, your poor breeches," Malcolm clucks, helping me stand up and slide down from the truck cab. "I owe you a pair, sweetheart."

He takes my bitten hand and holds it upright, his fingers pressing down on the cotton sheeting, and starts shuffling me towards the doors of Emergency. There is cold air blowing in my face, and bright lights, and a room full of miserable people. But all I can think about, dumbly hearing it over and over, is Malcolm Horsham calling me *sweetheart*.

Chapter Fourteen

"ONLY YOU," POSEY says, putting a takeout container on my kitchen counter. "The only shock is that it was day two, not day one."

"At least I managed to wreck myself in the first forty-eight hours," I suggest, cradling my bandaged left hand from my reclining position on the couch. "And earned myself this awesome extra day off. Thank you for coming over and feeding the kids last night."

Romeo, purring against my stomach, mews a quiet agreement.

"It was no problem," Posey assures me. "Everyone was very happy to see me. Although it was so weird getting a text from Malcolm's phone."

"Yeah, my screen needs fixed. He looked up your number online."

"Great to know I'm so easy to find," Posey jokes. "What time did you get home?"

"Two o'clock," I sigh. Malcolm drove me home after sitting at the hospital for hours. He must have been exhausted. "I feel really dumb," I confess.

Posey is taking down bowls from the cabinet next to my angry old refrigerator. She glances over her shoulder at me and shakes her head. "I don't think you stuck your thumb in that horse's mouth and begged him to bite down, did you?"

"No, obviously. But—who gets *bit?*"

She shrugs. "I'm sure it happens."

"Do you know anyone who has been bitten by a horse? Like, badly enough to go to the hospital?"

"Well..."

"You see!"

"Oh, wait!" Posey is triumphant. "There was a girl I knew at Tampa Bay Downs when I was a kid who was bit on the shoulder and had to have stitches. She stood in front of a colt's stall even though he had a safety cone out front to show he was dangerous. Everyone kinda thought she deserved it, actually."

"Well, that only proves my point," I sigh. "She got bit because she was stupid."

Posey just laughs. She's dishing out rice and sweet-and-sour chicken into the bowls. Romeo gets a whiff of the meat and hops up to investigate, his little paws brushing against my bandaged hand as he climbs across me and onto the back of the sofa. "Ouch, buddy," I say through gritted teeth. "Watch out for a girl's chomped thumb, would ya?"

"Well, anyway," Posey says, closing up the takeout container before Romeo can stick his nose into it, "you got an extra day off and it's not that bad, and I bet you're not even nauseous anymore now that you're coming off those heavy-duty drugs they gave you."

"No, I'm starving," I admit, pulling myself to an upright position. "But jeez, whatever they gave me last night had me feeling like I had the flu on top of everything else." I'd been so nauseous I could barely speak when Malcolm got me home this morning, letting him position me on the sofa with a trashcan nearby with hardly a second thought. Now, the memory is just one more embarrassment. The only good thing to come out of this whole ordeal was that I didn't throw up.

But hey, that's worth something. It's no fun being sick when you live alone. I mean, not that being sick is a party when you have a roommate or a family. But it's certainly better when you have someone to take care of you...and clean up.

At least I have Posey, who is snapping her fingers at me. "Come eat," she commands.

"Please don't snap your fingers," I say feebly. "The idea of the tips of fingers right now..."

"Oh, sorry." Posey hides her hands behind her back. "Didn't occur to me. But—the tip is *there*, right?"

"Just barely." The doctor had whistled when she saw my thumb—one of those long, low whistles to show her appreciation for such a nasty wound. But once she'd numbed the area and cleaned up all the blood and ragged flesh, she'd found I wasn't actually *missing* any of my thumb. I'd assumed Wesley's black-hearted horse had chewed up the end and swallowed it, so it was nice to know my hand was intact.

"Good as new once we get the stitches out," the doctor had said cheerfully. "Well...the nail is going to look a little wacky for a while."

That was fine, I assured her weakly. I just wanted that thumb sewn back together and under a bandage where I didn't have to see it again. Behind me, I'd heard Malcolm clear his throat. I was sure he found the entire situation disgusting.

I join Posey at the little kitchen table and we start on our late lunch. It's kind of lucky Wesley's horse got my left thumb instead of my right one, because I'm the opposite of ambidextrous and if anything happened to my right hand, I'd probably be unable to care for myself until the bandages came off. But with only my left thumb wrapped up and immobile, I should be able to do most of my work at the farm as well as keep up with everything around here...although moving into the apartment on Monday is going to be extremely challenging.

"Are you still planning on moving on Monday?" Posey asks, as if she hears my thoughts.

"Yeah." I look around at my cramped little mobile home. There's not much in it, but I know I could still fill a decent number of boxes if I took everything. "I think I'll just take a suitcase and not worry about my stuff. I'll have to drop by every weekend and make sure the place doesn't fall apart, anyway, since I'll be back by summer."

"Is it weird, moving fifteen minutes away? I would find it bizarre to have all my things still here but be staying in another apartment."

"I guess I'll find out. But I think it might be a little like a vacation."

Posey giggles at that. "A *vacation* at Malcolm Horsham's place? You're joking, right? Once he has you upstairs, he is *never* going to leave you alone."

Suddenly, my heart-rate seems to ramp up. "Never leave me alone?" I repeat, staring at Posey. "What do you—"

"I mean, he's going to have you working at all hours," Posey snorts. "What did you think I meant?"

"Oh, nothing," I fumble, catching up and feeling deeply embarrassed. Why did I think she meant—something else? Of course Malcolm isn't going to use my proximity as an excuse for... well, for coming upstairs and getting, I don't know, romantic. I can't even think of the right words to use. That's how silly the idea of it is. "Painkillers are making my head fuzzy," I say. "Some things just aren't registering right away."

"Good thing he gave you the day off," Posey remarks. "Or there's no telling what you might have done at the barn today. Tacked up a horse backwards or turned someone out in the arena while he was riding."

"Yeah," I agree weakly, thinking of the day in full swing without me. What is my absence doing to Alison's careful schedule? Maybe she doesn't miss me at all, and just went back to the way things were a few days ago, before I started. Or maybe she's furious, and she's telling Malcolm between every ride how inconvenient my absence is, how ridiculous it is that I went and got myself bit by a client's horse on my second day. "She's pathetic," I imagine Alison saying. *"Wah-wah, a horse bit my widdle thumb!* Meanwhile, the rest of us have to do twice as much work while she sits home and watches Netflix."

"Evie?" Posey is looking at me oddly, her head tilted. "Are you okay?"

"What? Yes, I'm fine." I scoop up some chicken and rice and stick it in my mouth to show her that everything is great.

But I know I drifted away just now, making up stories in my head about Malcolm and Alison.

I have to get it together. Or maybe it is just the residual effect of all those drugs, and I just need a nap.

"I think you need a nap," Posey decides, once again reading my thoughts. "Finish that and I'll tuck you in with Romeo. And then I'm taking your phone to get the screen fixed. Ah-ah!" She holds up a finger as I start to protest. "You don't get a say in this. Until your little brain fog passes, I'm in charge of your life."

"Fine," I grouse, "but I'll be all better by tomorrow."

"Good thing," Posey retorts. "Because then Malcolm will be in charge again, and either way, *you* aren't."

Chapter Fifteen

SIX DAYS AFTER I start working for Malcolm, I finally have a real day off. One that wasn't forced by doctor's orders, I mean.

On a sunny Monday morning when half of Ocala is down for the count after a raucous weekend of events, Grand Prix jumping, and polo matches, I pack up a pair of suitcases with clothes, a few books, and all of Romeo's toys. Breezy's life is already packed into my rust-bucket two-horse trailer, with his blankets and storage containers neatly stacked in the tiny tack room. With my bags wedged onto the floor of the passenger seat, and Romeo in his carrying case on the seat itself, I check the hitch of my old farm truck one more time before loading Breezy. He hops in happily, clearly missing his life as a show horse.

And so we're off.

My truck doesn't go faster than fifty miles an hour, with or without a horse in tow, so it takes nearly half an hour to get to Malcolm's. Romeo, distrustful of the trip, meows the entire time. The sound makes me wonder if I'm doing the right thing, even though I know my little cat is going to settle right into the pretty apartment above the stable.

It's just that we've lived at my little farm for a couple of years now, and it's *mine,* and the idea of changing it all up seemed appealing for a little while, but now I'm having serious second thoughts about the decision. I'm feeling like we were the happiest little crew in the world at my scrubby mini-farm, and now...we're *leaving*? So I can be at the beck and call of my boss? It seems crazy, and Romeo's constant meowing is just slamming that assessment home with every plaintive yowl.

But Breezy doesn't share the cat's opinion. He bounces out of the trailer with impressive agility for a horse who is permanently side-lined with a soft-tissue injury, then dances his way right out to the paddock Alison assigned him yesterday when we were finalizing arrangements. The other horses are turned out as well, since this is their day off too, and pretty soon the entire farm is rippling with whinnies and shaking with hoof-beats as excited horses put on a show to greet the new guy.

For a few minutes I stand and watch it all, half-afraid he'll step badly and hurt himself again. Or, in a possibly worse scenario, one of Malcolm's horses will be injured and I'll be to blame.

But eventually, everyone quiets down and goes back to grazing without any signs of lameness. I breathe a little easier, turning back to the truck to rescue Romeo. My cat has turned off the angry meow machine and huddles as far from the door of his little fabric carrier as he can get, his black tail wrapped around his pink nose. Two angry green eyes skewer me as I kneel down to peer in at him.

"You're going to like it," I promise him. "Give me five minutes to get my bags up there, and I'll let you out."

I'm just hoisting one suitcase when Malcolm appears, wearing jeans and a t-shirt. It's the most casual I've seen my famously stylish boss in the week I've been here, and the sight of him makes me pause.

He looks *really* good in jeans and a t-shirt.

Maybe it's just the change talking, but I can't help but admire the way the green shirt hugs his abs. Of course, he has the front tucked into the waistband, the sides and back of the shirt hanging loose. Of course, he'd take that extra time to make sure his shirt sits just right on his figure before he comes waltzing over to see his new working student moving into her digs.

I'm just amused enough by his vanity to give him a half-smile, despite the general terror I've been laboring under for the past work-week. Things after the bite didn't get easier, only tougher. Riding with my bandaged thumb held out of the way of my reins didn't make my daily requirement of three horses go away, or my lesson every other day. The only thing I haven't done yet is ride Bucky.

Malcolm rode him several times, though, and the sight of him on my horse filled me with an envy and jealousy I haven't been able to shake yet.

Maybe having Breezy here will make it easier to wait until Malcolm deems me ready to ride Bucky. I hope so. I need this strange, craving sensation to go away.

I'm sure as soon as I get on my horse, it will vanish.

"Let me take that bag," Malcolm insists, tugging the suitcase from my uninjured hand. "Can you manage the cat alright?"

"I've got him," I say, scooping up the cat carrier. "Thanks so much. I didn't expect to see you on a Monday."

"I'm never far away," he says, with a twist of his lips that is half-smile, half something else. As if he wishes he could put some distance between himself and the business. But that's not how being a professional horse trainer works, and we both know it.

"You live right over the hill, don't you?" I ask, as we head towards the staircase. The paddocks back up to a slight rise lined with trees, and a driveway goes past the stable and maintenance buildings before disappearing into their shade. I just assumed that's where Malcolm's house is; I can't imagine him living in an apartment somewhere in Ocala, or some little house in a subdivision.

"That's right, just behind the back paddock. Hidden enough that sometimes I can have a lazy Monday and pretend I'm not on call twenty-four seven," he adds.

"But when you hear horses running, you just have to check," I guess.

"Of course." He unlocks the door to my apartment with a key on his ring. I eye it as we step inside and he slings the keys onto the kitchen counter. Is that going to be my key...or will he have one on his key-ring even when I live here? "Here we are," he announces. "Home sweet home."

I look around the stable attic with appreciation. It's just as cute as I remember from a week ago, and I find myself excited all over again. It's going to be a nice change from my shadowy little trailer. Light is pouring through the open blinds, the whole place smells of lemon cleaner, and while it's mostly one room, I could never call it cramped. "This is great," I say. "Did the last working student live here? Or Alison?"

It's the first time I've had the courage to ask about either of them, and I'm immediately embarrassed with myself. I bend down and busy my hands with Romeo's cat carrier, unzipping it so the cat can poke his head out. He gives the apartment a cautious glare.

"Alison lived here back when she first started, three years ago," Malcolm replies, brushing some dust from a shelf. "But she moved to her own apartment last year. Or was it the year before? After that, I started giving it to the working students."

I notice the plural, wondering how many he's had living here. The last time Malcolm made the news at the feed store, it was for making a working student cry at Sunshine State Horse Trials. The girl quit on him, very publicly—they were standing by the jumping arena looking at the course map when she threw the reins of his horse at him and stalked away. Supposedly by the time Malcolm got back to the farm that night—with Alison, I suppose—the girl had already moved out and was on the road back to her parents in South Carolina.

We'd laughed about it at the time, but now, standing in the apartment where that poor girl must have lived, with the man who made her cry and give up her Ocala dreams standing right next to me with that secret little smile on his lips, I just feel a shiver of nervousness.

And something else.

Something I can't place.

"Well, I'll leave you to settle in," Malcolm says, watching Romeo creep out of the carrier with tiny steps. "I'm sure your cat would find it easier to get used to a new place without me in the way. Don't mind the sound of people down in the barn—the weekend stall cleaners usually show up around three, and they'll feed and turn back out at about five. You're *not* to go to the barn on your day off, got it?"

I blink at him. "What? Why?"

Malcolm chuckles. "Because it's your day off! Don't go get yourself burned out before you've even gotten started. I have big plans for you, miss."

I'm staring at him, wondering what on earth he could mean by that, when Romeo decides to leap out of the carrier at full speed and race between us, only finding out the floors are slick tile in the last scrabbling inches before he slides right into the wall dividing the living room and bedroom. "*Yowl!!*" the cat curses, shaking his little head.

"Oh, poor baby," I say, trying not to laugh. Romeo trots across the living room and dives under the sofa to pout. "He's going to make me pay for that later."

"Don't keep her up all night," Malcolm tells Romeo, opening the door to leave. "Your mother needs her rest." He glances at me on the way out and smiles. "Glad you're here, Evie," he says warmly, in a tone

I haven't heard since the night at the hospital. "Everything will seem easier now."

And with that, he's gone. I listen to his footsteps going down the staircase. Somehow, I resist the urge to peek through the blinds to see him walking up the driveway towards his hidden house beyond the hill. If I do, I'm sure he'll look back and see me watching him.

Or he won't look back at all.

Which would be worse?

"You're getting silly now, girl," I tell myself. "How about you just unpack, and not make everything weird?"

From beneath the sofa, Romeo agrees with a resounding *meow*.

Malcolm is right about one thing: Tuesday morning is a lot easier when I don't have to get up early enough to feed Breezy, get into my Jeep, and drive across the dark country roads to get to work on time. I grant myself an entire forty-five minutes of extra sleep, which feels like a ridiculous luxury considering ten days ago, I was getting up a full two hours earlier to get to work at the training barn, and still saunter down the stairs five minutes before eight, with Romeo asleep on the sofa and the pleasant knowledge that my animals won't have to wait until well after dark to be taken care of tonight.

The horses are already in for the morning, rustling in their hay after having cleaned up their breakfast a full half-hour ago. I'd heard the couple who fed and cleaned stalls down there while I was sitting at the round kitchen table, sipping coffee and eating cereal. This is the lap of luxury, I tell myself. Living at work is the best. I should have done this a week ago.

I pause to say hello to Breezy, who isn't used to staying inside all day. He runs his nose along the bars and nickers at me, expecting me to take him outside. I make a mental note to ask Malcolm if it's possible to leave him turned out. Otherwise, I might have to add ulcer medication to the long list of supplements he's already getting in his feed. Maybe this won't be the best situation for him, after all.

Next to him, Bucky is rummaging through his hay with enthusiasm. I wait for him to look up at me, but even when I try calling his name, Bucky doesn't bother lifting his nose from his hay-pile. I'm just not that interesting to him yet. I wonder if I'll ever be.

Of course you will, I scold myself. *You're being a big baby about this horse.*

But I can't help it. Breezy was my competition horse, the one I thought I'd go all the way with...but he has also been my best friend.

If I'm going to get anywhere with Bucky in the future, we're going to have to be buddies. I don't want this to be a get-on, get-off situation, the way Malcolm has to be with his horses.

"Ready to start?"

Speak of the devil, it's Malcolm, coming up the aisle behind me in sage green breeches and polished dress boots. As usual, he looks the part of thriving equestrian professional. But a little piece of me misses the casual guy in jeans and a t-shirt from yesterday.

"All set," I say as he walks up alongside me, nearly overpowering me with his unusually good mood. The satisfaction rolls off him in waves. "What's the occasion?"

Malcolm lifts an eyebrow. "Huh?"

"Oh, you just seem really pleased about something."

"I am! I've got you here now, so I feel like the team is ready for whatever the circuit is about to throw at us. It always makes me nervous when a new employee is still living off site. I don't know if I can trust them to show up every day. But now I know you will."

Right, I think. *Now I'm your captive.*

Silly, of course, when I can always throw my stuff back in a suitcase and drive right back to my own house. Malcolm doesn't own me.

And that makes me different from most working students. I'm not in the dependent position so many of them find themselves in, unable to get out easily. I'm an adult; I pay my own way in this world. I have a house and a savings account.

But I can't think of a tactful way to remind him of that. So I just nod and follow him down to the office.

Alison is behind the desk, tapping in the day's schedule. "We have three lessons this afternoon," she informs Malcolm. "Which means that Evie and I both have to ride four this afternoon to get you off horses by two."

"That's fine," Malcolm says, still sounding unusually jovially. "Take your pick. It's a dressage day for everyone."

I think of my past week in the dressage saddle. I feel much more comfortable in it now, but I'm definitely not up to par with my old self yet…and Malcolm seems to enjoy picking apart my form. Well, if it makes him happy… "Great," I say, adding my opinion to the mix. "Looking forward to it."

Alison flicks her gaze upwards and studies me for a minute. "You get all moved in yesterday?"

"Sure did, and the cat is settled in, and—"

"Super," she interrupts, her voice flat. "That makes late nights easier on all of us. You're taking over night-check, remember?"

Four nights a week, she'd said before.. "Uh, half the week, I think?"

"No," Alison says. "Every night but Monday. The stall-cleaners will do it Monday."

"Oh." She's changed the rules, but it doesn't seem like something I can fight. I glance at Malcolm, but he's already halfway out the office door, ready to start riding.

"Let's go, girls!" he calls over his shoulder. "The horses wait for no man!"

"The schedule's on your phone," Alison tells me. "Let's go."

And with that, Tuesday is off and running.

Chapter Sixteen

SUDDENLY, ALL MY days are blurring together. Between grooming, fitting in my own rides, and helping out the numerous students who are turning up in droves to get lessons before their first event of the season, the hours flash by. Twelve, thirteen, fourteen-hour days—I'm working easily twice as much every day as I was working in the racehorse business, and remembering why, just a year ago, I told Posey that I was in no hurry to become a working student in the eventing game ever again.

But here I am. Hustling, getting blisters, and shivering through cold fronts all in the name of making Malcolm Horsham as much money as possible.

At least, I assume we're making him money. Malcolm's style professor game is still strong, but I've noticed something interesting —he seems to only have three work outfits. And no, I don't think he's the kind of genius who spotted a bargain and bought five sets of something on clearance. Because I've noticed little things on his breeches. The same spot on one pair of olive-colored breeches, right above his left knee. A little snag on his slate-colored breeches, in the seam down the left thigh. And his sage-colored breeches are missing a button on the left rear pocket.

Yes, I'm far too aware of the details of his pants—I get it! But when you consider that for much of the day, Malcolm is on a horse, and that puts his knees at eye-level for me...well, it makes a little more sense, doesn't it?

Anyway, the realization that Malcolm isn't necessarily *loaded,* not weighed down with wealth the way we've all assumed, but is possibly just muddling through professional equestrian life with the same "make it pretty and put on a brave face" mentality that so many of us mere mortals have been living with for years—well, it makes me more sympathetic to him when he's barking commands at me or yelling at Alison about some minor mistake on the schedule or just sitting at his desk with his fists clenched, taking deep breaths to get him through some phone call with a client in which he blustered but did not come out the victor.

Actually, in those rare moments when he's sitting in there looking as if he's gone ten rounds with a heavyweight and just barely escaped with his life—those make me like him more, too.

Malcolm Horsham is *also* a mere mortal...imagine that!

I'd tell Posey about it, and she'd laugh at me, if I ever had a spare moment to draw breath and talk to her. But six days flash by in the blink of an eye, just hard work from dawn to dusk and then some, and before I know it, another week has passed, and it's Sunday night in the stable, waiting for Wesley to take home her demon horse.

By now I'm just wearing a waterproof little sock over the thumb her horse tried to mangle, and if you ignore the black-and-blue nail, you can almost pretend the jagged red seam of healing flesh on the pad of my thumb isn't anything serious. But I can't help feeling nervous around her horse, especially when she thrusts the reins at me after her ride and stalks up the aisle, typing vigorously on her phone.

Archer is breathing hard, too tired to try eating me this time. Alison takes a look at him and shakes her head. "Give that poor bastard a good liniment bath," she says. "I'm going to sweep the aisle and as soon as we get her out of here, we can be done for the night."

That's a relief; we're well past seven o'clock and I'd like to go upstairs, collapse on the sofa, and let Romeo purr on my lap for what's left of this evening. The prospect of a day off tomorrow is all that keeps me hanging on, even though it won't be very exciting—it's past time I went to the grocery store, and I have to get over to my house and make sure nothing else has moved in. In Florida, you can never be too sure.

I'm pouring a generous dollop of peppermint-scented liniment into a steaming water bucket when Malcolm comes stalking into the aisle. His dress boots are dusty and he's wearing the sage-green breeches tonight, the ones missing a button. I wonder if I can sneak a button onto the breeches, just to tie together his typically stylish look for him, and then dismiss the idea as insane. What am I going to do, break into his laundry room with a sewing kit?

He glowers at the black horse as if the animal has personally ruined his day. "I don't like you," he tells Archer.

The horse grinds his molars, making a squeaking sound, and tosses his head.

"He doesn't like you either," I quip, not paying attention to my manners.

Malcolm shifts his glare to me. He's been in a glare-y mood all day, getting more moody with every lesson that passed through the stable. I'm finding that weekends, when more of his amateur students show up and monopolize his time, are the toughest to deal with. He just doesn't like teaching that much. Rough, because that's how professionals make the most money per hour.

"What do you know about him?" Malcolm demands. "He clearly isn't your best friend, or you wouldn't have that little rubber condom-thing on your thumb."

"It's not a condom thing!" I retort, but I'm embarrassed, because the stupid rubber bandage looks exactly like a tiny condom on my thumb, and I've been sensitive about it all week. "Anyway, he bit me by accident," I go on, dipping a sponge into the hot water and savoring the feel on my own skin. "It was kind of my fault, even. I did an *all done* sign, and he didn't know what it was."

Malcolm quirks an eyebrow, suddenly interested. "What's an all done sign?"

"Oh." I slosh water onto Archer's back, feeling even sillier than when we were just talking about my finger condom. "It's a thing you can teach your horse to show when you're out of treats. You hold up your hands and say 'All done!' Do that often enough and they learn what it means."

I hazard a glance at Malcolm; he's grinning now. "When you say it like that, I feel like you're talking to a toddler. 'All done!'" he imitates in a sing-song voice.

"Don't make fun of me," I say. The horse is leaning into my sponge now; the warm water is soothing his tired muscles. It's like we're friends now—friends through the power of liniment and heat. "It works, and it's not like I came up with it on my own or something. I read it in a book."

"It's not the idea I'm laughing at," he informs me. "It's the way you sound when you say it. Like you're a kindergarten teacher."

"Honestly, isn't that what you feel like half the time?"

Malcolm's quiet for long enough that I lean around the wet horse and look to see if he's walked away.

He's just standing there, arms folded across his chest, looking at the horse as if he's never seen him before. He feels my gaze on him and forces a smile. "Yeah," he says, "I guess sometimes I do."

And then he walks away.

I can't help but feel like I said something wrong, but I'm not sure why that would have offended him so much. I was talking about the way we have to treat horses, who are like large, dangerous toddlers more often than not. But as I scrape the excess water off Wesley's horse and throw a cooler over this back, I wonder if he went somewhere else with my words.

I wonder if it's how he feels about teaching humans.

Maybe he's not happy about it, but honestly? The unhappiness makes him more human.

I make good on my promise to myself to stretch out on the couch with Romeo purring on my lap...but only for about an hour, because I have to go down the stairs again and do night-check at nine. Since the horses are turned out, night-check is really about walking along the paddocks and shining a flashlight across the fields to make sure that everyone is alive and accounted for. It's not a bad gig in good weather, but tonight there's a cold front rolling in and I can already hear thunder rumbling in the distance. The wind is picking up as well.

I decide to hop up early, earning me a dirty look from Romeo, so that I can get night-check done before the storm hits. It's eight-thirty, only a half-hour early...I think the slight deviation from the schedule can be excused this time, even by Miss Punctuality herself, Alison.

I glance down at my fluffy pajama set as I slide my feet into a pair of rubber boots. Nope, not changing into real clothes. It's bad enough that I have to go out before a storm to wake up a bunch of horses, who are probably already in their run-in sheds eating hay because they don't want to get wet in the coming storm front. I'm absolutely not going to get dressed again to do it. And yes, I *am* wearing white pajamas with cavorting rainbow-farting unicorns patterned across both the top and bottom, but what is wrong with that? No clients are going to see me...or Malcolm.

"Be right back, Romeo," I call, and open the front door. The wind tries to tug it from my hands, and it ends up slamming behind me. "Yikes," I mutter, running down the stairs. "Just a little dramatic out here tonight."

In the northwest sky, lightning is flickering through the clouds, and the wind carries the smell of rain. As I expected, most of the horses are in their run-in sheds already, eating their way through their hay and pretending they aren't going to be muddy monsters by seven a.m., after the rain has passed and they're able to roll in the puddles left behind. They look up at me as I shine the flashlight across their faces, blinking at the sudden glare. Breezy is one of the few horses who remains out on the grass, his tail blowing over his hindquarters as a big gust roars out of the northwest.

"Of course," I tell him, exasperated. "Mr. I Love All Weathers. Why don't you go into your run-in shed like the other horses?"

Breezy gives me an affectionate nicker, which can almost certainly be translated as "silly human," and goes back to grazing.

Bucky, in the next paddock, hasn't quite made up his mind. He's half-in and half-out of his shed, resting one hind foot while he snoozes. "Good choice, baby," I tell him, and try not to feel hurt when he doesn't so much as glance in my direction. I'll get to know my new horse eventually, I remind myself, and finish my walk down the row of paddocks.

Everyone's fine. Everyone is always fine. It's a perfectly acceptable monotony, because when you come down for night-check and find someone cast in their stall or trying to colic, that signals a long and sleepless night is ahead, and at this point in my week, I need every wink of sleep I can get.

As I climb up the stairs towards my apartment, I notice a new chill in the wind, and suddenly all I can think about is hot chocolate. I know I don't have any in my cupboards, but there's some in the office. I do a reverse on the stairs, listening to the wind roar against the eaves and jumping slightly when thunder rumbles much closer. The storm is almost here.

I'm hustling down the dim stable aisle, my mind on hot chocolate and the sound of rain against my windows, when I realize the office door is open and the light is on, its glow streaming into the aisle. My footsteps stutter and slow. Is Malcolm down here? Then I hear a low murmur of voices, both female. What on earth...

I would very much like to return to my apartment, but something tells me this is my job to handle. I am the one in charge. I am tiptoeing down the aisle, nearly to the open office door, when a woman comes out, looks at me, and screams.

I do the only logical thing: I scream right back. She *scared* me; what else could I do? We're both screaming and then she throws herself back into the office while I turn and pelt headlong up the barn aisle.

I make it all the way to the archway in the center of the stable before I get hold of myself. What just happened? Did I just have a terror-fueled screaming match with a woman in Malcolm's office—now that I think about it, a very well-dressed, middle-aged woman, who is probably not a robber but actually a client who stopped by after hours for some reason? I mean, it is the time of year when all the clients seem to think they own him, so the idea isn't that outlandish. I glance through the archway and see a gleaming silver car parked in front of the fountain. I must not have heard it come in because of the wind and thunder.

And then I hear a shout behind me. I whirl around and see Malcolm marching down the aisle. It's too dark to see his expression, but I can imagine it, and what I'm picturing can't be good.

I turn my back on him and start off down the aisle again, heading for my apartment as quickly as I can without running. Maybe I can just pretend none of this ever happened—

"Evie!"

Or not.

"Evie, stop!"

I make my legs stop scissoring and stand still. I'm next to Bucky's stall. The nameplate on the stall door glints dully in the half-light. I look at it for a moment, wishing it said "Owner Evie Ballenger" beneath his name. It's the least of my worries right now, but still I can't help wishing that horse really felt like he was mine.

"Evie, what on *earth* are you wearing?"

I whirl around and face Malcolm. He's still in his riding clothes, still wearing those breeches with the missing button. Even with that little error, he looks professional and put-together. I am wearing unicorn pajamas.

Unicorns farting rainbows, no less.

"I'm wearing my pajamas," I say, with all the dignity of a princess. "It's late and I'm tired, and I am wearing my comfy clothes."

Malcolm rubs his jaw, like he doesn't know what he's going to do with me. "In the barn aisle? Really?"

"How was I supposed to know there's anyone here? I came out to do night-check early because of the storm—" Thunder growls, deep and dangerous, to punctuate my words. "And then I wanted to get a hot chocolate packet because I wanted to be cozy."

His lip twitches at the word *cozy*. As if there's something hilarious about the desire to curl up under a fleece blanket, drink hot chocolate, and pet a cat while watching *Schitt's Creek* and listening to a storm rumble outside. Excuse me, that sounds like freaking heaven on a stick. He could do with a little cozy time, himself.

There's a flash of lightning outside, and thunder growls again. The wind whips at my pajamas. "If I don't go now, I'm going to get wet on the way up," I say petulantly.

Now Malcolm really grins. "Poor little lamb," he mocks. "But you didn't even get your hot cocoa!"

"I don't want it anymore," I inform him, although that's not true. I want it even *more* now.

"Lillian thought you were a ghost," he says. "She's down there recovering from her panic attack."

"What kind of ghost is covered with unicorns farting rainbows?" I demand, forgetting that this isn't my best defense. "Anyway, why is she even here?"

Malcolm shrugs. "She needed some paperwork signed. My time is her time. I do what I have to do."

"Well, I'm sorry about that," I say. *Lillian*, I think. That name again. The woman he was speaking with on the phone the first day I was here, that had been Lillian. The person Alison complained about wanting to sell Oceanus, that was Lillian. *My time is her time.* She's clearly important to the business, and Malcolm doesn't want her to be.

A few drops of rain patter on the roof overhead, reminding me that time's fleeting and storms wait for no hot chocolate. "Look, I need to go—"

"Wait," Malcolm says, and his hand darts out to catch my wrist as I am turning to leave. "Let me get your hot chocolate for you, at least."

I freeze, arrested not just by his grip on my wrist, but by the way it *feels*. My skin goes white-hot for a moment, then ice-cold in the same breath. Everything in my system is riveted on the feeling of his fingers wrapped around my bare wrist.

And then he lets go.

I watch my boss walk down the aisle again, his strides long and confident. By the time he's back with not just a packet, but an entire *box* of hot chocolate packets, an early shower ahead of the storm is already pattering on the roof. He thrusts the box into my hand and I find myself staring up at him.

He's so much taller than I am.

"An entire box?" I ask.

"Now you won't have to come down here and frighten all my business away."

"Oh, right." Embarrassment floods through me again.

"Go," he tells me. "Hurry, little unicorn ghost, before you get wet and melt."

I take the box and run.

Chapter Seventeen

THE FIRST EVENT I work for Fine Day Farm comes the following weekend, and by weekend, I mean a Thursday. That's the first day of a long weekend of horse trials—dressage, cross-country, and stadium jumping that all add up to one score per horse and rider team, commonly called "eventing".

On Thursday there is a one-day event for the riders who want to cram all that excitement into a single day. Malcolm opts to ride two of his younger horses in the Novice competition on Thursday and takes four students who also want to do the one-day event. But we have six more horses competing across the Friday-Sunday section of the event, with dressage on Friday, cross-country on Saturday, and jumping on Sunday. Malcolm has six students in that, as well.

Alison warns me ahead of time to expect chaos. "But you have to manage it with grace," she says primly, polishing a bit to a shine so high I can see my own face in the metal. "There should be absolutely no giveaway to the clients or to Malcolm that you're stressed."

"What about you?" I ask with mock innocence. "Are you allowed to know I'm stressed?"

Alison snorts. "I might know, but will I care? That's the question."

I give her a sideways grin and reach for the metal polish. It's my job to get the crud out of the brass clinchers of Malcolm's favorite bridle, the one that he'll ride his top horses in on the cross-country and jumping days. He's taking Artsy and Oceanus in the Advanced division, which is a pretty big deal. About as big as it can get before heading off to one of the three-day events that are considered the peaks of the sport's annual competition calendar.

Obviously, the bridle has to look like it's never been used, instead of giving away the reality: that Malcolm has been using it since the late nineties and considers it a good-luck charm.

I already knew about the Good Luck Bridle; it was something that makes the gossip rounds occasionally, when the conversation turns to superstitions and the unlikely trainers who suffer from them. Sallyann at OBS says that Red Woodford, one of the top racehorse trainers in the country, can't go anywhere without a lucky pocketknife he's had since he was twelve. "It makes air travel really difficult," she always says when she's recounting the story.

And I have heard on good authority that Marlene Beaufort, the world-champion barrel racing rider, has a lucky show shirt that keeps getting revamped to fit the changing styles of that flashy show circuit. She keeps a seamstress on retainer, people say.

I sigh. It feels like forever since I was able to spend some quality time propping up a feed store counter and chit-chat with the girls. Or have lunch with Posey, or see Kayla on one of her weekly trips into Ocala—now that she lives up in Alachua County, these things have to be planned.

I didn't expect this job to take over my life so thoroughly...or to feel so isolated by it. Even when there are a lot of people in the stable aisle, they're not there to talk to me, and I don't have time to stop and get to know them. And if I did, I feel pretty sure that kind of socializing would be discouraged. They're the clients; I'm the help. They're here for Malcolm, not me.

And frankly, I'm starting to wonder if I'm getting anything out of this job. It has been three weeks, and I haven't ridden Bucky even once. I see my horse when I pass him in the aisle, or when it's my turn to tack him up for Malcolm, instead of Alison's. And when I am his groom, I'm moving quickly and efficiently, not spending time rubbing his coat with a massager or feeding him treats while we get to know each other.

I'm just the help, even to my own horse.

There's nothing to be done about that part of things—he's under a training contract for five more months, and I have to respect that side of the bargain or I wouldn't put it past my aunt to find a way to take him back, rescind the entire offer, and pretend that Christmas party never happened.

So, that's why Bucky is here.

But why am *I* here, working my tail off, and seeing absolutely nothing for it?

My fingers slide on the metal polish and I bend back a fingernail on one of the brass clinchers. *"Dammit,"* I mutter, shaking my sore finger. "Is this bridle clean enough?"

Alison glances over it. "I think so, yeah. Why, got somewhere to be?"

Her mocking tone is getting on my last nerve. "Yeah, I need to figure out what I'm doing with my life," I grumble.

"What's that supposed to mean?" She sounds genuinely interested now, as if discovering a secret drama was exactly what the doctor ordered.

Well, as a former purveyor of quality drama, I can certainly understand her position. Still, she's Malcolm's assistant. I'm not going to give away the house. "I just need to make a plan for when this program is over," I lie, hanging up the bridle on its wooden hook. "You know, in June, the absolute best time to find a new riding job."

Hot, buggy, stormy June, when the biggest players in the sport are up in their summer digs, not sweating it in Ocala. If I *did* see some success in eventing and wanted to stick with it, I'd probably have to wait until fall for a job with another top barn.

Like this one.

Alison lifts her eyebrows at me. "So you're not going to stay here?"

"Is that on offer?" I ask skeptically.

"Of course, that's the whole idea," she says. "You apprentice for six months, and then you're all trained up and we can bring you on as a member of the team. That's how I got this job."

"No one else works here," I point out. "So, where are all the other successful working students?"

Alison's smile dips. "There aren't any."

"Exactly. What makes you think I'll *want* to stay?"

She shakes her head. "I don't understand why everyone leaves. What is so different here from every other professional barn? Malcolm is a top trainer. So he gets a little demanding...so what? That's part of the game. If you ask me, we've just been picking the wrong people, and we're weeding them out when they leave the program early. Not everyone is built for this sport at the upper levels," she adds, sounding self-important in a way that rubs me exactly the wrong way.

"What about the ridiculous hours?" I snap. "Have either of you ever considered that you're the only two people on earth willing to work six days a week, fifteen hours a day? Maybe the problem is *you*."

"What would you like us to do? Turn away business? Maybe we should be nine to five, Monday through Friday?" Alison laughs scornfully. "We exist in this business because we do whatever it takes to please our customers. They are paying massive sums of money to learn from the best, and place their horses with the best, and they get our undying devotion in return...or else they'll go to someone else who will treat them the way they expect. You've worked in racing for years—are you telling me that the owners in horse racing aren't given every little whim their heart desires?"

I don't have a reply to that. I know everything she says is true. The horse business is ridiculous for exactly this reason: the trainers need insane sums of money to run their barns and compete their horses, and the owners need to be cosseted and adored in return for all that cash. In return, they show some tiny modicum of loyalty...some of the time.

The long days aren't Malcolm's fault. They're part of the game.

But they're also not the only reason why I'm not sure I should stay.

"I want to ride Bucky," I confess at last.

Alison nods. "I can understand that. When Malcolm thinks you're ready, you'll get to ride him. Don't worry."

"It's like I'm a bad rider, though! I mean, I know what I'm doing on a horse. Maybe I'm not Malcolm, but I'm capable of not ruining Bucky in the first ten minutes on his back."

"It's probably not about you," Alison says. "It's about Bucky."

"But how would my riding him cause such an issue?"

Alison sighs and throws down her sponge. "I don't *know*, Evie. Why don't you go and ask Malcolm?"

My riding lesson on Diamond is an hour later, and it feels like the perfect time to ask when I'll be able to ride my shiny new horse.

After I'm past being yelled at for my position, obviously.

"Your *shoulders*, for god's sake!" Malcolm strikes himself on the forehead while I miserably trot a circle around him. We've been circling for what feels like forever, although I know deep down it has probably been all of five minutes. The problem is that he just keeps repeating himself, and every time he says the same thing, I lose one more inch of my ability to ride.

It's not just about my shoulders at this point; I feel like a lump of Jell-O in the saddle, quivering from head to toe while Diamond does his best to trot a round circle.

"Put your shoulders back," Malcolm says, having exhausted every metaphor and *Centered Riding*-inspired image imaginable. None of them have worked on me today. My shoulders want to slump forward and place me in my safe space: a rounded position just ahead of my horse's center of gravity where it's very hard for him to displace me in the event of an unexpected bolt, buck, or duck. It's something that's prefect for riding youngsters and racehorses, but obviously it's anathema to the classical riding position necessary for dressage.

And without dressage, of course, there is nothing. Not in eventing, where the best in class will always finish their three-phase competition on their dressage score, not picking up any jumping penalties along the way.

"Shoulders. Back."

It's not working. I start to feel a prickling behind my eyes. *I'm just tired,* I tell myself. *I'm just very, very tired and frustrated.*

"Oh, come on, Evie!" Malcolm shouts.

Diamond snorts at him. I feel myself hunching over, as if I'm trying to make myself small, as if I can escape his notice if I just shrink into my horse's mane.

And then Malcolm says, in a strangely quiet voice, "Evie, tighten your stomach muscles. Make them taut."

I take a breath and obey. I feel my ribcage lift as my abdominal muscles contract. I have decent abs. Racehorses will give those to a person.

"Right," Malcolm mutters. "Evie—"

There's something about the way he's saying my name right now, in a cool and calm tone, that makes me sit up a bit straighter.

"Evie," he repeats, like he sees he's found my magic switch, "lift your chest."

I take a breath and lift my chest.

"That's it," Malcolm says, amusement tinging his words. "Evie—"

His voice caresses my name. I feel a little shiver run up and down my spine. And *that* makes me sit up straighter, too.

"Evie, *tits out!*"

I gasp and raise my chest higher, flinging my shoulders back and my chin up, and Malcolm exclaims, "That's it, Evie, that's it, you've got it!"

Diamond snorts and pushes forward, his hind hooves digging into the soft ground as he shows his appreciation for my new, improved seat.

After the lesson, Malcolm lays a hand on the flap of my saddle, so close to my knee I can almost feel the heat of his skin. "That was pretty funny," he tells me, "the way you sat bolt upright when I said 'tits out'. Not exactly kosher, but it did the job, right?"

Suddenly, I'm blushing. I'm desperately embarrassed. I ought to be able to see the humor in it—I know Kayla has shouted 'Tits out!' at me from across the arena back when we used to ride together. It's a funny thing to say because it's *true* that the right riding position should have our chests held out high and proud.

But I don't know how to cope with Malcolm talking about my chest like that.

He sees my blush and pats the saddle flap, his fingers brushing my knee ever so slightly. My skin does that hot-cold flash again, and without thinking I tighten my fingers on the reins, moving Diamond back a single step. Malcolm slides his hand onto Diamond's warm neck without a second thought. "I think you did amazing today," he says. "I'd like to see you take Diamond in the next one-day we can get you into, okay? Novice, just to get you out there."

Closing dates for events are two weeks in advance, so theoretically, I could be showing in the next three weeks. I swallow, then ask the real question. "What about Bucky?"

Malcolm lifts his eyebrows. "I'm still getting Bucky ironed out. He has a few kinks from his last rider that need to be fixed."

"I can ride a horse with kinks," I inform him. "You know I came from racing. I rode problem horses every single day."

Malcolm takes his hand back, wipes it on his breeches. "But did you fix them," he asks pointedly, "or did you just make sure they can make it around the track as fast as possible?"

He has me there. Any fixes I made on those horses were lightning-quick, perfunctory, and probably wiped out by the next exercise rider to get on their backs. I try to think of a reply that isn't just agreeing with him, fail, and settle for chewing my lower lip.

Malcolm watches my face for a long moment, as if he wants to be sure he's made his point. That's a trick he has with me, and I don't know if I love it or hate it. Right now, I think I hate it. And him.

He just negated the past year of my riding life.

"Fine," I say at last. "I just got them around the track."

Malcolm nods shortly and turns away.

As he starts to walk back to the stable aisle, he says, without turning around, "I'll have you on Bucky next week. After this event weekend, okay?"

"Okay," I reply, because there's nothing else I can say, and it's better than nothing. Better than a full denial.

Survive this weekend, and I can ride my horse.

I'll take it.

In the barn, Alison is waiting with a list of tack and supplies that need to go into the horse trailer for the first run over to the event grounds. "As soon as Diamond is clean and cooled out, get this done, okay?"

It's not a request, obviously, but a demand. I take the list from her and stick into my pocket. The only real surprise is that it isn't a PDF I have to use my phone for. Alison's a real tyrant about keeping everything on our phones. She says that way we can't say we lose everything she gives us.

Diamond gets his bath and a liniment rub-down, and then it's back to his stall and his hay. I run my fingers along the rails of Bucky's stall as I walk back to the tack room to start packing for the event. As usual, he doesn't look up, but I'm used to that now. Things will change, I tell myself, as soon as I start riding him. Then we can bond, and everything will be different and better.

I walk into the tack room, and Malcolm is waiting for me, his hands behind his back, his face full of conflicting emotions. "Evie," he says, "are you interested in riding *this* weekend, instead of waiting for the next event?"

Chapter Eighteen

MY FIRST THOUGHT is *absolutely not,* but luckily, I'm old enough to know better than to blurt out my first reply, especially to a boss. I know that *no* is the wrong answer. He expects me to say yes. What working student would ever turn down the opportunity to compete sooner than expected?

Me, an older and wiser person than most working students.

One of the problems of working a job like this at my age is that I'm doing the work of a fearless twenty-one-year-old...nearly ten years past my prime fearless years. And past my peak slavish-devotion-to-trainers years, too.

That's why the hours are so tediously and wearingly long to me; that's why I felt like it was okay to blow up at Alison about working so late six days a week; that's why I get frustrated when I'm not allowed to ride my own horse.

Because I'm too old to revere my trainer as a king and my apprenticeship as a gift from the eventing gods.

But that age also works as a gift now, so that I can swallow my initial balky reply—youthful foolishness!—and instead smile weakly and say, "Well, of course."

Give the boss what he wants.

Malcolm nods briskly. I have to admit, he still looks conflicted, but maybe he's just working through this new plan in his head.

"Unless you don't think it's the best idea," I suggest, seeing a potential way out.

His brow furrows. "Why would I suggest something that I didn't think was a good idea?"

His tone isn't exactly icy, but it isn't warm, either.

I opt for a shrug.

"The thing is, I got a call from one of the students and they won't make it—some work thing is keeping them from flying to Ocala. So we have an extra spot in Training and I can get the secretary to move you and Diamond into it."

Wait a second. Press pause. All riders hold on course.

"In Training? But you said we were going to go Novice." In three weeks, not in two days. Now he wants me to bump up a level?

Not that Training Level is insurmountable—but the cross-country course certainly won't be as straightforward as a Novice course. The jump to Training is pretty nerve-wracking for most people, and I've been out of the game for a year—I think I count as *most people*. Plus, I've never even taken Diamond cross-country schooling, either. We've only jumped together in the arena.

"Diamond's a reliable horse," Malcolm reminds me, looking at his phone instead of me. "And you've competed through Prelim, right? That's what you said in your interview."

"Yeah, that's true, but it was more than a year ago."

"Well, it'll be like riding a bike. Unless you'd rather not..."

The challenge is unspoken, but it hangs in the air between us. There's absolutely no way I'm going to back down in front of him. Age is just a number, after all. It can't help me now.

All the good sense in the world can't convince me that I should tell Malcolm I'm not ready to ride Diamond at Training Level.

"Of *course* I'll do it."

"Perfect," Malcolm says, looking genuinely pleased. "I'll have Alison call the secretary and ask her for this favor—it won't be a problem. Make sure your show clothes are ready to go, yes? And add everything you've been riding in to the trailer-load you're taking over. Tomorrow is about bathing and braiding—no riding."

Great, so I won't even get another practice ride on Diamond. Everything I did today has to carry with me until our dressage test on Thursday morning. That's in less than forty-eight hours. I realize I don't even know the dressage test and start sweating. There's no way Malcolm will allow me a caller, so I'm going to have to find out which one they're asking for at this event and make sure I know the moves. I haven't done Training in two years. They'll probably have changed a few things about it...

I realize I'm wringing my hands in an empty tack room; Malcolm is gone and it's just me, a dozen saddles, and the looming fear of disaster now.

Great job, Evie, I tell myself. *Not in over your head or anything!*

Alison takes the news that I'll be showing this weekend with calm acceptance. "Do you have a black coat for dressage?" she asks, not looking up from her eternal schedule.

"Yes," I say. "And a blue one for stadium. And a purple and navy jumper for cross-country—"

"Nope," Alison says. "You'll be wearing our colors in the cross-country. I have a long-sleeved tee you can wear under your vest—please tell me your vest isn't purple."

"No, it's navy," I retort, annoyed. I *like* my purple and blue cross-country jumper and I haven't worn it since the last time I was able to event Breezy.

"Navy vest is fine. Helmet cover?"

"Navy and purple," I admit.

"I'll give you a navy one," Alison says. "I have some extras somewhere. And you'll use a farm saddle pad. Green for cross-country, but white for dressage and stadium. No colors in the arena. Malcolm's rule. And mine," she adds, enjoying her authority a little too much.

I take my medicine laying down—the only way I can—and focus on packing the trailer. By four o'clock the sun is sinking towards the horizon and I've got everything on the list shoved into the tack room and the horse area, including hay, feed, and rubber storage bins with the farm signs and silk flowers I'll be adding around the stalls and the tack stall. Alison hands me the keys and waves me away. I can only assume I'm on the truck's insurance. There's another thing that a twenty-year-old working student wouldn't think about, I think with a private smile, as I trudge out to the dually truck.

Malcolm is riding past on one of the client horses; he reins back and waves me over. "Heading to the horse park?"

I hold up the keys. "Looking forward to putting your pretty green truck through her paces," I tease.

"Oh lord, watch out for the red-light cameras in Ocala," Malcolm groans. "My last working student actually got my license suspended. I had to jump through all kinds of hoops to get that fixed."

I laugh, pushing aside the usual (and completely unnecessary) surge of jealousy that always roars into my brain when my nameless predecessor is mentioned. Whoever she was, clearly she was more trouble to Malcolm than she was worth. Whereas I am...

"Well, see you later," Malcolm calls, riding away.

I am just the next working student in a long list of eager young girls, I remind myself.

Well, maybe not so young.

* * *

There are other grooms like me at the horse park, prepping the show stabling for their employers. I pass women in jeans and ball-caps, long sleeves tugged down against the chill settling with sunset. We nod and smile when we bother to make eye contact. But mostly, we are too busy for chit-chat. We are the staff, the prep team. We have bosses to please and work ahead of us back at the farm. But there are coolers and buckets of ice sitting around. Drinks come later, for those who can sit and stay.

Wheelbarrows creak, hay bales crack open, and drills scream as grooms make new holes for the bucket holders, stall guards, barn signs, and whatever other accoutrement each barn feels is necessary for their comfort on a long horse trials weekend. The place needs to feel like home, to the horses and the students.

All the showing I did last year was at the very fancy Legends Equestrian Center on the other side of town, when I was riding Breezy with the equally fancy dressage trainer I'd started with after eventing was out of the question. I feel good back at an event, which is a wilder, woolier kind of horse show. More casual, more friendly, more, "I just cracked open a six-pack, want one?" than your typical dressage or hunter/jumper show.

For a long time I thought I wanted to get out of eventing and specialize in jumpers, which is exciting and tends to pay more in prize money. But eventing is always where my heart has been, I think, and working in racing has just been a job, not a passion.

Understanding that about myself has led me here, and to working with Malcolm, and I'm going to make the best of this.

I'm hanging up the green-and-navy signs for the farm when a short, friendly looking woman stops and takes a look at my work. I step back and grin, happy to show off all my hard work. In the late evening light, my section of barn aisle looks very professional: tack trunks lining the walls of the tack stall, bridles hanging from hooks along the walls, silk ferns and flowers in pots on either side of the door. The stalls all have our stall guards in the farm colors across the open doorways, and inside, fluffy beds of bright shavings await the horses who will arrive tomorrow afternoon. Including Diamond.

Taking it all in, I feel proud to be the representative of Fine Day Farm. It's a big deal, and I've set us up like the powerhouse we are.

We. The word feels good.

"Looks great," the woman declares, hands on hips. "I'm Candy O'Rourke. You must be Malcolm's new girl?"

Candy O'Rourke. I know the name. Sifting through the side of the brain where I keep my feed store gossip, I hold out a hand. "Evie Ballenger," I say. "Yeah, working student of three *very* long weeks."

Candy laughs and gives my hand a firm shake. "The few and the brave, Malcolm's girls," she says. "Funny how the guys always steer clear of him, too. I don't think men can handle being yelled at. Their loss," she adds, shrugging. "You're going to learn a ton from him. Showing this weekend?"

"Thursday, in the one-day," I say. "Training Level."

"Oh, very nice! Well, tell Malcolm that Candy says hello and reminds him to check his buttons." She grins and strides off down the aisle, leaving me blinking after her in confusion.

Remember to check his buttons? All I can think of is that missing button on his sage-green breeches. But he wouldn't wear those breeches here, and anyway, how would Candy know about that?

I turn back to my work, and while my fingers are busy with knots, I remember who Candy O'Rourke is. I can practically hear Sallyann talking about her now: "One of the richest women in Ocala, but you'd never know it to look at her. She's just a big old softie, but her dad started some clothing company back in the seventies and she inherited every dollar of it. She events because she loves it and doesn't have to lift a finger, but she does all her own work. Absolutely the best person in town, if you ask me."

That's why her name didn't register with me at first. Because there was no gossip about Candy O'Rourke. She is the rarest diamond in the horse business: a person no one had a single bad thing to say about.

I know even *I* don't have that honor, tiny little fish in this great big pond that I am.

But now I want to know everything there is to know about Candy, starting with how she knows Malcolm...and what the deal is with her buttons comment.

It's full-dark by the time I leave the horse park, listening to the grumbling about early sunsets and doing some complaining of my own as I go back to the truck. Malcolm doesn't have anything to worry about when it comes to red-light cameras; I drive like a granny, even with no horses in the back. It's past six when I finally park the trailer behind the barn, but I have to groan when I see all the light streaming from the outdoor arenas. Malcolm is out in the jumping ring, teaching.

It's like the champagne bubbles have finally stopped fizzing, and all I'm left with is flat, tasteless wine. Yes, I repped Fine Day Farm tonight, and it felt good when I was done setting up, but what's the real pay-off? Endless days with a man who never stops working?

I used to have set hours, I think rebelliously. And my own house, and my horse in the yard.

Suddenly, my old life seems like heaven. A paradise I had and squandered in the name of endless hours grinding away for someone else's fame and fortune.

Oh yes, I feel very sorry for myself.

For a moment I lean my head against the truck steering well and for myself to take a few deep breaths. It's fine. I'm just exhausted. I'm just wiped out. It's only natural. I've been going since eight a.m., and in the span of eleven or so hours, I have ridden multiple horses, I have just set up twelve stalls at the horse park, and to come back and find the workday isn't over yet...well, it's demoralizing, that's what it is.

I don't *want* to keep going. I don't want to spend all day tomorrow bathing and braiding and driving horses to the horse park, either.

And I can't even imagine how I'm going to balance all my responsibilities here, at the event, and *ride* three phases in one day on Thursday, with the whole weekend of work stretching ahead of me before my one precious day off.

This was a mistake, I think, not for the first time, but certainly with the most certainty.

Maybe eventing feels like home, and there's no denying all the good feelings that rose up while I was at the horse park this evening.

But it could be I'm going about it the wrong way. I could always just have a project horse that I bring up through the levels while making money on my own terms at Posey's farm. Wouldn't that have made more sense?

"Maybe you should quit," I say to myself, knowing it's mainly the exhaustion is talking, but still there has to be a wisp of truth in there. "Maybe you're too old for this."

But quitting would mean giving up Bucky. That would be crazy.

And, although I don't know why I even care, it would also mean giving up Malcolm.

Chapter Nineteen

A RAPPING ON the truck window makes me sit bolt upright. I gasp and look around, confused. I have a sore spot on my forehead and my right hand is asleep, pins and needles tingling up my forearm.

I glance left, trying to figure out why I'm in the pickup truck, and I see Malcolm peering through the window. His expression is the odd mix of concern and irritation that I've noticed a few times when I'm interacting with him. Like he's not saying what he wants to, and it's killing him. I'm still not sure why he saves his temper for Alison, his faithful barn manager, and mainly leaves me be with little more than a hint of gruffness. It's not what I expected; I suppose I should be grateful.

"Open the door," he says, his voice muffled by the glass. "Are you okay? What's going on?"

Oh my god. I fell asleep in the truck. What time is it? I steal a glance at my phone, face-up on the seat beside me.

It's eight o'clock.

I've been asleep for nearly an hour.

Certain I'm about to be fired, I open the truck door and stare at Malcolm, humiliation and horror coiling in my stomach. Maybe I'm on the fence about continuing to work this job, but this is not the way I planned to exit it.

Malcolm leans into the truck, his hands on the door frame. Encircling me like a fence. "Are you okay?"

I shrug and shake my head at the same time. "I don't know what happened. I parked the truck, and I was going to get out and then..."

"You just passed out." Malcolm rubs his face with his hand, looking chagrined. "I didn't even know you were back yet. Alison was on the way out and she sent me a text that you were sitting in the truck. She was in a hurry and couldn't stop, I guess."

I wonder if Alison saw that I was asleep with my head against the steering wheel, and just left that part out, as a fun surprise for Malcolm.

"I'm really sorry," I stammer. "I swear I didn't mean to fall asleep. I'm just—" I stop myself from whining the word *tired*.

But it's like Malcolm heard it, anyway. He nods, and suddenly his expression softens. It's a welcome change, all the lines that usually gather around his lips and eyes smoothing out. Tension adds years to his face, I realize. He's always handsome, but now his skin fairly glows beneath his leftover summer tan, and his green eyes seem to glitter at me.

I find myself taking one long, unsteady breath.

Malcolm doesn't notice that I'm having a moment. He just says, "I know you're tired. I am, too. This schedule is for the dogs. You want to come up to the house and have dinner with me? I feel like I need to win you back after this day."

I blink at him for a moment. *Win me back?* "I—uh—sure?"

He smiles and gives me a friendly pat on the knee. My skin does that hot-and-cold thing again. As tired and confused as I am, my body seems to have no problem coming alive every time Malcolm so much as brushes against me.

"Go get into your comfy clothes and then come back to the house," he says. "You can drive if you don't feel like walking, but it's just five minutes. The hill makes it look farther away."

"My comfy clothes?" I ask, remembering the night I scared his client and he gave me a box of hot chocolate.

Malcolm's smile is as bright as the moon. "Unless you think rainbow-farting unicorns isn't formal enough for dinner. But I'm going to be in *my* PJs. Not as cute as yours, just fair warning...it's late and I'm done with zippers and buttons for the day."

Buttons, I think, but he's already turning away and walking up the driveway. Just over the rise, five minutes away.

The only question now is: will I really wear those pajamas to dinner with the boss?

Well, at this point, I kind of have to. It's practically a dare, right? And when does Evie Ballenger stand down from a dare?

Upstairs in the barn apartment, I change out of my dusty barn clothes, take a lightning-fast shower, and tug on my silly pajamas. I pause to give myself a hard stare in the bathroom mirror. The mirror isn't enough to show me anything below the waist, but the view of my top is pretty hilarious. Rainbow-farting unicorns for the win, right?

The night is turning chilly, though, so I add a fleece jacket on the way out.

I'm halfway down the stairs when I notice a ruckus going down in some of the paddocks. I sigh. My plan had been to go eat, then come back and do night-check, but it's obvious these horses aren't going to survive on their own for another hour. I turn right instead of left, heading for the paddocks. When I hear another bang and a horse squeals, I break into a jog. There's no telling what those dummies are getting up to without human supervision!

And sure enough, it's trouble. In the dim light thrown from the barn, I can see that Oceanus has his blanket strap caught on a water trough. It's one of those "how on earth" moments that only seem to come to the top horses. A plow horse could have been turned out with fifty straps dangling off him and never gotten hurt, but a top-level event horse worth six figures can't stay out of trouble even with his blanket done up perfectly and his legs wrapped in cotton wool.

Oceanus is a smart horse, though, and he isn't panicky yet. Just kicking at the water trough as if he thinks he can convince the heavy rubber trough to let go of him.

"Hold still, buddy," I say, slipping between the wooden slats of the fence. Sometimes it's nice to be the tiniest girl I know; it saves the effort of climbing fences or finding gates. I jog over to the trough, my fleece jacket open to the evening chill. "Look," I call to Oceanus. "I'm wearing unicorns. Cute, right?"

Oceanus looks at me with pricked ears. Then he nickers. It's a tiny, adorable *save- me* request that makes my heart wring. "Poor boy," I tell him. "I've got you. Mama Evie has you."

I put a hand on his neck, feeling the heat of him, his rapid heartbeat, and lean down to twist the blanket buckle free. The little metal clip caught on the lip of the water trough somehow; he must have been rubbing on it. Horses will rub on just about anything, I've found.

The stupid little buckle has gotten itself caught on the lip so well, you'd think it was made to fit there. I have to fiddle with it, and while I'm still trying to unhook it, Oceanus concludes that since I am here, the problem is solved. He starts to back away. When the blanket buckle catches and resists, he completely loses his cool.

Oceanus snorts and gives another tug—a hard one. Then he starts to thrash. This water trough, he has decided, needs to die.

"Ho, buddy, ho, ho, ho, ho!" I cry, getting more shrill by the second, but it's too late to stop him. Oceanus flings himself backward with all the strength he's got—and it's a lot, because this horse is Olympic-level-fit—and as he rears back on his hindquarters, the water trough actually tugs forward. Good grief, what is the buckle made of, titanium? I scramble to get out of the trough's way, but it turns out the trough isn't going on a rampage. It's just going to flip over.

On me.

Water floods over me, unicorn pajamas and rainbows and all. It's ice-cold, and I can't help but scream. Luckily, by now the buckle has finally snapped, so I don't scare Oceanus with my shocked cry. He's already galloping away, his breath sharp and loud in the quiet night.

Did I say quiet? I actually mean in the *riot* of sound that erupts now, as every other horse who was sweating it out now decides to either panic or celebrate Oceanus's great escape. Panic and celebration look pretty similar when you're a horse, so I can't be sure which. They're spinning around their paddocks, they're squealing and kicking, they're whinnying and snorting. It sounds like a three-ring circus with every ring going at once.

There's no way Malcolm won't hear this, I think, trying to wring water from my fleece pajamas and coat. Half of Marion County can hear this.

A sharp wind finds its way into my open jacket as I trudge across the paddock after Oceanus, who is bouncing around in the far corner, snorting at Bucky, the closest horse to him, and therefore his best friend on this exciting night. I start to tug my sodden coat closed, then stop as the water makes everything worse. All I want it to go inside and forget this night ever happened. But, true to form, this day *won't* end.

Now, I have to find a way to tie up that dangling strap on his blanket, and then I have to text Malcolm and tell him I won't be coming to dinner. A stab of disappointment runs through me, but there's nothing to be done. I'm drenched, cold, and dirty. My skin goes hot and cold every time my skin meets Malcolm's. I'm on the fence about even working for him anymore. Facts are facts: I need a hot shower, fresh clothes, and a forty-year nap before I'm ready to face that man again.

"Evie?"

I've finally caught up with Oceanus and am reaching for the dangling blanket strap, but I pause as I hear my name. So does Oceanus; he turns around, ignoring my presence completely, and trots across the field. I watch the loose strap bounce around his hocks as he heads for Malcolm, a shadowy figure on the other side of the paddock. Silhouetted by the lights on the barn behind him, he looks reassuring: a tall and strong figure come to save me.

But of course, that's not his job.

Oceanus stops at the fence and nickers to Malcolm. The horse is now back where we began. With a sigh, I cross the paddock yet again.

By the time I reach them, Malcolm has already climbed the fence and is tying up the broken blanket strap.

"I see you had a bit of excitement—" he begins to joke, and then he does a double-take. "Evie! You're soaking wet!"

"I'm aware," I answer shortly, because the cold is starting to seep into my bones and I'm too frozen to be polite. "I need to go inside and get—"

I almost say "out of these clothes" but something about Malcolm's face as he looks me up and down stops me from speaking so intimately. He shakes his head and tears off his coat, one of those beautiful waxed leather coats like the one Posey inherited from her

Irish racehorse trainer father. "No, no," I demure, but he's already on me, wrapping the coat around my shoulders and tugging it close over my chest.

"You're freezing out here," he says urgently, buttoning it up. There's no tenderness in his actions, only speed, but the feel of his fingers brushing my neck as he pulls the coat close to my cheek is enough to send shivers racing up and down my spine. Or maybe that's just the intense chill entering my system. My teeth are chattering now and it's hard for me to tell what sensations are what.

"To your apartment, let's go!" he commands, marching me towards the paddock gate. With Oceanus still sniffing excitedly at us, I find myself being maneuvered like a doll, straight out of the paddock. There's a pause to close the gate ("Get back, Oceanus, for heaven's sake," he says, shoving at the horse, who is loving all of this) and then he is guiding me across the driveway to the barn, up the stairs, and to the door...which is locked.

"Where are your keys?" Malcolm asks.

I'm shivering all over despite his coat, and it's all I can do to chatter, "In my pocket."

"In your pocket—which one?"

"Pants," I reply, writhing inwardly.

He has me wrapped up in his coat like a burrito, so my hands aren't free to dig out my keys. A thinking person might have concluded that since we'll be inside in a moment if the keys are procured, he might as well open the coat and let me fish out my keys from my own pocket. But I guess he's not thinking straight, probably because he caught me chasing around his top horse in the moonlight and he wants to get back out there and check on him properly, so Malcolm just feels along my thigh, plunges his hand into my pocket, and grabs the keys.

If I wasn't chattering my teeth so hard, I'd gasp. His fingers feel like they're burning right through the cold fleece, leaving their mark on my skin. And just as quickly, his hand is gone, and he's reaching past me, his chest brushing my shoulder. He sticks the key into the door lock with what seems like unnecessary effort.

Romeo is waiting on the sofa, his accusing face on, but there's no time to apologize to him for leaving him at night; I'm being marched across the room to the bathroom. "Get out of those clothes and into a hot shower," Malcolm says, in a tone which expects immediate compliance.

"Okay," I mutter, too cold to bother complaining about how mean he's being.

While I'm standing under the hot water, my wet clothes scattered over the tile floor outside the bathtub, my brain slowly starts to work properly again. Wow, I think, I was *really* cold out there. Like, hypothermia-cold. Pretty incredible. I turn my face to the shower and let the hot water beat down on my skin. This is good. Arousing, even. The way it feels when a finger traces down your—

My eyes fly open, which is a mistake, because I'm looking up at the shower-head. I shriek and close them again, swiping at my eyes as soon as I've turned around and gotten my face clear of the water hammering down. Most barn apartment don't rejoice in water pressure this powerful. I'm still blinking the water out of them when Malcolm's voice is at the door.

"Evie? Are you alright?"

He's *really* close, I think, with a shiver that's definitely not from the cold anymore. This bathroom is tiny, that door is basically made of cardboard, and right on the other side is a tall, authoritative, handsome—

Malcolm. My boss. Who just wrapped me up in his coat, his fingers brushing my skin, before he ran his hand down my thigh—

I slap both my cheeks. *Snap out of it, Evie.*

It's official. The lack of sleep is destroying my reason. I was just feeling all warm and sexy about *Malcolm.*

"Evie, do I need to come in? Answer me!"

The command in his voice does something to me. Something... inappropriate.

It shouldn't. I don't like being bossed around. I have spent most of my life man-free because I don't like being told what to do.

But the way Malcolm's voice dips down into his chest when he's barking out an order—well, that voice seems to seek out all the most willing, embarrassingly humble parts of me.

Not good, Evie.

The door handle turns and I shriek again, terrified he'll come in. Hopeful he'll come in? *No,* terrified! I stammer out, "I'm fine, I'm fine, I'm fine!"

There's a pause. Then Malcolm rumbles, "For god's sake, you just had to *say* so," and I hear his footsteps as he walks away from the bathroom door.

After that, the shower ceases to feel like a safe space. I'm out, dripping on my wet unicorn pajamas and wrapping a towel around my chest, when I realize I have no clean clothes in here.

My bedroom door is about six feet away. With Malcolm still lurking in my apartment, that six feet feels like six miles. I look down at my towel and wish I had spent a little racehorse money on larger, more luxurious bath-sheets. This skimpy thing barely covers my unmentionables.

Well, there's only one thing I can do. The heat is already retreating, and I know enough about getting really cold to know I need to bundle up before I take another chill. I open the bathroom door a half-inch and call, "Malcolm, I—um—I'm going to my bedroom to get dressed."

A pan clatters on the stovetop. *What is he doing?* I can't see him through the tiny opening I've given the door. "No problem," he replies. "I won't peek."

"Okay," I squeak, and then I take a breath, fling open the door, and scamper for my bedroom. Romeo looks up from the center of my bed, where he has retreated to complain that there's a stranger in the apartment. I close the door behind me; it feels as flimsy and ephemeral as a curtain of beads. I'll just keep this towel tucked up to my chin while I find some clothes...

Under my cat's disapproving stare, I find a pair of fleece-lined riding breeches, some thick gray socks, and a black-and-white checked flannel shirt, then wriggle into everything as fast as I can. There's a draft in the bedroom window, and I pause to stuff the towel against the windowsill to block it out. Then I take a look at myself in the mirror.

Not bad, actually. Sort of lumberjack-chic. My soaking wet hair is a mess. I wind the whole ridiculous length of it into a bun. Better. And not so cold.

"Here I go, Romeo," I tell my cat. He closes his green eyes, fed up with me.

Malcolm turns from the stove as I pad into the apartment in my thick socks. "Well, you look warmer," he says pleasantly. "Supper's almost ready."

I blink at the mess he's made of the kitchen counters. "What are you *making?*"

Chapter Twenty

"Well, I had limited ingredients to work with," Malcolm says. "And don't worry, I'll give you a little something in your next check to cover everything I'm using up. I know what it's like living on a working student stipend." He chuckles. It would be funny if he wasn't the one paying me a starvation wage, but he's also boarding my horse and giving me free housing, so, whatever. It's my own fault I don't need it and still have a mortgage payment. That's the joy of doing the work of a twenty-year-old.

"Anyway, it started out as chili out of a can, pretty simple, but now I think it's kind of a chili-beef-nacho-salad," he continues. "Because I couldn't find any cornbread mix. Do you really not have cornbread mix? It's like thirty cents a box. I thought it was a must in any working student kitchen."

"I'm all out," I say, astonished by the fact that he's decided to make me dinner. I look at the discarded wrappers and boxes on the counter. "Did you use *all* the cheese?"

"There was only half a bag of shredded," Malcolm says defensively.

"It needed to last me the rest of the week."

"Right, well, I *said* I'd pay you for everything."

We look at each other for a moment. Malcolm's jaw has a mulish set to it, as if he knows he has been naughty and he's not going to admit it.

160

"Okay then," I sigh. "I appreciate it."

"Well, sit down," Malcolm blusters like a fed-up housewife, "and I'll bring you some food."

"Let me get you a beer, at least," I offer.

"Can't say no to that."

With beers cracked and the kitchen table laden with plates of a very interesting looking—Taco? Chili? Salad?—we sit across from one another and dig in. I find that Malcolm is a very liberal hot sauce user, which I appreciate in a person. I also enjoy burning my tongue relentlessly with pepper for no apparent reason. It's just a personal pleasure. He watches me tip some extra sauce onto a lettuce leaf which has offended me with its nakedness.

"You can take the heat," he says appreciatively.

"I have been slowly deadening my tastebuds since I was eighteen," I explain. "I was vegan for a while and I thought food was boring, so a boyfriend introduced me to hot sauce. The vegan thing went out the window, but the heat remains my best friend."

"What about the boyfriend?"

I glance up at him. Malcolm is grinning. "Long gone before high school graduation," I tell him. "I'm not good at relationships with humans. Just horses."

"Well, no one expected you to keep your high school boyfriend forever," he says mildly.

"Turns out Ryan was gay, too, so that was kind of a bummer," I recall. "I think he might be married to a nice man in Chicago now. He designs expensive water faucets, according to his Facebook."

"Ah-ha!"

"Ah-ha, what?"

"You stalk your ex boyfriends on Facebook! I knew you were just like everyone else, Evie Ballenger. Underneath that cool, professional exterior, you're—"

"Underneath that *what?*" I put down my fork and stare at him in genuine confusion. "Who here is cool and professional? You're one of those things, anyway, but me? I'm neither."

"Excuse me?" Malcolm stares at me, his smile edged with incredulity. "You're the most professional employee I've ever had, and that includes Alison. I never have to wonder where you are. I never have to worry if you're going to talk back to a client. I never see you come sneaking in late or taking a long lunch break so you can fit in a phone interview with some other trainer you're thinking of ditching me for—"

"First of all," I laugh, holding up a finger to stop him mid-compliment, before things get ridiculous. "First of all, you've only had me on the payroll for less than a month, so we are still in a honeymoon period. Second, how could you say that about Alison? While she's running the place with the precision of a Swiss clock, I have forced you to drag me to the ER, rescue me from certain drowning and/or freezing in a paddock, and I'm sure there have been some other shenanigans I'm not proud of..." I trail off. He's looking at me with genuine affection now, and the light in his eyes is almost too much to bear. Did I know Malcolm had such beautiful, sparkling, expressive eyes? What am I going to do with this knowledge now?

"If this is the honeymoon period," Malcolm says quietly, "I hope it never ends."

I bite my lip.

He's still looking at me with those bright eyes, and all at once it's too much. I duck my head over my food and poke at the salad, shoving some lettuce aside in favor of some beef. Naturally, a little fleck of hot sauce slips from the wet lettuce and hits my cheek, just below my left eye. I stifle a little shriek and swipe at it with a fingernail, closing my eyes tight to make sure I don't end up with habanero blindness, a malady that probably doesn't exist but which would be the perfect ending to this pleasant dinner with Malcolm.

"Easy there," he murmurs, and I hear his chair creak as he gets up. In a moment Malcolm's warmth is next to my body, his chest just touching my shoulder and giving me full-body shivers. I gasp as something cool and damp touches my cheek—Malcolm has wet a napkin and is gently brushing against my face. "All gone," he says. "Close call, though. That was almost in your eye."

"I should wear goggles," I chuckle nervously, opening my eyes. His face is very close to mine. I can see the faint stubble of a day's beard. He has an unfairly chiseled chin. From this close, it begs to be traced with one fingertip.

"You'd look very cute in them," Malcolm says, and then he's heading back to his chair, leaving a wintry chill in his wake. I feel like I'm back outside in the teeth of that north wind, wet clothes weighing me down. He sits down and picks up his fork, smiles at me, goes back to eating. As if nothing happened.

None of it did happen to him, I realize bleakly. Those shivers, that warmth, the white-hot feeling that flashes across my skin when he touches me by accident—*that's all me.*

And I need to get over it.

Malcolm Horsham is my boss. He's not some guy I met at the feed store; our hands didn't touch over the same bucket of electrolytes, we didn't blush at one another while carrying our purchases out to our trucks, only to find we're parked too close to each other to open our doors at the same time. There was no meet-cute, and this is not a rom-com.

Just a woman of twenty-seven who made some questionable decisions with her employment and who is trying to survive those choices now, and a professional horse trainer who has a reputation for scaring his employees out of his employment more quickly than anyone else in the business. Just because he hasn't turned on me yet doesn't mean it isn't coming.

I resolve to keep my head down, finish my dinner, and get this guy out of my apartment before I can do anything else stupid in front of him.

"Tomorrow should be easier than today," Malcolm says eventually, as if he knows a new level of quiet has settled over us and he's not entirely comfortable with it. "No riding, so the schedule shouldn't be so tight."

"Are you kidding?" I can't help myself. "With Alison cracking the whip? I am guessing I'll have thirty minutes to bathe and condition, forty-five to braid manes, and there will be beatings if I go over any of my marks."

"Oh, she's not that bad," Malcolm says with a chuckle. "Alison is a godsend, honestly."

"I don't dispute that, but she needs more staff."

He lifts his eyebrows. "*She* needs more? I think you mean *I* do."

"No, Alison is your barn manager. She needs help working for her. Like, three more of me, for a start."

"Three more of you," Malcolm says fondly. "Imagine that. We'd have to have our own dedicated wing at the hospital."

"Oh, that was low," I inform him.

"Only joking!" He holds up his hands in self-defense. "I'm sorry! Well, let's just see what happens this weekend, shall we? I think the two of you have things well in hand."

I nod and go back to scraping up the rest of my salad, which really is good despite the odd pairings. Malcolm does the same, and afterwards we drain our beers in silence. Is it a companionable silence, I wonder, or is he just finishing up so he can get out of here? "Thanks so much for making me dinner here," I say finally. "I didn't expect that, obviously."

"Well, I promised you supper, and I wasn't going to drag you back into the cold night," he says, his voice oddly impersonal. "But I guess I better be going now."

I nod slowly, feeling disappointed. We were getting along so well, and now...maybe I shouldn't have started talking about work, I don't know. Male bosses can be so weird when you criticize them, even just slightly. All I did was say we needed more staff to keep Alison from going crazy...

"Do you really think we need another working student?" Malcolm asks, as if that's what he's been pondering in silence. "I think I could get someone for the rest of the circuit."

"Oh," I say, flustered. "I mean—I think the days would be a little *easier*, but maybe that's not what you want to hear—"

"No, it's fine." Malcolm stands up and picks up his coat. "Let me talk to someone this weekend. I might have some help for the two of you, after all."

"Well, that's great." I stand up as well, wondering if I should get the door for him, or shake his hand, or even give him a hug.

Wouldn't *that* be delicious, my devious brain whispers.

I end up standing still, awkwardly gripping the back of my chair, while he pulls on his coat and heads out into the night. He waves goodbye right before the door closes behind him. But he doesn't look back. Doesn't meet my eyes. Doesn't give me another look at the sparkling personality he revealed so briefly.

I sit down and look at Romeo, who has hopped down from my bed and is in the bedroom doorway, tail wrapped around his forepaws, gazing at me impassively. "Well, what do you think?" I ask my cat. "Did I make a big enough idiot of myself?"

Romeo opens his pink mouth and mews.

"And he left me the dishes," I realize, looking at the mess of my kitchen. "What a guy, Romeo. What a guy."

Sighing, I pick up our plates and carry them to the sink to start clean-up. Nothing like washing dishes and staring out a window into the darkness, wondering where it all went wrong, to close out a weird evening.

Chapter Twenty-One

THURSDAY MORNING WOULD be a lot tougher if Posey didn't show up, giving me a boost of solidarity on an otherwise unfriendly morning. Alison is in a mood, Malcolm is tense, and the horses don't want anything but food, so they're hardly any help.

When she arrives, I'm midway through tacking up the first horse of the day. I leave the girth on the first hole and hold out my arms to her. The crushing hug she offers in return is exactly the squeeze I need to feel human again.

"Oh my god, I miss you, Pose," I moan.

"Ugh, I miss you so much, girl!" she exclaims. "How is eventing life treating you?"

"Not quite as good as racing life," I admit, stepping back. I already miss our hug. Am I that starved for human affection? No wonder I was getting weird ideas about Malcolm. But we'll keep that under wraps for now. Just the business details for Posey. "For one thing, I'm doing about ten times as much work, and getting paid less than a tenth of what I used to make."

"And that's just *one* thing?" Posey looks concerned. "Are you thinking of coming back? I've got a groom on your old barn detail, but he won't mind if you take over."

"I can't, not yet. I mean, yes. Sometimes I think of quitting this—" I lower my voice and look around, hoping Alison or Malcolm won't

167

overhear. But they're off doing their own things. "And then something draws me right back in," I finish, aware that it lets Posey know some things are being left unsaid.

I can't tell her everything, though.

Because I don't want to admit, even to myself, that dinner with Malcolm two nights ago is what slowed my roll when I was thinking of quitting. Even though there's no denying that I was thinking of leaving, warming up to the idea of returning to my old, comfortable life, and then he put his coat around me and made sure I was safe and warm, and made me dinner, and sat and ate with me, and showed me a little something of himself that wasn't on display during work hours.

The other part I thought about a lot was the ending: the way we had a warm, real conversation for the first half of our dinner, and that things got stilted and weird after that. It was so disappointing.

Yeah. I've been thinking about that way too much, actually. I wish I could just let it go.

I can't explain all of that to Posey, not right now. I glance at the horse next to me. Fidget is on alert, watching the rest of the stabling area as horses come and go. "I better finish tacking him up," I say.

"Okay. Well, Kayla's coming, too." Posey seems relieved that I feel good enough about my job to not walk out and leave it all behind. "She just has longer to drive than I did, so, expect her in another hour, I think."

"That's perfect timing. My dressage test is in about an hour and ten, so just bring her over to the warm-up and you guys can catch it!" My stomach jumps, a little flip of nervousness. But it should be fine. I am pretty sure I know my dressage test. Just to practice it, I think, *Enter Working Trot, Halt a X, Salute the Judge.*

But that's *all* the tests until like, way upper-level stuff. Knowing the first move doesn't prove anything.

"We'll be there," Posey promises. She runs her eyes over the horse I'm supposed to be tacking up. "Who is this?"

"Oh!" I realize I'm going to fall behind if I don't keep moving. "This is Fidget," I say, tightening the horse's girth another few holes. "He's going in the Preliminary Level one-day event today, with Malcolm."

"Pretty," Posey says. "Dutch warmblood?"

"Yeah, is it obvious?"

"Not really," Posey laughs. "Lucky guess. He honestly could be Thoroughbred except for his height, and that shoulder—va-voom, he must get *some* extension with that thing, huh?"

"He really does. I've seen Malcolm do some pretty incredible stuff with him at home." I pick up his bridle and Fidget lifts his head immediately. I'm short, and Fidget loves that about me. Slows down the bridling process by whole minutes. "Of course, he does the giraffe routine."

"Tall horses," Posey commiserates. "Well, I'll let you get to it. I don't want to slow you down. See at the dressage!"

"Great," I say, already trying to convince Fidget to lower his head. By the time I get him bridled, Posey is long gone, but Alison is stalking over, phone in hand. She's wearing dress boots and white breeches, her show shirt collar sticking up above a sage-green sweatshirt with the farm logo on the chest. Not a good replacement for one of my best friends, especially with the taskmistress expression she's wearing.

"We need this horse at the dressage warm-up now," she informs me. "Is he ready?"

"Ready as soon as this noseband is fastened," I grunt, leaning beneath Fidget's head, which he has now lowered to knee-level, just to be as annoying as possible. "Malcolm is over there already?"

"He's talking to some owners," Alison says. "They always show up at the worst possible moment."

All day will be the worst possible moment, I think. This is a one-day horse trials. It's go-go-go until the last horse comes out of the stadium jumping arena.

"Off you go," Alison says as I straighten up. She's still examining her phone. As I walk Fidget past her, I glance at the screen, expecting to see her schedule. But it's actually the dressage test she has to ride in an hour. She runs her hand through her hair, and I realize her fingers are trembling ever so slightly.

Alison's scared. That knowledge gives me an unfair little buoy of confidence as I set off across the show-grounds. At least I'm not the only one from Fine Day Farm with nerves. Yeah, we've both done this before...but that doesn't make it any easier, does it?

The dressage warm-up area is cordoned off with white rope and some helpful orange cones at the corners. There's a sand arena and a wide grassy area just beyond. Hot horses are bouncing around, their eyes wide and their nostrils flared.

Warm-up arenas tend to have any anything-goes feeling, especially at the lower levels, where skill sets tend to vary wildly. But this is a ring full of Preliminary riders, and there are quite a few big-name trainers like Malcolm here today, along with hungry amateurs getting ready for the spring circuit, so there's a similarity to the horses out here: mostly tallish, mostly bay, all of them fit and savagely ready to head out to cross-country so that they can *gallop*.

But first, they have to maintain some level of decorum for their dressage tests. And that's why the warm-up is so very, very full. These horses are getting a very solid riding-in, as the English eventing manuals call a warm-up.

Malcolm is standing off to one side by the in-gate, looking incredibly dashing in white breeches and polished dress boots. He's already in his black dressage coat, a blindingly white shirt collar poking above the lapels, and as he leans on one leg, his arms crossed across his chest, I get such a rush of attraction that I feel like my eyes must be bugging out of my head, cartoon-coyote style. This guy is *fit* —and yes, I meant that in the British sense of the word, too.

There's no shame in feeling attracted to an athletic man in his dressage habit. I know I see him in riding breeches and boots every single day, but there's something about the tuxedo-like formalwear of dressage, along with the secret knowledge that two days ago he was sitting across from me in my apartment, eating dinner with me, that gives my heart a few minor palpitations.

Okay, Mama, I tell myself. Let's be logical. You're attracted to Malcolm. That's natural and normal. He's a thirty-two-year-old, very fit, quite famous equestrian. You would be attracted to him even if you didn't really know him. Possibly you would be *more* attracted to him because you would be missing important information about his personality, like that he's gruff and demanding and thinks that just you and Alison can do the work of ten men. Or that he still hasn't let you ride your own horse. Or that he rescued you from the freezing cold, wrapped you in his coat, and made you dinner...

Stop that, Evie. Enough of that. Concentrate on the dirty dishes he left all over your kitchen. It took you half an hour to clean up after his little chili-taco-salad innovation.

I bring Fidget to a halt about five feet away from Malcolm and the owners. Malcolm glances at me, nods, and continues his conversation with the woman across from him.

He's not going to cut them off and get on his horse?

Fidget, hot and bothered by the commotion and the realization that he's going to have to do more dressage than he wants to on this fine, cool morning, starts turning in anxious circles. His hooves tear at the damp sod and a clump of mud flicks onto one of his white stockings.

"Can you stand him *still?*" Malcolm demands, in a tone so harsh that even his owners look startled.

I look at my boss in shock. What, he's going to embarrass me in front of the entire eventing community today? Attitude problems are one thing at home, but in public, I would expect a *little* civility, if only to keep up appearances.

"He's not going to stand still," I say finally, when it's apparent I'm not going to get an apology for being spoken to like that in front of another human. "He's ready to go."

"Then just walk him around," Malcolm says brusquely. "Use your head, Evie."

I bite my lip before I say something really offensive in front of a paying client. But he's got a real nerve. I had to rush over here with poor Fidget, and now Malcolm won't even get on? This is absurd.

Time ticks away. Still, Malcolm is speaking to the middle-aged couple as if he has all day. I feel like pulling my hair out. He's running out of time for a thorough warm-up, and there's nothing I can do about it. Eventing rules say that no one can warm-up a competing horse except for the registered rider. I could get on Fidget with a very loose rein and walk him, but that wouldn't accomplish anything more than what I'm doing on the ground. He needs to be *worked*. Trot, canter, transitions, all of the above.

Finally, with only about twenty minutes before his test, the owners wave goodbye to Malcolm and he comes over to get his horse, buttoning his coat up as he walks up to me. "Hold him still so I can mount," he says. "Is his girth tight?"

"It was," I hedge, "before we walked over, but—"

Malcolm already has his foot in the left stirrup. He leaves the ground with a little jump, and as his weight hits the stirrup in full, the saddle slips a good two inches to the left. He aborts the mount, kicking his foot free and hopping backward to regain his balance on the ground. Then he rounds on me with a face like a thunderstorm. "What the *hell*, Evie?"

"It was tight when I got here!" I retort, just barely holding back from a full-fledged shout. "But he's been walking, and he's sweaty and tucked-up, and now it's not tight enough to support mounting. Why didn't you *check* it, you idiot?"

Malcolm stares at me. His eyes, which sparkled so beautifully at me on Tuesday night, now seem flat and dead.

I'm fired, I think, and the realization hits me with more dread than I would have expected.

I clench every muscle in my body, waiting for Malcolm to say those awful words. But he just whirls around, straightens the saddle, and pops the girth up two holes. In another ten seconds, he's on the horse, gathering up the reins and turning in a tight circle around me.

"Meet me in front of the dressage arena in fifteen minutes," he hisses. "Wet cloth for boots, a second one for his mouth and nose. If you don't have them, run and get them now."

"Of course I have them," I snap, back on the defensive, but he's already riding away, nudging Fidget into a trot.

I watch him rising with each stride for a few moments, feeling like I should be observing him closely, learning, but I really can't bear to look at him right now.

And also, I realize, I've forgotten the little grooming bucket with the wet cloths.

I know better than to run headlong across a show-ground, screaming and waving my arms, but honestly, it would feel so good. Instead, I have to settle for a stiff-armed power walk, racing between the throngs of horses and riders and kids on mopeds who feel like they can't walk between the individual arenas. The stabling area seems to be a ridiculous distance away from the dressage, and by the time I get back, Alison is grooming the next horse to go out. She looks at me, then at the bucket sitting on the ground near the tack stall, and raises her eyebrows.

"Seriously?"

I don't answer her. I just grab the bucket and launch myself back into my power walk. Someday, when I am old and gray, I will be the fastest retiree at the mall.

For now, though, I just have to survive this day without getting fired.

Somehow I make it back to the dressage area within the fifteen minutes allowed to me—and before Malcolm gets to the arena, so he probably doesn't know I forgot the bucket. I'm ready and waiting as he walks Fidget up, the horse already impressively calm and cool on a loose rein, as if fifteen minutes was somehow all he needed for warm-up after all.

I silently wipe off Malcolm's boots, trying not to feel like the act is weirdly intimate...but it is, it really is.

He backs his left foot out to the stirrup so that I can more easily get the dust off. I feel his foot inside the Italian leather, which seems as thin as a glove. Without thinking, I give it a little squeeze.

"Hey!" he exclaims. "What was that for?"

I look up at him, surprised at myself, and suddenly we're both smiling. "I just thought you deserved that for being so rude to me before," I tell him boldly. "Anyone would think I'm your working student and you can say whatever you want to me."

"Yeah, we wouldn't want that." Malcolm's smile widens into a grin, and that sparkle is back in his eyes. I feel myself warming up, as if the chilly morning suddenly turned into a summer afternoon, and then a ring steward calls, "Horsham on deck," and Malcolm's face becomes all business again. He slips his boot back into the stirrup. "Get his mouth, okay?" he says, looking at the dressage arena instead of me.

"Okay," I mutter, pulling out the other tea towel. I wipe the extra drool and foam from Fidget's lips and make sure his nostrils are clear. "You're all set, boss," I say, adding a little emphasis to his title.

Just to remind us both of where we stand.

Malcolm doesn't even glance back at me as he trots Fidget around the white boards of the dressage arena, using up the minute between the preceding rider's final salute and the bell signaling for the next rider to enter the ring.

That's fine, though.

I don't need lingering stares and constant upheaval on an event day, I think. And neither does he.

Somehow, an hour later, I'm mounted on Diamond and riding around that warm-up myself. Alison and Malcolm are in the ring too, and while we've ridden like this back at the farm, it feels good on a different level to be a trio at an event. Like we're really all on the same team, instead of three very differing levels of authority, with me on the bottom.

Malcolm even finds time to yell at me—I mean, give me some pointers—as I bumble around the warm-up on a revved-up Diamond, feeling as if I've never ridden this horse before. The Diamond of the farm and the Diamond of an event are two different creatures, for sure.

"You have to raise your hands and sit deep," Malcolm tells me as I bounce past him at an entirely over-expressive trot. "He needs to sit back on his hind end and you're the one who has to put him there. Do some trot-halt transitions a few times and really sit him down, okay? And remember—tits out!"

A few heads turn our way, and I hear some chuckles. A blush runs up my face, but there's no time to think about it. In a few minutes I'm going to have to ride over to that arena and check in with the steward, and then I'm going into the arena to ride between those boards, and—

"Relax," Malcolm says. "It's not life or death, Ballenger."

And there's something about the humor in his tone, or the way he uses my last name instead of calling me Evie, that helps me shake the nervousness out of my muscles. At least, enough to ride like a normal human who has been on a horse before.

Posey and Kayla are waiting near the dressage ring, waving at me as I ride over. Kayla holds up a blue and yellow box that can only have come from Donut King. What a freaking godsend good friends are, I think, waving back. The knowledge of a glazed blueberry donut at the finish line will get me through this test.

Well, not the finish line. We aren't racing today. It'll carry me through the final salute and exit on loose rein.

"Remember," Malcolm says, bringing his horse alongside me, "you're going to sit deep through this. Push him along. Don't let him pull you, okay?"

"Okay," I breathe. That's what I'm doing now. I'm breathing. Deeply, rhythmically, as best I can. I figure if I just keep breathing in a slow, careful cycle now, my body will remember how to do it all the way through my dressage test.

"You've got this," Malcolm says, leaning over to pat me on the knee, and I instantly forget how to breathe.

Chapter Twenty-Two

"HE SEEMS NICE," Kayla says, watching me tear through the blueberry glazed donut with slightly widened eyes. We haven't seen each other in a while and she must have forgotten how I can eat when I'm tense. Posey once said it was like I had an auxiliary stomach I switched to in emergencies.

"He really does," Posey agrees. "I thought he had such a bad reputation."

"Oh, he deserves the reputation," I tell them, coming up briefly for air. "Because he can turn on a dime. He's a grump, then he's a nice guy, then he's a grump again, and you never know which way it's going to be. It's exhausting."

As I say it, I wonder if it's true, or if I'm just parroting something I heard at the feed store. But no, he does make me very tired. So it must be true.

"Anyone can be grumpy," Kayla argues. "I can be grumpy. We heard Malcolm was *mean*."

"That's true," Posey says. "He doesn't seem mean."

"He's mean to Alison sometimes, but she just snaps back at him."

"Oh, really." Kayla seems to find that interesting.

"And he yelled at me in front of a client this morning," I go on, wishing I hadn't brought up Alison. "I might have yelled back a little bit. In front of people. I'm lucky he didn't fire me on the spot."

Posey laughs. "I can just see you doing that, though. Getting bossed around is so not your thing, Evie! I mean, you've quit over less before."

She's right. Kayla and I once quit working at the racehorse farm back before Adam and Posey took over management, because we didn't like working for Adam's father. And I'd do it again, too.

"Seriously," Kayla says, "why do you put up with him being disrespectful to you now? Is it just the riding lessons? Because I can probably get you lessons with Pete when he comes to work with Basil," she adds. Her boyfriend, Basil Han, is training horses in partnership with Pete Morrison of Briar Hill Farm. Pete's kind of a big deal in eventing; his wife Jules even more so. It would make a lot of sense to run with Kayla's offer.

And yet even now, presented with an easy way out, I shrug it off.

"I don't know." I reach for another donut. "Bucky's under contract whether I work for Malcolm or not, you know. So, working there is still my best bet to get ahead with Bucky, even if I haven't ridden him yet. Malcolm said I can ride him next week, so we'll see."

"Okay," Kayla says. "Well, you let me know if you ever change your mind."

Kayla and Posey start chatting about a horse they both know over in the dressage arena while I tear through the second donut. It doesn't taste as good as the first one. Probably because I'm realizing that I've just spent several minutes trying to convince my best friends to believe three things that aren't true: that I want to leave Fine Day Farm, that Malcolm is the monster everyone says, and that I'm only sticking around so I can ride Bucky.

And maybe that all felt true to me before. A few days ago. Even earlier this morning, when he was snapping at me in front of his clients.

But if I'm being very honest with myself, things feel different now.

I feel like I'm heading up a very different path than the one I expected when I signed on as his working student.

Maybe something a lot more dangerous, a path that ends with me in tears, but that's the chance I take every time I get into the saddle. So I guess I'm used to taking big risks.

My phone buzzes and I swallow the rest of the chocolate-iced I just started chewing ten seconds ago. "That's my alarm to get the next horse ready for cross-country," I say. "Gotta go."

"Oh, boo," Kayla pouts. "But you just got here."

"What can I say? It's a one-day event. All mayhem, all day. You've done this, you know the drill."

"Yeah, I know." Kayla pushes the donut box to Posey. "*Maybe* we'll save you something for later."

"Please do," I say, prepping for my mad dash out of the shady tent and into the January sunshine. "I probably won't have anything better for lunch."

But as soon as I get back to the barn, I find myself pleasantly surprised. A well-dressed woman I recognize as Wesley's mom is setting out a big picnic lunch on a folding table in front of the tack stall. There's a long sub sandwich cut into little pieces, perfect for grabbing on the go while getting a horse groomed and tacked, and bags of chips, plastic-wrapped brownies, jugs of iced tea and lemonade...basically, the perfect school lunch for a bunch of twelve-year-olds, or the ultimate treat for a bunch of eventers. We are simply not that discriminating in the middle of a horse show day.

"Thank you so much, Miranda," I gasp, reaching for one of the little ham sandwiches. The two donuts somehow made me hungrier, but I didn't realize it until I saw actual protein in front of me. I'm already cramming the sandwich into my mouth as I head for the tack stall to grab the saddle and bridle I'll need for the next horse.

So, naturally, who do I run into but Malcolm?

He takes one look at the sandwich half-hanging out of my mouth and bursts into laughter. "You know, if you face any clients looking like this, I'd have to discipline you pretty seriously," he says when he finally has control of himself.

I've swallowed most of the sandwich by now; the rest is in my hand. "Why would you have to *discipline* me?" I ask sourly, putting absolutely no innuendo into the word—neither did he, I note.

"Because some level of professional decorum is a must in a barn of this level?" Malcolm suggests.

"Oh, shut up," Alison snaps, moving past both of us. "You can flirt back at the barn. For today, can we just *focus?*"

And she heads back out of the stall with a bridle over her shoulder.

Malcolm looks at me with a half-smile. "Did she just say we were flirting?"

"Ridiculous, right?" I want to walk away from him, but my stomach is clenching in a weird way which suggests I should stand still for a moment to avoid further embarrassment. Maybe I shouldn't have eaten half a ham sandwich on top of two donuts in quick succession. Or maybe it's the way Alison just publicly called the two of us out—and now I have to stand here and see what Malcolm thinks about it.

If I think we've been flirting, and maybe I do, a little, that's fine.

If he thinks we've been flirting, does that mean...does that mean something might come of it?

I resist the urge to bend over and groan, but the butterflies are really ripping into my stomach lining right now. Shouldn't butterflies be softer than this?

Malcolm rubs his jaw. That chiseled, roguish jawline that I've been having thoughts about for several days now...or let's be real here, for weeks. "Yeah," he agrees after a moment. "Ridiculous."

My stomach stops clenching and simply falls to my feet. Then I see his smile curving his lips.

"Absolutely crazy," he murmurs, a husky edge to his voice.

And he brushes against me, just enough to set my skin on fire, as he leaves the tack stall.

Somehow, I survive the day.

Diamond and I have a passable score to end on, including just one rail down in the stadium jumping, to finish in sixth place. I'm not jubilant in front of Malcolm, because that would be embarrassing, but inside I'm full of joy. I haven't evented in over a year, and some mornings out there on the training track, I'd wondered if I was ever going to find my way back to the cross-country course and the arena. To stand here at the horse park, just over three weeks into my time with Malcolm, and hold this green ribbon means a lot to me.

Malcolm seems pleased that I have pinned but not ecstatic with the color, so I put the ribbon to one side while I start packing up the supplies that will go back to the farm tonight. All the one-day horses will go home to enjoy a few days of turnout and leisure, while the three-day horses who are already here will become our priority.

I run a dolly laden with tack trunks out to the trailer and when I come back, I notice my ribbon is now hanging with the other ones alongside the tack stall.

My heart does a little skip of joy.

The show days slip by in a blur, made more complicated by the number of students and owners constantly crowding Alison and me. Wesley's mother brings us lunch every day, but she's really no better than the rest when it comes to questioning our every move, making sure we're doing the best we can to get her daughter into the spotlight this weekend. I understand the impulse, but I also wish that there was strict security and regulation about who was allowed to come into the barn. It would be a lot easier if it was riders and grooms only.

Wesley herself is surprisingly low on nervous energy, especially on cross-country day when I expect her to be beside herself. Her horse Archer is a tough ride, but she sits around the aisle and looks at the course map while I'm tacking him up, looking shockingly Zen and comfortable with herself.

"This is just like Malcolm's favorite bridle," I notice as I take her new cross-country bridle from its bag. "Did you order it that way on purpose?"

"Yeah, I really like his," she says. "But it's not exactly the same. Look at the contrasting stitching. Isn't that sharp?"

"Uh-huh." I don't have the heart to tell her that contrasting stitching turns brown with oil and grime after a few years. Her bridle will eventually look exactly like Malcom's battered old lucky charm. "Looks really good on your horse, too."

"I know," she says, gloating a little. I let her have it. Everyone gets excited for a new bridle, and it's her show day, besides. "Go get 'em," I say encouragingly. "Have fun out there."

Wesley rolls her eyes as she takes the reins, like she can't believe how weird her trainer's ancient working student is being.

That's fine, I think. I don't have to cart around your horse for you, so think whatever you like.

With Wesley off to the mounting block, I pull out my list and see who is next. It's another of Malcolm's horses, Regent.

Nice, I think. Regent is a super chill ex-racehorse who lives for cross-country day and naps. I pull the chestnut horse out and get busy cleaning up. After Regent, I'll have a few minutes to pick stalls, and then I'll be ready to bathe Wesley's horse after his cross-country run, and then I'll have to get Malcolm's last horse of the day ready.

Alison is over at the finish line to catch hot horses and bring them back, so it's my job to stay in the barn.

Easy-peasy, I think. I got the bargain on this one.

The last horse to go is not easy to tack. His name is Dragon, and that seems both unfair and unwise. Why not name a horse Lamb or Sweetie Pie? It can't *hurt*. There's just no reason to tempt the fates by calling a horse after a fire-breathing creature of doom and destruction.

The fates really sat up and listened with this one, too. Dragon tramples all over everyone at the farm; he's practically a steamroller at the event. He stomps and paws and shakes and nips and does everything he can to get under my skin. "You're a monster," I tell him, finally slipping on Malcolm's lucky bridle and getting it buckled just as fast as I can.

"Is that horse ready?" Alison demands. "I want to get him over there and finally be over this day."

"Here you go," I say. "Take him away, please."

She pockets her phone and snatches his reins, barely looking at him. Belatedly, I realize neither of us gave him a final look-over, so I pause to watch him walk away, checking that he's wearing all his galloping boots and the saddle isn't on backwards or something. I know it seems unlikely, but it has been a really long day, after two other really long days. After several long weeks. At this point, very few mistakes would surprise me. And none would be acceptable, but I'm pretty sure a screw-up now would cost me this job.

Malcolm has been on the warpath all day, according to Alison and Wesley, who came back from her cross-country looking completely wiped out. She said it went well, but judging by her exhausted expression, I wasn't so sure. I took her horse and gave him a soapy bath, followed up with a liniment soak, happy I hadn't been the one to stand at the warm-up all day, sweating in the sunlight and listening to Malcolm's terse commands.

"Barn duty is the best duty," I hum to myself, walking into the tack stall. I'll just get started on the mound of tack that needs cleaned—

Oh—

"Oh, no."

My voice seems small, as if the great event circling around me has turned me into a tiny fraction of a person.

Or maybe it's just that my life is now over, because on top of the pile of bridles hung on the tack hook, is Malcolm's brown padded bridle with a brass clincher brow-band. The bridle he uses on all his cross-country runs.

His lucky bridle.

The one I just put on his last horse...I *thought*.

Oh my god. I start shuffling through the tack, looking for Wesley's bridle, but I'm going cold all over, because it would be here, it would be halfway from the top, but it's not—

Because I sent out his last horse in Wesley's bridle.

How did I not see the difference? Yes, they're identical down to the bit, but Wesley's is at least a decade newer, and it has the contrasting stitching—

And then I remember the look on Wesley's face as she wordlessly handed me her horse's reins, and the mud splashed on her jersey and over her horse's front end. I figured he'd stumbled in the water...it happens.

But I hadn't thought about the muddy water staining that sparkling new white stitching. I'd been in such a hurry to cool Archer out, I'd just pulled the bridle right over his ears and tossed the wet dirty tack in a pile.

And then I'd picked that bridle up, and it had gotten mixed up somewhere along the way, and now—

"Oh god," I say. "Oh no. Oh god. Oh please no."

But the eventing gods never listen.

This time, I run.

I ignore the dirty looks and a couple of shouts of "Slow down," and "No running around the horses!" I don't have time to be polite or pretend that these hardened, tough event horses have never been exposed to a quickly moving human in their lives. If someone's horse spooks because I ran past, well, that's a shame. Maybe they should expose their horse to more scary things in life.

But anyway, my problems vastly outweigh theirs. I'm about to get fired.

The cross-country warm-up is about as far away as it can be without being hosted on a neighboring farm, or in the next county. This is to keep the all-day rumble of galloping hooves from upsetting the horses in stabling, or so I assume. But right now it's just a hindrance, in my way as I race to save my job.

When I finally get there, I'm winded and I can barely speak, but I see Alison standing near the grassy area where horses and riders are careening in circles, getting warmed up for their gallops. She looks back at me, her eyes widening in shock. "What are you *doing* here?"

"Malcolm—bridle—" I wheeze.

"What's wrong with his bridle? Spit it out!"

"It's Wesley's," I gasp, overwhelmed with shame. "I put Wesley's bridle on Regent."

Alison narrows her eyes at me, then looks out at the cross-country warm-up. I see Malcolm cantering Regent towards a warm-up fence. The horse coils and springs at just the right time, his ears pricked, his expression happy. There's no sign that I've got him in the wrong tack.

"He looks correct," Alison says. "Are you sure?"

"Sure I'm sure," I blather. "It's the same bit—it's practically the same bridle—but it's Wesley's, not Malcolm's. Not his lucky bridle."

"Oh." Alison nods slowly, still watching him canter the horse around the warm-up. They head back to the practice fences. "Well, it's too late to change it out now."

I put my hands on my knees, feeling light-headed. "I ran over here as fast as I could—"

"We're not changing anything," Alison says. "You hear me?" She looks at the bridle hanging over my shoulder and I watch her nod to herself, building up her own resolve in the matter. "He's riding with the bridle he's got on the horse, and that's final. Take that old thing back to the barn and hide it before he sees it, you hear me? And never say a word about this to anyone."

I look at Alison with a new respect unfurling in my chest. She's willing to keep this screw-up—which is a surprisingly major deal, considering that Malcolm is a pretty smart guy and shouldn't have a lucky bridle at all—a secret. A secret she and I will share.

I wonder if it will bring us closer together.

Probably not. Alison is cool and all, but I wouldn't put it past her to hold this over my head as blackmail if she finds it necessary in the future.

Well, I don't have any choice...and giving Alison potential power over me feels more palatable than stopping Malcolm to explain that I put the wrong bridle on his horse.

"Okay," I say, turning to leave.

"Thanks for coming over here, though," Alison says.

I look back at her, surprised.

She nods and waves me away. I guess that's the only compliment I'm going to get.

Well, it's certainly more than I deserve.

Chapter Twenty-Three

IT'S A RELIEF to get home that night and walk out to check on the horses enjoying their three days off. They've been brought in, fed, and turned out again by the stall-cleaners. This is basically their idea of paradise.

Bucky ignores me, as usual, but Breezy has a lot to say and I find myself standing out in the moonlight for a good twenty minutes, rubbing his neck in all the right places while he curls his lips around the belt loops on my jeans and rubs his head against my shoulder. I don't mind at all. The night is warm, as if the freezing-cold wind of a few days ago never happened. These up-and-down weather swings are part of Florida in winter, but they can make a person feel half-crazy sometimes.

Or maybe that's just the job and lifestyle I have committed to.

"I wish you'd been there today," I tell Breezy, laughing as he tickles my fingers with his wiggling lips. "You would have loved galloping cross-country in this weather. So dry, no humidity to make you all hot and miserable." It's the humid, hot summers that I blame for Breezy's anhidrosis, even though most vets are hesitant to give any real reason for why some horses simply stop sweating. Does it show up more in horses who compete in Florida, or do we simply see it more because more horses compete in Florida than in other places? It's just one of those cases which hasn't been cracked yet.

Meanwhile, it has put my poor Easy Breezy out to pasture before his time. He places his chin on my chest, leaving a trail of warm green horse slobber on the sage-green farm shirt I'm supposed to wear again tomorrow. Looks like I'm doing laundry tonight.

As I walk back to the barn, I see a figure in the aisle. Malcolm. The realization gives me a little shudder of anticipation, as if I've been waiting to see him again.

So silly.

For a moment, I think about ignoring him and just going upstairs. Then I give in to the simple pull I feel in his orbit and walk down to see him.

Malcolm is leaning against the office door, looking at the dark gloom of the covered arena.

"Something in there?" I call.

He glances back at me, surprised. "I would have thought you'd be in for the night."

"Long night-check," I explain. "Breezy thought he needed some extra scritches."

"Looks like he really appreciated your company," Malcolm says, his gaze settling on the green stain above my left boob.

"What can I say? The boys love my boobs." I feel myself blush the moment I say it, but fortunately, the barn aisle is very dim. I'm sure he can't see it.

Malcolm chuckles. "I love barn girl humor," he says. "No one ever talked like this when I was working in finance."

I mime falling backwards in shock. "Wait, you worked in *finance?*"

"Very briefly, right out of college. I only lasted a year before I went back home and told my parents I was going to do horses full-time."

"Were they disappointed?"

"A little, but I think I've made it up to them."

"That's what it's all about, right?" I think of my mom, who has given up hoping I will grow out of the horse girl phase. "I haven't managed that yet, but I figure I'm young yet."

"You've got time," he agrees. "But once you're on this treadmill, you can't get off. That's the thing about knowing a lot about money management—you realize pretty quickly that you've picked the wrong livelihood once you've run an eventing barn for a few years. That's why I keep things so tight around here. This place runs on a fine line between breaking even and utter collapse."

"Oh, I know." I can't help but wonder why he's telling me this. "I've been doing it a long time, too. I know it isn't profitable for anyone. Except maybe the vets."

He grins. "And the tack stores."

I shift, wondering why he'd bring up tack. Random, or—

"I know about the bridle," he says.

"Oh."

"It was a pretty honest mistake. I'll have to order some of those rings for them, the little ID tags? If Wesley's going to be here more often, I mean, it could happen again."

"Is Wesley going to be here more often?"

"Didn't Alison tell you? Wesley is going to help you guys out for the next two months. Her mother agreed to let her be a working student. Part-time; she still has schoolwork to do, but she'll be here a few days a week."

He can't be serious. I asked him for extra help around the barn and he came back with Wesley? A sixteen-year-old girl-child brought up with a silver spoon in her mouth and a silver snaffle for her ponies?

"Um," I say. "Uh."

There's no good reaction to this.

Malcolm's frowning. "That's what Alison said, too. *Um.* Is she not —do you guys not like her? I thought a teenager would listen to you

189

guys better than just hiring another groom who has their own way of doing things."

"She's just—uh, I'm not sure she's used to working," I suggest, as diplomatically as I can. "Has she ever had a job before?"

"Well, probably not. She's sixteen. But it's not like she needs to learn to count change or answer phones or something. She just needs to tack up horses, and she already knows how to do that."

"Does she, though? Seriously, Malcolm, if she knows how to do it, why is it my job when she comes for lessons, or at the event?"

Malcolm can't answer that.

And this, I think, is what happens when a trainer gets too removed from the day-to-day operations in his own barn aisle.

"Jeez," he says, rubbing his face. "I really didn't think about it. She must know, though. She's riding at Prelim, for god's sake."

"Malcolm, it is entirely possible Wesley has never tacked up a horse in her life. I'm not saying that's the case, but it's possible. Did you happen to *ask?*"

"No, but—" he gives me the most sheepish smile imaginable. "Her mother did say it would be good for Wesley to understand what happens when she's not in the saddle. I didn't think—"

It's my turn to rub at my face. "Maybe it's not as bad as that," I say. But I think it is. I think it's exactly as bad as that. "Listen, it's late. We can deal with this another time. Busy day tomorrow."

"Yeah." Malcolm looks at me for a moment. The moonlight falling through the ceiling's translucent panels picks out his high cheekbones, and lets his eyes fall into shadow, but I imagine I can see that sparkle in his gaze. My skin seems to tingle. But his next words are only work-related. As they should be. "Can you be at the show-grounds early tomorrow? Go over with me, maybe, and we'll let Alison sleep in a little. She seems a little, I don't know, tense."

I'm annoyed again, just like that. I'm not tired? I'm not tense? "That was probably just the news about Wesley sinking in," I say meanly.

"Yeah, I get that now," he replies. "But just between you and me? I mean, I seriously don't want her to find out—"

Oh god, another secret. But this one is with Malcolm. I lean forward, suddenly on pins and needles. "Yes?"

"You're an amazing braider," he says. "I want you to do the braids before stadium tomorrow."

"Instead of Alison," I reply, biting back a sigh. What did I think he was going to say? Not that.

"Please?"

I gaze at Malcolm Horsham, boy-man, pro trainer, famous jerk, style professor, creative chef, unwitting heartthrob. I think about telling him he's wrong, that Alison does better braids and we'll both be at the show-grounds at the regular time to get the horses ready together.

But then the unassailable pleasure of being complimented by him, of being told I do something better than the queen of the barn, the perfect Alison, takes over my stupid brain, and I say, "Yes, I'll go over early with you."

Malcolm's smile warms me from head to toe, and I know I'm going to spend a few sleepless minutes in bed tonight, just thinking about it.

Idiot that I am.

It's while we're halfway through the second horse's braids that I realize I want Malcolm to kiss me. It's ridiculous, embarrassing, and completely out of bounds, but there it is.

To be fair, we've been standing very close together for the past hour. Malcolm was outside the apartment at six a.m., two large steel travel mugs full of what proved to be excellent coffee in the console of his car, and he drove me to the show-grounds in a silence that was more, "Yes it's early and we shouldn't be talking, that would be barbaric," than, "I'm only your boss and we don't need to talk."

There is a difference, and when you are crushing on your boss as hard as I suddenly am, you can feel it. It's a relief to get to the stables and start lifting heavy buckets and tossing hay bales around. I have too much energy for my own skin right now.

The horses are pleased to see us, and we divide and conquer to get breakfast fed—the full hay-nets I stuffed last night with the last of my dwindling energy reserve are hung up to replace the empty ones they devoured overnight; the individual baggies of grain I made back at the farm are dumped into feed pans and distributed. Everyone eats up; everyone is bright-eyed and bushy-tailed. These horses are used to going out overnight, so keeping them inside at the horse park just gives them a pent-up energy which works to the rider's advantage on the third day of competition, when they should theoretically be tired from cross-country the day before.

They *will* be sore and stiff. At a racing barn, we'd pull everyone out for long walks as soon as their breakfast was eaten up, to stretch those muscles. But the first thing Malcolm wants done this morning are braids.

I feel rebellious on behalf of my sore fingers. There's no need to braid for stadium jumping; we took the braids out after dressage two days ago and I combed out all the frizzies to make sure their manes weren't wavy on cross-country day. But Malcolm, reverting to style professor mode, insists that his horses are *always* braided on stadium day.

So, less than five minutes after Oceanus has licked his bucket clean, I'm standing on a stool next to him, all up in his personal space, while Malcolm holds his lead-rope and watches my fingers pull his big horse's mane into slim braids.

"I'm going to space them a little wider than usual to save time," I mutter, thinking of the five other horses who will need braids this morning.

"No big fat balls of braids," Malcolm warns.

I glance down at him, my fingers full of mane, and wonder tiredly if I'm actually attracted to him or if that was a passing fancy, maybe created through sheer exhaustion. Maybe delusions, I think hopefully. My gaze lands on his craggy line of jaw and those bright jade eyes and no, sadly, it's all too real.

He lifts his eyebrows, inadvertently making himself even more adorable. "Everything okay? Do you need me to get something?"

Oblivious, like all men, always. It's for the best.

"No, it's fine," I say, and get back to work.

Braiding is a quiet ritual, especially when there's someone holding the horse, and when the horse is as experienced and amiable as Oceanus. It gives the braider entirely too much time to think. A chatty handler is helpful, but Malcolm is quiet this morning, evidently lost in his own thoughts. And so I have plenty of time to meditate on the strangeness of my life, how I got from there to here, and wonder what I'm going to do with myself now.

Of course, I mean my love life, which is non-existent with good reason. I have dated exactly three men in my life, and one woman, and none of it ended well. Horses come first, and that's a fact most people don't understand. Even horsemen don't seem to understand it, in my experience. Like all men, they think *they* come first. As Cher would say, as if.

One by one, I have shut people out of my life because they tried to stand between me and my career as a horsewoman. And even now, when I have been floating on unsteady waters since I had to retire

Breezy, not sure what I'm doing with my own life, I know that I would never let a man distract me from working with horses all day every day.

But Malcolm wouldn't be that man, I think.

Of course he wouldn't, but that's no great act of selflessness on his part. It's just that he's too wrapped up in himself to think about me for a second. A wry grin creases my lips at the idea of Malcolm even noticing that I might be ignoring him in favor of horses. He barely knows I exist outside of his personal valet and groom. My entire position in his life is that of a servant, and not even in a sexy way...

"Why are you smiling?"

Malcolm's voice has an amused, curious tone. Like he's been watching me for a while and I hadn't noticed, too buried in my braiding.

I straighten my neck, realizing I've been bent over this horse's neck for ten minutes without pause, and glance over at him. "Smiling? Oh," I flounder. "No. Probably just thrilled I'm halfway through this horse and there are only five fabulous necks to go."

"It does seem really exciting when you put it that way." Malcolm's grin is more pronounced now. "I guess this is the riveting stuff you expected when you signed on with me."

"Well, it has only been about a month." I focus on the next braid, gathering the wiry dark hairs together. My hands are dry and cracked in a few places, but I'm used to the pinpricks of rough horsehair and barely notice the pain. "In another month, who knows? Maybe I'll get to clean the sheaths of every gelding in the barn. Heady stuff, grooming for you."

Malcolm snorts. "You'll be happy to know we use that crud-buster lady who travels around the county cleaning sheaths for a living."

I allow him a small smile. "Actually, I *am* really happy to hear that. Of all the jobs I do with horses, reaching my hand up to coax a penis out of its sheath is probably my least favorite."

"Not a penis fan, eh?"

Eventually, all equestrians will engage in this conversation. It's not inappropriate. We just can't help ourselves. Sheath-cleaning is a necessary evil and we have to joke about it. "I love a good penis," I declare. "A nice, clean, coconut-oil-scented penis. I just want someone else to get it that way."

Malcolm snorts with laughter. I tie off the braid and start work on the last one. Are they wider apart than I would like? Yes, for sure. But I'll lie and say it's on purpose, to make Oceanus's neck look longer in photos.

"Here we go," I murmur. "Almost done, and this fine horse can get back to his morning hay."

"You're very good at braiding," Malcolm says. "Where did you learn?"

"Oh, picked it up as a teenager, I guess. I've always had quick fingers, and you know the small ones are best at this kind of work."

"That's true," he rumbles, and I hear innuendo slipping into his voice.

It's too early for quick-witted repartee, but we've already played the penis game, so I decide I've opened that door and it's too late to close it. So I just bite my tongue, concentrate on slipping the last braid into place, and tie it off. "There," I announce. "One braided horse, ready for stadium jumping."

"Awesome." Malcolm holds out his hand and I take it, suddenly and painfully aware that my fingers are grimy and my cuticles are black with grime. Yes, the horse was clean when I started—as clean as horses can get. Somehow, that's never enough to keep hands clean, though.

Malcolm doesn't flinch at my coal-miner's manicure. And why would he? We're the same kind of people.

Warmed by this thought, I grant Malcolm a big smile as I step down from the stool and land right in front of him. For a moment, my chest is nearly touching his—and then I step away, before he can see the pink flush creeping across my face and neck.

If he would even notice that sort of thing.

I'm ahead of him as we head to the next stall, my little Tupperware of braiding supplies in one aching hand, so it's a surprise when he reaches around me, his hard chest pressing against my shoulder, to open the next stall guard. The horse within pricks his ears, interested to see who is coming to visit so early in the morning, but for once I just turn my back on the horse and instead look up at Malcolm. He looks back at me, his eyes so close I can see his pupils dilate. For a moment I lose myself in the rush of sensation that comes with that involuntary movement, with the realization that he's as attracted to me as I am to him, and then I take a single step backward.

Malcolm's face clouds, as if he is just waking up from a dream and he isn't sure he likes reality. Then he's penitent. "Oh, I'm sorry," he says. "That was—I should not have—"

"No," I say gently. "It's okay that you did. But—we can't."

I know it like I know my own name—there's no future here if we start canoodling. He's Malcolm Horsham, a man with a reputation for bluster and berating that isn't exactly un-earned. And while I'm not sure I'd call Malcolm the worst I've ever worked for, I know that we can't be involved romantically if we're still employee and employer. He'll try to be nice for a while, but eventually I'll do something that sets him off, he'll rage, and my feelings will be hurt. Things will get messy.

And just like that, I'll have put a man before horses.

Chapter Twenty-Four

MAYBE I DON'T let things get serious at the event, but there's no doubt that something has changed between us. And it starts to affect life at the farm, starting the very next day we all work together.

Tuesday dawns, a dark and rainy day. Before I even open my eyes, I hear the rain battering against the windows and wish I could stay in bed all day. For a moment, I even consider texting Alison and Malcolm to tell them that I'm sick. Ate something bad on my one and only day off. Went a little wild at the seafood buffet. But before I know it, I'm flinging back the covers and hopping out of bed to get my day started. Horse girl habits die hard, and even though the horses aren't waiting on me to feed breakfast, I can't just stay in bed when I'm expected in the barn.

"But the horses were in all night," I tell Romeo, "so they're going to be very dramatic today."

Romeo flicks a paw at the drawstring on my pajamas bottom and yawns, showing me his extraordinarily sharp teeth.

After toast and coffee, I head downstairs and find I'm the first one there. Impressive, I think, heading into the office to get the morning's coffeepot rolling. That's usually Alison's job, just like making the schedule. I wonder where—

My phone buzzes.

Alison: *Not coming in today. You handle things.*

Oh, my god. I stare at the message for a moment longer, only to be surprised by Malcolm striding through the office door. My eyes sweep up his rainy-day horseman ensemble: brown country boots, slick with rain; beige breeches in a heavy-looking knit; a sage-green jersey—all topped off with the same brown waxed raincoat he wrapped around me in the paddock last week.

As my gaze reaches his face, our eyes lock and for a moment neither of us moves, neither of us blinks. I'm aware that my heart is pounding wildly in my chest, and there's something weird about my skin. Oh, it's goosebumps. Goosebumps all over, from head to toe.

"Hi," Malcolm says, his voice sounding oddly strangled.

"Um, good morning," I manage, pretending I sound better than he does.

But I don't. My voice sounds odd even to me.

"Uh," Malcolm says.

"Yeah."

We're still staring at each other, neither willing to break eye contact first. It's Malcolm who finally looks away, pulling his phone from his pocket. I know what he's going to see and I wait, watching as his face falls.

"Looks like it's just us," he says at last, looking at me without lifting his chin. It's like he's deflecting, using his eyelashes to shield himself from fully looking at me.

And I sigh, because it's weird anyway, and we didn't even do anything.

How's that for fair?

I force myself to turn around and fiddle with the coffeemaker, which seems to be making coffee ridiculously slow this morning.

We can do this, I think, but I don't bother saying it out loud. It's too silly.

Behind me, Malcolm settles down at his desk. I feel his warmth just a few inches away and wonder why he didn't let me get out of the way first. Or leave the room. Or vacate the farm. Maybe move to Virginia. They have big eventing farms and he could probably put in a good word for me at one of his friends' places...

"We'll just hack everyone today," he says, in a voice that's surprisingly normal. I stiffen, annoyed that he could put himself back together so quickly, while I'm still cracked and out of sorts. "Between the two of us, we can give everyone twenty minutes in the covered ring. I'll just make a list really quickly and we can run through it. I'll groom my own, keep it simple."

I remember something. "What about Wesley?"

"Oh, god, Wesley."

"Okay, I'm guessing you forgot her."

"I can't take her today. She's—she's so young—"

"Well, isn't that something you should have thought of before you hired her?" I snap, pushed beyond all reason. "I mean, you were going to foist her on Alison and me and her youth was fine, but the minute *you* have to work with her, it's a problem? How is that fair?"

Malcolm's chair creaks; I assume he has spun around to look at me, but I leave my back to him. I *won't* look at him. Possibly ever again. That way, madness lies.

"I wasn't *foisting* her on you. I was doing exactly what you wanted, which was hiring extra help."

"We already had this discussion." The coffee pot is nearly full; I watch it trickling towards the fill line. "I'm not going to argue with you about it now."

"What do you want me to do about her," Malcolm says flatly, no question in his tone. Only demand. *You do it better than me, then.*

"I want you to call her and tell her to stay home. Tell her it's raining and there's not enough work for her to come in today. We're just hacking."

"If she came and took over grooming and tacking, we could do some actual work."

"Not if I have to teach her to groom and tack," I remind him.

"We still don't know—"

"Do whatever!" I shout, suddenly overwrought and too furious to continue talking to him. "Just make yourself happy, Malcolm. You always do anyway."

I stalk out of the office and stand in the empty barn aisle, listening to the rain roar on the roof. I'm Alison now, apparently. Bickering with Malcolm over the way things should be done. Funny how quickly that happens.

Does she argue with him constantly because they have a history, though? That's the question. If we share a few meaningful glances and suddenly the air is so thick between us that we can barely handle one another's presence, are we just repeating some foolish dance he's already waltzed with his barn manager?

Ugh, Malcolm shouldn't have a reputation for being a jerk. He should have a reputation for being a relentlessly attractive flirt. My boots rap a pounding pattern on the pavers of the aisle. I'm halfway to Bucky's stall, thinking that if I can't have a nice morning with my only colleague, I'll at least try to make friends with the horse that doesn't want me, when Malcolm catches up with me.

"What was that supposed to mean?" he demands.

He's hot and he's close and his eyes are shining with a fierce light. I realize that I've already broken my most recent promise to myself, the one where I never look at him again. Why can't I show a little more loyalty to myself?

"I just meant that it's your barn and you can do whatever you want."

"That's *not* what you meant," he insists. "And it's not fair. Talking to me like that—like I don't care what happens to you or what your day is like—come on! I'm not the one who wanted to pass up on this, Evie."

"This?" As if I don't know what he means.

"*This,*" he repeats, his gaze raking my face from my eyes to my lips, and when his eyes linger there, I know what he's thinking.

He's going to kiss me, right here in front of the horses.

And I want him to do it.

Everything in my brain is fighting this. I know that the moment we kiss, I forfeit everything I am here to accomplish. Because it won't last. And when it all falls apart, there goes Evie's job. There goes Evie's return to eventing. There goes Evie back to her lonely little house and her mornings galloping babies and her afternoons feeding yearlings. There goes Evie, taking back her old life exactly the way she wanted to, before she realized that her old life was *stupid*.

While everyone else in the world keeps moving up and on, acquiring horses and victories and relationships, Evie Ballenger will still be alone on the stupid tiny farm she never should have bought, looking out the window as her childhood horse grows older and her dreams grow fainter.

I can see a glimmer of bright green in the corner of my eye; it's my sixth-place ribbon, hanging on Diamond's stall door. Everything has changed. I want more of it—more of everything.

Everything.

"Evie," Malcolm says harshly, his voice catching in his throat, and that's what turns me, that's what changes my mind, that's what decides it all for me. That little catch, that says he's nearly lost control, that says he hurts as long as I'm still two feet away from him with my arms across my chest and my chin lifted to ward him off.

So I give in, clumsy with misgiving. He's too tall for me, that much is obvious. I give a little lunge, half out of frustration and half out of hurry and maybe a little bit out of fear that we'll miss our moment. Our chins bump as we reach for each other, and we aren't sure what to do with our arms and they end up sort of wrapped up in each other, and his raincoat is getting me wet. So what? Add it to the list of complaints I simply do not care about right now.

We kiss without hesitation, without pause, without breath, without thought, and when we both come up for air—reluctantly, gasping, unsexy—we look at each other and there's no regret.

Not yet, anyway.

So begins what I start thinking of as Evie and Malcolm's Best Day Ever (At Work).

He nearly forgets to text Wesley to stay at home, but once that chore is managed, we have the whole barn to ourselves for the rest of the day. No one to watch us. No one to lecture us. No one to be horrified at the mockery we're making of workplace relationship clauses I've probably signed in my hiring paperwork.

Just the two of us working our way through a lot of horses who need to be stretched out after their long weekend of eventing and a day off, and a lot of kissing which needs to be done—urgently, at times.

Sometimes even when we're both on horseback.

It's while we're doing that particular little move, giggling like teenagers, that I realize how very, very happy I feel. Content, even. It's the same feeling I got that day last week when I was loading in all the supplies for the event, wandering the horse park and seeing all the other members of the eventing community out in full force, knowing that I was part of it.

And as our horses start to walk again and we're forced to end our silly little kiss, I feel a little quiver of worry, piercing through all these good feelings.

What if my happiness with eventing is wrapped up with this newfound obsession with Malcolm?

And what if we really do end this thing badly—will I simply hate eventing forever?

The fear of being without a path yet again is enough to chase the happiness away, but only for a few minutes.

Because the next time our horses circle around one another, Malcolm is sitting in the saddle laughing, his eyes fixed on mine, his craggy jawline mine for the stroking, his thin lips mine for the kissing, and I decide that for once, just once in my life, I should throw away all my good sense and just follow my other senses, instead.

The bad ones.

We kiss until our horses sidestep and pull us apart.

"I like this side of you," Malcolm says as we untack our horses in side-by-side grooming stalls.

"Which side?" I ask, throwing a little wiggle into my walk as I sashay around my horse, arms full of saddle, pad, and girth. "*This* side?"

He leers at my bottom. "Well, yes, although I meant the fun, laughing side I've seen all day. You're usually so serious, Evie. Sometimes you make me nervous."

I stare at him, all sexy pretense forgotten. "I make *you* nervous?"

"Yes!" he laughs. "I mean, you're just so clearly here for one reason, and that's to get your ass onto that big-time horse before I claim him for myself—"

"Wait," I interrupt. My smile is gone now. "Before you *what* now?"

Malcolm makes an impressive effort to recalibrate his expression. "I mean, not that I would—"

"Would *what?*"

"I'm just talking about the competition clause in the training contract," Malcolm says. "You know, the contract I have with your aunt?"

"That means you're training him for the next six months, yes," I say impatiently. "Five months, now. And I *still* haven't been on him—"

"Right, I'm training him, but it also says that if I want to compete him, she'll pay his expenses for an additional six months with an option to re-up the contract at the end of the twelve-month period, so, you know. I figured you knew about that. Am I wrong? Evie, I'm sorry."

I shake my head, flabbergasted. "How did I miss that?"

"I don't know. Maybe you didn't read the contract all the way through? It's long, most people wouldn't."

I'm sure I didn't. Contracts are full of boring legalese about who is responsible for injuries or damage to property, and that's the kind of stuff you have to overlook with horses because injuries and damage to property are basically inevitable, a built-in expense no matter which side of the signature you're on.

"Evie, I don't want to take that horse away from you. Please don't get me wrong about this. And I'm going to put you on him next week. We're going to start prepping the two of you for competing, okay?"

I have a choice, I think. I can believe him, and we can continue on with this wild, wonderful day and whatever it leads to. Or I can apply the same natural distrust I have of my aunt and most other things in life, and believe that he's just as likely to claim Bucky for himself for the rest of the year and leave me out of it.

But why would he do that, now that we're—well, *canoodling?*

"Okay," I say, making up my mind. "Thanks for telling me about it. Sorry I over-reacted. It was just a surprise."

"Hey," Malcolm says, walking to me and taking my hand. I feel my skin flash hot and cold, and I draw closer to him without a second thought. "Hey," he says again, tenderly this time, pushing my hair back from my face. "We're in this together, okay?"

"Okay," I whisper, giving in, utterly. What choice do I have? It's just the two of us here, and I'm only going with my bad senses.

He brings me back to his house for dinner that night.

The rain is long gone, but the cold is intense and the horses are once again inside, their blankets no match for the forecasted hard freeze. Horses up north might have stronger constitutions for cold weather, and have blankets that cover them from ears to tail, but Florida horses have thinner blood and less robust clothing to protect them from frosty nights. We help the stall-cleaners load them up on hay to keep their metabolisms firing on high. The barn is closed up, but it still feels sharply cold as we finish up for the night. The horses turn restlessly in their stalls, annoyed at the change to their routine.

"They'll have to work their faces off tomorrow or they'll tear the barn down," Malcolm remarks as we pull the aisle doors closed for the night. It's the first time it's been cold enough to have to seal the barn up since I started, and the doors groan with disuse. "It's going to be a rough one, especially if Alison doesn't make it again."

"Are you saying I'll actually have to put up with Wesley tomorrow?" I ask, getting to the core of the matter.

"I think you should at least try her out."

"I don't know." I lean against the staircase to my apartment, loathe to say goodnight to him, even though we've spent the past ten hours together. "I had a nice time just working with you today."

He laughs and wraps an arm around my waist. "I feel the same way about a day with just you," he agrees, "but if we try to give everyone a twenty-minute hack tomorrow, they're going to launch us into the rafters."

He's right, of course. And I have no business trying to let our newfound passion for kissing one another all day get in the way of our horses and our work. That's exactly what Evie Ballenger *doesn't* do. What is it about this guy that has me throwing out all my own hard-won knowledge about life, love, and the idiocy of dating anyone, let alone your boss?

"Fine," I sigh. "Well—goodnight."

"Wait," Malcolm says. "Come up to the house and have dinner with me."

Dinner, so soon? I think.

A ghost of my good sense pops up long enough to shout *No* and for once I decide to give her a shot.

"No," I reply.

Well done, Good Sense whispers, relieved.

"Not for that!" Malcolm exclaims, holding up his hands in mock terror. "Just dinner, I swear. I have these gorgeous steaks..."

I'm hungry, and my mouth waters instantly, all thoughts of Malcolm's potential aim to get me into bed completely rushing from my brain and replaced by the mental image of a filet, nicely crossed with grill marks, resting alongside a cloud of mashed potatoes and a roll the size of my fist. I haven't eaten anything that nice in months. My budget didn't extend to steak *before* I gave up three-quarters of my income to work for this guy.

"Fine. But only because it's steak."

"Understandable," Malcolm says gravely. "I'll go start the grill."

"I'll shower and feed the cat and put on clean clothes," I reply.

"Such a sexy little to-do list," Malcolm replies, grinning. He plants a kiss on my cheek and heads for the driveway.

He only makes it two steps before he turns around, slides a hand under the nape of my neck, and kisses me silly.

I look up at him after we've both come up for air. "What was that for?"

"Oh, I just didn't think the other one was good enough," he laughs, and then he leaves me blinking after him.

Malcolm's house is not what I expected. Everything about his personality says English leather and dark wood, but the house is a light-colored Floridian stucco, with shining bamboo floors and a pale blue palette that seems completely at odds with the man I know. He opens the door to my knock and I see he's already showered and cleaned up as well. True to my guess, he's wearing plaid flannel pajamas. I shrug out of my heavy coat and he laughs happily at my unicorn pajamas.

"I see they survived their dunking!"

"Yes, luckily water doesn't stain," I joke, flinging my cold coat onto the rack by the door. I look around the cathedral-ceilinged living room, taking in the light colored furniture and deep plush sofa. "Did you inherit this place from your grandma?"

Malcolm's still laughing, so he nearly chokes at my insult to his decor. "I didn't, actually! But I admit I haven't changed much since I moved here. I don't really have the time and everything's comfortable."

I follow him through to the dining room, where at least the walls are white instead of robin-egg-blue, and a sliding glass door opens onto a pool deck. A lovely little pool shimmers invitingly, and for a moment I forget that the temperature is in the thirties and falling fast. "I bet it's nice out there in the summer, huh?"

"I hope you packed your swimsuit," Malcolm says. "Summer's only a few months away."

"Gosh, that's right. It's hard to remember when it's this cold."

"I bet we get some nice hot days in February. We always do."

"The pool water will still be cold, though." I am the voice of reason here. That can be my role in our relationship. The one that knows better than to leap into a cold pool on a hot day.

"The pool has a heater," Malcolm counters, in the most salacious tones a person has ever used to describe a piece of industrial equipment.

"Oh!"

"Mm-hmm."

Left alone while he finishes with the steak grilling out on the cold pool deck, I pull my phone from my fuzzy pocket and flick through the texts I've been ignoring today while I was busy having Kissing Day with Malcolm. Kayla and Posey and I have been on a group chat for over a year now, and it gets heavy use on wet days like this, because Kayla's farm up in Alachua County doesn't have a covered arena, and Posey likes to curl up in a ball on her sofa all day when it rains. She calls this "boyfriend is the owner of the farm prerogative" but argues it isn't taking advantage of her position because she gets a lot of online work done.

There's a lot of silly banter back and forth that I don't see any need to address head-on, so I just type, *y'all are so funny,* as a way to prove I haven't died somewhere and am still in possession of my phone, complete with its new and improved screen.

Kayla immediately replies, *She emerges!*

Posey: *She is risen!*

Me: *Sacrilegious!*

Posey: *Haha, well.*

This is the kind of thing we do. We just chat nonsense at each other. It's like we're having coffee together.

And then Kayla takes it into serious-land by texting: *hey how are you resisting mr. sexy pants? I know he's been mean a lot, but goddamn that man can wear a pair of breeches.*

I look at my phone, trying to think how to answer. I can't decide if I should be truthful or not. And as the seconds tick by, I realize that every moment I don't reply quickly with a *haha no way* or some similar denial is incriminating me. Every moment of silence equals another tick in the *She's definitely into him* column. In fact, it will probably stagger straight into the *She's definitely already involved with him* column.

The column that shouldn't even exist.

Haha, I type, and then I delete it.

Worse and worse. They'd have seen I was stumbling over a reply and gave up on it. Stupid text bubbles, giving me away!

Kayla's bubble pops up again. *Hey I was just kidding.*

I sigh and reply: *Oh I know.*

Then I look at the *Oh* for a few moments, driving myself crazy with whether that word changes the meaning of my reply. If I'd left it out, would it be jokier? With it in, does it make things more arch? Like, big nod, oh I know—is that anything?

Am I losing it?

Malcolm comes in with the steak, and the smell of it drives all thoughts of texting voice out of my head. I pocket my phone. Let them wonder what's going on. Let them sidebar and text each other in a private chat, which is almost certainly what they're doing right now, about how weird Evie is being about Malcolm.

Because I'm sitting across from him, looking at his face smiling at me above his flannel pajamas, and I know I've got the best seat in town.

All innuendos implied.

Chapter Twenty-Five

ALISON, WESLEY, AND a phone call from a dressage show organizer all happen at the same time this morning, throwing the office into some sort of overdrive of personalities and chaos. It sucks, because Malcolm and I both arrived in the office a few minutes early to fit in some post-morning-mouthwash kissing, and to catch up on what happened in the eight hours since we'd last been together. I'd already filled him in on the thrilling moments after he walked me back to my apartment, so full of steak and mashed potatoes and rolls that I could barely move, and yet so cold that I was afraid our lips would freeze together as we kissed goodnight—was that a thing, seemed like it could be a thing—and he was describing the riveting moments in which he thought he couldn't fall asleep, so he got out a book and then the book fell on his face and mashed his nose, could I see the little cut—yes I could—and then *boom,* the entire world seemed to be in the little office with us.

I resent everyone and everything except for Malcolm.

And judging by his expression, he feels the same way.

Well, we both knew yesterday was an aberration, not something we'd likely get to repeat. And the horses are being absolute monsters in their stalls this morning, outraged about the no-turnout situation last night and hopped up on cold air, which is like a dangerous street drug for Floridian horses. There's no doubt that today is going to be extremely hard work.

Hopefully, though, we can still sneak in a few kisses.

Alison is the one to answer the phone, making angry eyes at Wesley and Malcolm while she puts on her most polite business tones. "Oh, of course Hardy, I'll let him know..." She puts her hand over the speaker and looks at Malcolm. "Hardy wants to know if we can bring some horses to the dressage show this weekend at Keystone Farm. Apparently, they're really light on entries."

I bite back a snort of derision; how is that *Malcolm's* fault? But to my surprise, Malcolm takes the request very seriously. "Definitely. Tell her to email the entry form to your address and you can get in some horses to her by this afternoon."

Alison nods and relays the information to whoever Hardy is. Then she hangs up and says, "That changes this week entirely."

"You want the desk?" Malcolm was just sitting down, but now he gets up and moves aside.

Alison takes the desk and the tablet and starts hammering away at the schedule. "As soon as I'm done with this, you can sign off on the dressage horses and we'll be rolling," she says without looking up.

Malcolm and I exchange a humorous glance: *look at Alison the Queen Bee working away!* And then I blush, because I realize it's the first time we've shared a look like this since we started kissing, and it's suddenly a million times more intimate. Like we are a club of two, removed from Alison, and instead of me being the newbie who hangs on the edges of the farm group, I'm the one in the inner circle.

Wow, such great heights.

Wesley, of course, sees everything, because she is a teenager and the only thing they see, besides their phone screens, are relationships in the balance. I glance over at her and see a knowing smile crease her lips.

Well, that's not great.

Alison glances up at us. "What is everyone still doing here? Malcolm, you'll have Artsy first. Wesley, put Artsy in the brown Stubben dressage. I'll take Adventure out first, so you get her for me, Evie—"

"Adventure goes in the brown Stubben, too," I remind her quietly.

Alison stops and looks at her schedule for a moment. "Oh," she says. "Wow, okay."

And that's when I realize Alison isn't her usual self, either.

Something's going on with her.

I'm dying to know what it is.

Five minutes later, we're all dispatched to the correct horses. Wesley looks nervous as she lifts Artsy's halter and peers at the massive horse lurking within his stall.

"Relax," I tell her. "If you can survive your horse, you can handle anything."

It's meant to be a joke, but Wesley gives me a wary glance that includes a very pointed look at my thumb. "My horse is a monster," she admits. "But I don't do much with him. Sal does."

"I assume Sal's your groom," I say, unhooking the latch of Mr. Toad's stall—he's the horse Alison decided to ride first, to improve the distribution of saddles.

"Yeah," Wesley says, still running her fingers over the smooth leather of Artsy's halter. "She's an ex-jockey who knew my mom years ago, and when we moved to Ocala for the winter, she came to work for us. We only have a couple horses but we have a lot of dogs and stuff. She likes them."

"That's nice. Are you going to get Artsy out?" I'm watching her from Mr. Toad's stall door; jury's still out on whether she doesn't know how to groom and tack up herself, but it's crunch time now. I

213

can always coach her through grooming while I'm doing Mr. Toad; Artsy is a nice boy.

"Yeah, I'm doing it," she says, taking a deep breath. Then she plunges in Artsy's stall. The big horse is a little startled, but he takes everything in his stride; that's why he's a top event horse, after all. Wesley slips on his halter with an acceptable level of expertise.

"Take him down to the grooming stall and I'll be right next to you," I call, turning my attention to Mr. Toad. "Now, you, sir, are going to be ridden by Miss Alison. How about that?"

Mr. Toad rubs his face on my shirt and sneezes. That's kind of his way of saying good morning. I wave at Breezy and Bucky as I walk him down the aisle. Breezy nickers; Bucky ignores me.

I'm used to it by now. Still sucks, but now I'm grateful Bucky brought me here so I can make all of these new, interesting mistakes with my life.

We're all lined up in the grooming stalls and Wesley seems capable around Artsy, running through a basic grooming session without hesitation and making good decisions, like spraying detangler on his tail before she combs it, and adding polo wraps without being asked. I watch her wrap his legs with one eye while finishing my own wraps, and I'm surprised at how capable she is. They're actually a little tight.

"Did Sal teach you to wrap legs?" I ask, sliding a finger under one bandage to make sure they're not too taut.

"She did," Wesley says, standing back. "How'd you know?"

"These are racing bandages," I explain. "Really neat and even. You should be proud of yourself. Just do them *slightly* looser next time. The wrap should sit in the same place if you do it right. Just give the leg a little extra room, okay?"

"Okay," Wesley agrees, smiling. It seems like the first time I've seen the girl do something for herself, and she looks pretty happy. That's how it is when you get your polo wraps just right. Like Christmas morning.

I'm happy to see she saddles pretty efficiently as well, maybe even a little too quickly; Artsy is surprised by how tightly she draws the girth, but other than popping his eyes a little, he lets her do what she wants. Such a good boy. I remind her to take it a little easier on the next horse and finish turning out Mr. Toad.

"Thanks," Alison says, taking his reins as I finish his bridle. "How'd the newbie do?"

"She's actually a decent little racetracker."

"Well, who would have expected that?"

"Not me."

Wesley is holding Oceanus's reins, listening to us. "You think I'm okay?" she asks timidly.

I'm tempted to tell her she's *just* okay, because I like this tentative version of her a lot more than the cocksure rich bitch she presents when she's here as a student. But Alison just goes for it. "You're doing *great,*" she tells the kid. "I'm *very* impressed."

"Damn, Alison," I say, slightly hurt. "You never said anything that nice to me."

"You're ten years older than she is," Alison says, shrugging. "I would expect you to know your job."

Across the aisle, Malcolm comes out of the aisle. My eyes are drawn to his as if we're connected by magnets. Alison sees my gaze flick over her shoulder and she turns her head. There's a pause while Alison holds our lives in her gloved palm, and then she shrugs.

"Well, let's get started," she tells Malcolm. "If we're going to get out of here before seven, we can't stand around."

"Hustle, hustle," Malcolm chides, in the lightest voice I've ever heard him use around Alison. "When are you going to take a breath and relax, Alison?"

Alison draws in her breath so sharply we all hear it; even the horses prick their ears at her. "Well, *sorry*," she snaps. "I didn't realize that my desire to work normal hours was so unusual."

"Come on, Alison, we've never worked normal hours," I kid, unable to help myself.

Her face, when she looks back at me, is unreadable.

Or maybe I'm just telling myself that, because I don't want to believe that Alison could have just turned against me so quickly.

Wesley looks after the pair as they walk their horses out to the covered arena. Then she turns back to me. "Alison seems mad at you."

"Yeah, I should keep my mouth shut," I agree. "Let that be a lesson to you."

"I didn't realize how scary she was before," Wesley says thoughtfully. "I guess there's a big difference between being a student and being an employee, right? But you and I are *working* students, so we're both...um, I don't really understand how it all works."

"It's everything and it's nothing," I tell her wearily, pulling out my phone to see which horses to tack up next. "Just remember, you're at the bottom of the food chain now, and you used to be at the top. You'll catch on pretty quickly."

"I guess so," Wesley says. "I mean, *you* did."

I glance at her sharply. "What does that mean?"

Wesley's grin is all the answer I need.

"There's nothing going on," I tell her.

"Nope," Wesley says, still grinning.

"Seriously, nothing. Whatever you're thinking, forget it."

"Relax," Wesley says, flicking through her phone like I have suddenly ceased to exist. "I don't sell people out. No matter what you think of me, I can keep your secret."

"Okay," I say tentatively, not sure how to reply to that one without confirming everything she's thinking. But then I realize that Wesley's

216

so deep into social media she literally doesn't know I'm still standing there. I leave before I can allow myself to feel insulted. She's sixteen.

And while our sport tends to treat sixteen-year-old riding wonders like they're the stars of the world, she's just my coworker now. I don't owe her anything.

Right now.

Alison orders sandwiches for lunch, and sends Wesley to pick them up from the driver when it arrives, the delivery app chiming on her phone while she's riding. I'm between horses and I follow Wesley down to the archway, where the driver looks suitably impressed by two slim women in breeches coming to collect their food. He's eyeing Wesley like she's a sandwich he'd like to sink his teeth into; I nudge her aside and tell him she's a teenager. The guy frowns and drives off.

Wesley grins at me, her teeth shiny white in the cold sunshine. "Thanks for protecting me from the UberEats guy, Mom," she says.

"Oh, shut up," I tell her. "Or next time I'll throw you in front of his car."

Wesley just laughs.

We set up the food on the desk and then go out and catch the hot horses, letting Malcolm and Alison head in to eat first. It's hard not to rush through cooling them out, knowing there's food waiting on the desk, and the knowledge of Malcolm sitting in that room just across the aisle makes me even hungrier. I want to be in there with him, the person he's conversing with, instead of leaving it all to Alison.

Oh god, I'm so jealous of Alison right now I could just scream. And that's a problem.

But it's a problem I'm going to have to live with. Because there's no way I'm giving up what Malcolm and I have started. I don't even

217

think I have a choice in the matter. If we tried to quit this thing now, while our blood is still running so hot, this barn's orderly operations would simply fall apart.

No, better to keep on kissing behind closed doors and hope for the best.

I don't know what the best would be. I don't have an end-game here. Just pure, unadulterated stupidity. And I suspect Malcolm is in the same boat.

At least we can sink beneath the waves together.

Wesley finishes her horse before me and throws on his cooler, walking him to his stall before disappearing into the office, all while I'm still rubbing liniment into my horse's tired muscles. I start to rinse him, feeling grouchy about the party of three in the office while I'm out here alone. This morning, for just a moment, it was Malcolm and me; now it's Malcolm and everyone else.

They're all pretty much done eating five minutes later when I walk into the office, dripping wet and smelling sharply of spearmint. Alison glances up at me and wrinkles her nose. "Did you drop a bucket of water on your own head by mistake?"

"Yes, that's what I did," I grouse in reply, reaching for the last unopened sandwich. "I thought it would feel good to soak myself in liniment water on a freezing-cold day."

Wesley giggles. Her eyes are locked on her phone, but I glare at her anyway. I'm sure she's enjoying the drama I'm providing her, even if she's acting like she's just watched the funniest video on earth and is ignoring the world around her.

Alison narrows her blue eyes at me.

Just stop, I warn myself. You can't go making enemies with your manager just because you're jealous of the time she's spending with Malcolm.

Anyway, it's silly to be jealous of Alison. They've worked together for three years and they're not together.

Not that I have any proof they haven't been together in the past...

I fill my mouth with roast beef and will myself to not be such a jealous idiot, but it's hard. Once an idiot, always an idiot, right?

Malcolm is flicking through the tablet, completely ignoring the silent drama playing out between his employees. "Oh, Alison, I have one more to add to this dressage line-up."

She looks at him, annoyed. "Who else could be going?"

"I have to go pick up this horse tomorrow afternoon. Mastermind. You can add him in for First Level, Test Two, okay? He's been schooling through Second Level with Mackenzie Phelps."

"Since when is there a new horse coming? How did I not know this?"

"I just got the email," Malcolm says cooly. "Literally just now, Mackenzie said she wants me to take him on for the rest of the season. She's already full at her place and she just found out she's expecting, so she's parceling out some of the horses in her barn. Is that okay, or do you want to drive over to her farm and check the sonogram first?"

The harshness in his tone surprises everyone. Even Wesley looks up.

I realize that except for a few outbreaks at the event, Malcolm has been abnormally calm for the past few days. Yesterday, he never raised his voice at me, which isn't that much of a surprise. But thinking back to the event weekend, the last time I heard him say something truly thoughtless was...

It was when he shouted at me in front of the owners at the dressage warm-up on Thursday.

Could he be keeping his well-known temper in check—for *me?*

If so, Alison just unleashed it again.

She has her jaw set now in a way that says she doesn't appreciate the way he's spoken to her. But her voice is still convincingly meek when she replies, "No, I believe you. I was just surprised."

"Good," he says brusquely. "So you'll tell Hardy—"

"I'll put in his entry," she says.

"Good." Another pause. "And I'm taking Evie with me to pick him up. Remember that when you're making tomorrow's schedules."

"We have lessons starting at four tomorrow," Alison says, her voice slightly strained.

"We'll be back. We'll head out at eleven. That's plenty of time."

Eleven? I think, surprised. That's a lot of time to pick up another Ocala horse. "Where is Mackenzie Phelps' barn?"

"New Smyrna Beach," he replies. I must look startled, because he adds, "The inland part, not the beach part."

"Oh, right. I forgot there are a lot of farms over there. It's what, an hour away?"

"More or less. We'll just hustle over there, get the horse, come right back. Keep Alison's day on track." His grin doesn't quite reach his eyes; he's still angry with her for talking back to him.

I suddenly wonder if all the effort of being nice is going to bottle up Malcolm's energy in a way that will lead to more volcanic eruptions when previously a simple sharp word or two might have done. It's kind of disappointing to think that his being pleasant with me could make him worse, overall, with everyone else.

Typical, though, I think, polishing off my sandwich as I glance at my phone to see what Alison has listed next—then instantly wishing I hadn't eaten so much roast beef. The next horse on the schedule is Bucky, and I'm the one named as rider.

Chapter Twenty-Six

BUCKY IS A big horse. I knew that already, but actually getting into the saddle and feeling the width of him between my thighs, and the distance down to the ground—that's sobering stuff. At seventeen hands, he's not quite the tallest horse I've ever ridden, but he's pretty close. And his width is nothing like the slab-sided Thoroughbreds I've gotten used to over the past few years. This is a horse with *substance,* a horse who "takes up your leg" in horsemen's parlance. Something that shrimpy little me definitely does not need.

"Do I look ridiculous on him?" I bleat, feeling the big horse's long stride lurch me in the saddle as he walks away from the mounting block.

"You look like a child," Alison says helpfully. "An adorable little leadline toddler. On a Clydesdale."

"No, she doesn't," Malcolm scoffs. "Don't make her uncomfortable. You look fine, Evie. He takes a lot of leg, so you'll just have to stretch longer to fit him, that's all. Maybe drop your stirrups a hole, too. So that he feels your calf and heel where he's used to feeling pressure."

I've been riding with my stirrups a hole short and Malcolm has been graciously ignoring that fact, but I guess today is the day he makes me lengthen them. The emotional blackmail of *so your horse actually feels your tiny, stubby legs* is a bit hard to swallow, though. I didn't ask to be this short.

I hunch over and lengthen my stirrups, begging my legs to stretch long and accept this new position. Fortunately, Bucky's stride is so big and airy, my hips are loosening immediately and it's easier to get into the right position. It's hard to believe a month ago I was barely able to sit with my back straight and my shoulders back. The progress was a little harder to clock when I was primarily riding Diamond or hacking some of the other horses, but on Bucky, I can feel that I'm a different rider now.

I sit a little taller at the thought. All this drama will have been worth the trouble, I think. I'm already a better rider. And there are still five months to go.

"There you go, that's really nice!" Malcolm calls. He's circling his horse while he watches me ride, simultaneously giving me an impromptu riding lesson while suppling his mount for a dressage ride that will be ten times tougher than anything I throw at Bucky this afternoon. "Get a nice swinging walk on him, now. He can be a little lazy when you first get on, so I want you to warm up his back and get a nice march forward. Leg on either side as his hind leg comes up and forward—left, right, left, right, left, right—"

I know the drill, but it's a struggle to catch Bucky's leg on the upswing when he's moving me so much in the saddle. I feel like I'm flopping around in the tack, and suddenly I'm annoyed at the old brown dressage saddle I've been riding in since I got here. Just once, I would like a thigh block and a knee roll and a deep seat to keep me in place instead of having to rely entirely on myself to do all that work. All the pro riders have dressage saddles with so many bells and whistles they practically cage them into place, so why can't I have that?

Surely I need help with my position more than an Olympic rider does!

"Left, right, left right," Malcolm is droning. I hazard a glance at him. He's still circling his horse, his eyes on the horse's ears as he waits for the horse to give and flex at the poll. He's not even looking at me. "And start to ask for a slight bend to the inside. Close your hand on the inside rein, then relax it, and bring your hand out slightly, so that you can just see his right eye. Keep the leg on, left, right, left, right, and squeeze the rein, and relax, and keep the walk marching forward, don't let him fall in off the rail, you want a *bend*, not a turn—"

At this point I have stopped Bucky completely and am just watching him ride his horse while calling out instructions to me. He is entirely in his own world, on some kind of autopilot. Across the arena, Alison glances over to see why I've stopped and then she looks at Malcolm, too. She laughs. "Evie's on to you, boss!"

Malcolm looks up from his horse's ears. "What? What are you talking about?" He glances back at me. "Evie! Why aren't you warming that horse up?"

"I'm sorry," I chortle; Alison's laughter is catching up with me. "But you're just over there on Planet Dressage, giving me a riding lesson with absolutely no idea that I wasn't even walking anymore. I could have taken this horse in and given him a bath and you'd still be teaching."

"I would have noticed if you'd gone into the barn," he protests, but he's starting to grin, too. "You know," he realizes, "I had no idea I could do that. But now I see what you mean. I was completely wrapped up in getting Vinnie here to give to my hand, and I just stopped looking up at you."

"It's good to know I'm completely forgettable," I tease, picking up the reins and preparing to start working with Bucky again. In all the laughter, I've forgotten to be scared of him or overwhelmed by his size and big gaits, and when he starts walking again, I simply sway with him, a hundred times more balanced than I was a few minutes before.

"You're not forgettable," Malcolm is protesting, but then he catches my eye and he shuts up before he says something incriminating in front of Alison. "Your horse looks good," he says instead, changing the subject. "Let's see that flexion to the inside, for real this time."

"Of course," I reply, bringing my hand slightly in to guide his nose towards the center of the ring. "Kids' stuff."

I try to focus on my work, but as I urge Bucky to bend to the inside, I'm aware that someone is watching me. And that person isn't Malcolm.

It's Alison.

It's another cold night, but there's no chance of freezing and the horses would tear the barn down if we kept them in again, so everyone gets blanketed and turned out after dinner feeding. Wesley and I help the stall-cleaners, because for once we're actually finished on time. Alison is smug as she closes her schedule for the day, but I know that good feeling won't last through tomorrow. Picking up a horse always takes longer than planned, and New Smyrna Beach is probably more than an hour away.

But that's tomorrow's problem. Wesley waves as her mom pulls up, hopping into the SUV with a grin.

"She seemed to have fun with us," I remark.

"I'm really glad she worked out after all," Alison says, speaking candidly to me for the first time all day. "She turned out to be a big help. And look at you! You got to ride Bucky!"

"I know, and it was amazing." I'm still glowing after that ride, nearly four hours ago now, but fresh in my mind. We ended up doing walk, trot, canter, and some circles—nothing thrilling, but a perfect first ride on a horse very different from any other horse I've ever ridden.

Any horse I've ever *owned,* I remind myself. It's hard to believe that in a few months, this horse and I will go to an event and our names will be paired. *Owned and ridden by Evie Ballenger.* God, I can't wait.

"Hopefully Malcolm gets back on him tomorrow, though," Alison goes on, "because I have him in that show on Saturday doing First Level. Not hard, but it would be better if he's fine-tuned by the rider he's used to."

My balloon of good feeling loses just a little helium. I knew Malcolm would be showing Bucky this weekend, but maybe I'd conveniently forgotten...or hoped that he'd switch out his name with mine, and let me ride him instead.

"Do I have any horses in the show?" I ask.

"Diamond, Frolic, and Timeout," Alison replies, naming three horses I ride almost every day. "Frolic and Timeout are only doing Training Level Test Three, so you don't have to do anything serious. No one likes it, but I think the toughest thing in that test is the stretching circle."

"That's the truth," I say, relaxing a little. Training Level at a dressage show; Novice Level at an event...they're practically the same test, just with different names. The horses just have to move with a modicum of respectability; at that level, it's about what the horse *will* be able to do, not about what they're doing already. It's preparation for the big asks at the higher levels: obedient, listening to the rider, able to give a little when asked.

"I'd like to see a big showing from Timeout, if you can get it," Alison goes on. "It's really time for him to step up."

"I'll see what I can do," I promise. "Who are you riding?"

"Oh, just Adventure and Mr. Toad," Alison says carelessly, looking at her phone. "Nothing exciting. First Level tests."

"Well, that's nice." I wonder a little why she's not riding more horses than that. Malcolm said to fill the show up, for whatever reason, and she's capable of showing half the horses in this barn.

"Yeah."

"You didn't think of doing a few more?" I venture.

Alison shrugs. "I have enough on my plate, and frankly, it's not my favor to return. Malcolm is the one who owes Hardy a good turn, so when she comes calling, I don't mind giving him five or six to ride... but I'm taking it easy this weekend. And you should remember that," she adds seriously. "Don't let him toss his workload onto you, or get you all caught up in promises he's made to other people."

I blink at her, confused by that last line. Somehow, the intensity of her tone makes me think she's talking about more than owing favors to show organizers.

"You get me?" Alison prompts. "Malcolm's life is not your problem. Trust me when I tell you that you don't *want* it to be."

Okay, this is definitely about way more than the dressage show. "Um, okay?" I reply, making sure she can see I would like an explanation.

But Alison isn't going to give me anything else. "Good," she says, glancing back down at her phone. "I think you might just survive this working student gig. If the first month is anything to go on."

"Well, thanks. I feel like I'm just barely hanging on, but it's good to know I appear to be making it."

She grins at me. "Okay, I'm leaving."

I look up, surprised to see we've walked all the way back to the office. The light is still on, which means Malcolm is inside. Of course he is; he's waiting for me. There's no way he'd go back to his house without saying goodbye to me. Or maybe just making out with me for the next half-hour or so.

Oh, that's what is coming, alright.

I feel my heart start pounding; the anticipation of being left alone with him after an entire day in the company of coworkers, hardly able to look at each other for fear we'll give away our secret, has me suddenly fiercely thirsty for his touch. I realize that my skin has been tingling, to a certain extent, all day long, and now it's raging with the desire to feel and be felt.

"Okay," I manage to say, and Alison gives me one more of those thoughtful looks, like the way she was watching me in the riding ring, before she waves and heads back down the aisle, purse over her shoulder, never glancing back.

I let her car head down the driveway, then count to three before I go into the office.

Malcolm is standing next to his desk, his eyes wide and light.

"Well, *finally,*" he breathes, as if he's been holding his breath for hours, and I fall into his arms.

Chapter Twenty-Seven

I'M UP AT a ridiculous hour on this sunny February morning, so early that Romeo took one look at the clock and went back to sleep. At least, I assume he checked the time. How do cats know when to get up? For me, it's all about the alarm...but I didn't need an alarm this morning.

I feel like a herd of wild horses is thundering through my chest. Falling back asleep would be impossible.

So here I sit, at my kitchen table, drinking coffee and flicking through my phone and thinking about the drive to New Smyrna Beach today. Hours, alone with Malcolm, in his truck. What if we have nothing to talk about? What if we sit in silence? What if he has terrible taste in music? What if he puts on a podcast about vigilante justice?

That's the thing about horse-people; they can seem so debonair and classy in their tweeds and breeches, but take them out of the barn and talk about something besides horses and they can reveal some *very* untidy obsessions.

And of course, it's always possible he'll think I'm the one with a terrible taste in music. I don't, obviously, but I've heard these things can be a tiny bit subjective.

Like dressage, I think, looking at my calendar and the words *Dressage Show* written across Saturday. I guess I better make sure I know my test. Seems like a decent use of waking up too early.

But after reading through Training Level Test Three six times, I have no better knowledge of what I'm supposed to do after halting at X than I did before I started.

There's only one thing on my mind this morning, and he's taking up so much room in my brain, I can't wedge in anything else.

"Ready for the road-trip?" Malcolm calls, swinging into the barn with his long stride. He's wearing the beige breeches today, the pair with the missing button. Except for that tiny flaw, he looks like a million dollars. Literally.

"Those are *some* boots," I reply, staring at his feet with real appreciation. He's wearing a pair of slim jodhpur boots in a chestnut leather that glows beneath the barn lights. They look new, expensive, and cut to fit his feet perfectly. If I had boots that nice, I'm not sure I would wear them into a barn. Or ever, actually. I would just set them in my closet and peek in at them once or twice a day, to reassure myself they were still there, still pristine.

"Oh, these boots?" Malcolm does a pirouette, sliding on the toe in a way that terrifies me—what if the leather brushes the pavers and *scuffs?*—and flashes me a toothy grin. "They are pretty nice, aren't they? I ordered them at a show a few months ago and forgot all about them. Arrived yesterday. I didn't even see the box last night, though." His grin turns wolfish.

I feel a blush coming on and look around. No Alison, no Wesley, and the stall-cleaners are outside scrubbing water buckets. I take a step closer to him, suddenly daring when there's no audience to catch what's going on. "I'm sorry. Were you *distracted* last night?"

Malcolm turns down his chin and looks at me hungrily. "There's a certain girl in my employ who can't keep her hands to herself," he murmurs.

It shouldn't sound so saucy. I am a modern woman; I know bosses and employees are a recipe for disaster, a three-course meal of disrespect and advantages taken and boundaries crossed. But it's also a fairly common fantasy, if we're being realistic here, and it's also absolutely out of my hands, beyond my control, decreed by the universe, etc. etc. etc.

I can't help my attraction to this ridiculous, beautiful man and not to get too puffed-up about myself, but I'd like to think he can't help being attracted to me. Nothing about this feels like a power trip on his part.

Except maybe we shouldn't flirt like it is.

"Less said about my employment, the better," I tell him, taking a careful step back.

A shadow of worry crosses his face, which makes me feel infinitely better. "Oh, I didn't even think about that. Sorry. Will do better and try not to be a sexy boss anymore."

"Thank god," I sigh, batting my eyelashes. "If there's one thing I can't deal with, it's a guy who is so delusional about his looks, he thinks he's a sexy boss."

"My looks?" Malcolm scoffs. "I thought I was just being delusional about being the boss."

"Well, that's probably true."

We start towards the office together. Not hand in hand or anything crazy like that, but companionably matching strides. My knuckles brush his. There's a pleasant thrill to the touch.

"Alison is the boss, after all."

"I'm learning that," he mutters. "You bring a lot of uncomfortable truths to the table, Evie."

"I know. You'll get used to it." I pause at Bucky's stall and peer in. The horse is eating his hay. He flicks his ears towards me and for half a moment, I think he might actually walk over and say good morning. Then he just takes another mouthful. I sigh.

"Still beating yourself up about a horse that doesn't love you?" Malcolm asks teasingly.

I look at him.

"Oh, you are! I'm sorry. But you're going to get him, eventually. Just wait until I'm through with him."

I don't tell him that's what I'm worried about. That I'll have to wait until he's through with him—and that wait might be a lot longer than another five months. Malcolm's showing him this weekend, without offering me the ride. There's every chance his competitive nature will win out and he'll keep showing Bucky under my aunt's contract, even if it hurts my feelings.

Instead of spilling all that, though, I shrug and walk over to Breezy's stall. My retired horse gives my fingers a gentle tug through the bars, his lips soft and enquiring. "Now, this is how I like to be greeted in the morning," I tell him.

"Really? Maybe *I* should suck your fingers—" Malcolm shuts up abruptly.

I glance over my shoulder and see Alison waltzing into the barn. I can't help but smirk at Malcolm, who has a pleasing tinge of red on either cheek. "Better watch your mouth," I whisper.

"I'd rather watch yours," he whispers back, and then he raises his voice and calls, "Alison! Get down here and let Evie's crazy horse slurp on your fingers. It's the latest and greatest in horse training."

"You're insane," Alison says cooly, walking past without pausing. "Don't you have to get to New Smyrna today? Stop clowning around and get on the road."

I hazard a glance at Malcolm. He's staring after Alison, a slightly dazed expression on his face. "Alright?" I ask him.

"I'm just realizing it's not even a joke," Malcolm responds blankly. "She *is* in charge, isn't she?"

I pat him on the arm. "She sure is, boss."

That's the last time I call Malcolm 'boss'. Because once we're seated in his truck and he's put on some decent music that doesn't make me hate him, heading east on the long, straight highway through the Ocala National Forest that will bring us out to the coastal communities, I know I don't want anyone to think of me as this guy's employee anymore.

For one thing, it's hugely frowned upon, obviously. The balance of power between a trainer and a working student is basically nil—the trainer has all the power, the student has none.

But we feel more balanced now, I think, staring at the distant horizon as the truck slides between acres and acres of ramrod-straight longleaf pines. For one thing, I can talk back to him, and not worry he's going to yell at me or fire me. I definitely hold more power than I did a week ago. Maybe the scales have even tipped in my favor.

"I should've made you drive," Malcolm grumbles.

Or maybe not.

"I didn't want to drive," I reply lightly.

"Well, neither did I."

"Why didn't you ask me to, then?"

"Because this is a very expensive rig, and I feel better with my own hands on the wheel."

"I drove it to the horse park," I remind him. "That included the *interstate*."

"I was a nervous wreck the whole time. Jitters, sweats, the whole nine yards."

"Liar," I say comfortably. "Oh, watch out! A squirrel!"

Malcolm's hands don't move. "Did I hit it?"

I look in the mirror. "You missed it. You didn't even try, though."

"You want me to swerve? With a six-horse trailer behind me?"

"No, I guess not."

"That's why you can't drive it. Unless it's a last resort. Because you might wreck my entire rig for the sake of a *squirrel.*"

"That squirrel has a family," I inform him, struggling to keep a straight face. "And *dreams.*"

"That squirrel had a death wish, and on this road, he's going to get it."

"I suppose Alison wouldn't swerve, either," I remark.

"She might swerve to hit it," Malcolm says, his voice reflective. "A bit of a shark, our Alison."

"Just realizing that now?"

"A little, yeah." He glances at me, a twist to his smile. "Alison has been running things for me for so long, I must have missed when it stopped being me in charge. Having you around has kind of underscored that for me."

"But you had a working student before me," I remind him. "Why didn't you notice when *she* was around?" I can't help the emphasis on *she.* I'm not jealous of a girl I never met. I'm not.

Malcolm hears it, too, the dirty rat. I can see it in his face. "She wasn't like you," he says. "She didn't last very long."

"You scared her away."

"How do you—who told you that?" He looks at me longer this time, and the truck tires hit the rumble strip along the side of the road. He guides it back into place, fingers taut on the wheel.

"People talk," I say lightly. "Gossip gets around. You have a reputation."

"I do?"

Now it's my turn to stare at him. Luckily, I don't have a truck to steer. "Are you serious, Malcolm?"

"You're making me nervous. What are people saying?"

"People say—" I pause, trying to think of how to word this, with the least sting. I seriously can't believe he doesn't know he's considered a terror in this town. Possibly in several states. "They say you're a tough boss," I say finally. "A bit of a—erm—shouter?"

"A *shouter?*"

"Yeah, like right now, when you're shouting at me?"

"Oh," Malcolm says, in a more normal voice. And then: "Oh," again.

More quietly, this time.

The radio warbles gently. A truck overtakes us, narrowly missing an oncoming car, and barrels ahead, its engine roaring. The Florida sky wraps over the pine forest around us like a blue dome on a vast terrarium. And still Malcolm says nothing.

"Are you...okay?" I venture after a few minutes have passed.

"Yes, I—" he pauses. "Do I shout at you?"

"You *have,*" I say truthfully. "But not since the event."

"Really? What did I shout about?"

"I interrupted your talk with a client to get you on your horse for dressage."

"I don't remember that."

"Well, you did."

"I'm sorry."

I look at him, and he gives me a quick, furtive glance in kind. "Thank you," I say, as his eyes flick back to the road. "You didn't have to apologize, but thank you."

"I think I did," Malcolm replies. "In fact, I'm afraid I may have more apologies to make, if this is true. Will you call me out on it?"

"What?" Is he asking me to be his own personal Jiminy Cricket? "You want me to stop you when you're rude to people?"

"It would be *nice,*" he says, an edge to his voice.

"Well, you're about to be rude to me, so stop and think about that."

Malcolm chews at his lip for a moment. "You're right," he says. "I'm sorry. But it really would be helpful, if you don't mind."

"Well, I'll try," I say.

"Are you hungry?"

I look at him, perplexed. "I guess?"

"I know a place," Malcolm says. "Let's have an early lunch."

Chapter Twenty-Eight

I NEVER EXPECTED the beach, but when we speed through the farms and suburbs on the west side of New Smyrna Beach, then cross the interstate and keep going east, it becomes more and more apparent we're driving all the way to the end of the pavement. When we eventually reach the barrier island lining the coast, I'm wondering where the hell Malcolm thinks he can park a six-horse rig and a dually truck, but of course, he's already there in his head. He pulls into a Publix parking lot and lines the rig neatly along the farthest row of spaces.

"Publix? You shouldn't have," I say. "No, really, it's too much."

"Oh, shut it," he laughs. "I didn't bring you all this way for a Pub Sub. We're on foot from here."

"Even better. A forced march to the sea."

"We are one block from the Atlantic Ocean and the best little beach bar in Florida and *this* is the thanks I get!" Malcolm raises his hands to the sky.

"I just want you to know I'll never pretend to be happy," I tell him, hopping down from the truck. "I'm a straight shooter. If this walk is longer than a block, I'm going to complain. *All* the way there, *all* the way back."

"I appreciate that," Malcolm says gravely. And then he holds out his hand.

I wait half a second, then I take it. His fingers wrap tightly around mine.

They feel good there.

The walk to the beach is longer than a block, but the morning is cool and the breeze is pleasant, so I decide not to complain—too much. We pass a few wood-framed houses surrounded by palm trees, and a 1950s-era motel with a pelican painted on the front wall, a cheerful fish waving from its open mouth. Lizards scatter across the cracked sidewalk in front of our feet, and there's a heady scent of jasmine mixed with the salt in the air. In the distance, a roar tells me the Atlantic is in one of her tempers.

A shack at the end of the road turns out to be the bar Malcolm had in mind, its leaning wooden doorway barely distinguishable from the boardwalk disappearing over the dune. He takes me around the staircase, past a few mop buckets and a sink, and onto the covered patio of a very battered beach bar. A deeply tanned woman on the far side of fifty offers us iced teas, margaritas, or a bucket of beer. Malcolm wisely chooses the sweet tea for both of us.

"Ordering for me?" I smirk, settling onto the creaky chair he pulled out for me. The table rocks beneath my elbows, sticky with salt.

"I need you alert on the way back," he says. "In case we get lost."

"Oh, I thought you knew the way to her farm!"

"I do from the west," Malcolm grins. "Not from the east."

"Great." I look around the patio. We're the only ones here. Suddenly it strikes me—this is the perfect place for us. No one here, and even if anyone else comes, they won't know he's Malcolm Horsham, or that I'm Evie Ballenger, his working student.

This is our secret spot, I think.

"Yes," he says, smiling. "Exactly."

"I didn't say anything."

"I can hear you thinking." He reaches across the table, strokes a finger across the back of my hand. The touch raises a rush of sensation across my skin. "I thought for an hour we could just get out of the horse world bubble, be different people."

"I'd like that," I say. "Yes. Are you a beach bum in disguise?"

"You know, I am, kind of." He's still stroking his finger along my hand. I hope he never stops. "My father is from Jamaica. I lived there until I was six."

"Wait, what? I didn't know that." How did my gossip girls fail me on this? "You're *Jamaican?*"

"My father is. My mother is from Miami." Malcolm grins. "And we moved back to south Florida because she said I'd have more opportunities here. But I think she really missed her job. My mom's in tourism, some kind of financial analyst, which is how I ended up in finance for a while, too. But she's happy with it. She likes her desk, her view from the sixth floor. She's the breadwinner of the family, and she likes that, too."

"Did she buy you horses?" I ask. "Was that her thing, too?"

"Horses are my *dad's* thing," Malcolm says. "I guess it runs in the boys, in our family. The old style. He grew up riding horses all over the place, horses on the beach, horses in town, horses in the garden. He bought me my first pony when I was seven. Put it in the garage. The neighbors raised hell. We had to board him. I think my father was mad about that. He grumbled every time he mowed the lawn. Said it was a horse's job, not a man's."

"So you grew up with horses," I say. "Showing?"

"Catch-riding," Malcolm replies. "Ponies, mostly. I was a late bloomer. That was good, because I got to ride ponies until I was about fourteen. They paid more than horses, and they were tougher, too. So I was riding all winter at Wellington, essentially working full-time when I should have been in middle school, bumming lessons from the homeschool tutors so I could pass the tests and get moved to the next grade."

"Oh, you were the full horse show orphan," I exclaim, clapping my hands. "Raised by your trainers?"

"Essentially," Malcolm laughs. "But since we lived nearby, I didn't have to live in an RV by the show-grounds with some people I barely knew, or my coaches. It wasn't so bad. A lot of keeping up with the Joneses, though. And it was all my own money, going into the clothes and everything. The new boots every season. The latest helmet, the best jacket. I spent half of what I made on clothes to wear in the next class, easy."

"And that's why you're so stylish."

"Oh, you think I'm stylish?"

"Malcolm, do you have *any* idea what people say about you?" I ask, frustrated.

"Until this morning, Evie, I didn't realize people were talking about me."

I stare at him. He's dead serious.

The waitress puts sweet teas between us. "Can I take your order?"

Just once, I would love for a server to recognize a heated silence between two people. "A fish sandwich," I say, exasperated. "Fries, not chips."

"Fries are extra," she drones.

"Pay the woman for fries, Malcolm."

He forces a chuckle. "I'll have the same. *Yes,*" he adds, before she can say anything. "We'll have fries." He smiles at me as she stalks off. "They're very good fries."

Such a distraction, I can barely remember what we were talking about. Oh, right. This is the man who doesn't know how gossip works. I start to fill him in, but he interrupts me. "How did *you* start riding, Evie?"

"The usual way," I say, waving a hand. "Begged mom for riding lessons, got riding lessons, begged mom for horse, got off-track Thoroughbred, yada yada yada, here we sit today."

"Fascinating."

I stick a straw into my tea and bang the ice around the cup. "I'm no A-circuit brat, but I do okay."

"You're an excellent rider. I think you're going places."

"Oh, yeah? I'm almost thirty and I've been dead in the water since I got to Ocala," I counter. "A couple events, a couple dressage shows, and I might as well have quit before I got here and stayed back in Maryland. My mom was right. Ocala didn't have the secret sauce I thought it did. Just another place with horse shows." I've never realized how angry I've been about this until right now. "I had a good horse, the *best* horse, and what happens? He stops sweating. Then he tears a ligament. And I had all my eggs in that basket. It was all Breezy. Without him—"

I try to stop myself before I lose my cool, but maybe that's already come and gone, because Malcolm is gripping my hand tightly, like I'm standing on a ledge and he's trying to pull me back.

"I'm sorry," I mutter. "Now you know why I needed Bucky so bad. But it still feels too late, sometimes. I'd basically given up. Just another horse girl with five-star dreams that aren't coming true."

He holds my gaze. "You just weren't in the right place yet," he says softly. "Your dreams can still come true."

I want to kiss him. It's such a strong desire that I'm considering getting up and walking around the table and tugging him to his feet and—

"Fish sandwiches," the server says.

"That was fast," I mutter as she drops the plastic baskets on the table.

She side-eyes me. "Fish cooks fast."

"And also there's no one else here," I mutter, although I wait until she's disappearing into the kitchen.

"Well, it is eleven in the morning," Malcolm says mildly, investigating his sandwich. "Most of the locals aren't awake yet."

"So, you think I still have a chance." I decide to be light about his words, like there wasn't a wealth of emotion in them. "I'm not going to ruin Bucky once you finally hand him over?"

"You're not going to ruin Bucky," Malcolm chuckles. "I'll make sure of that myself."

There's really no time for a stroll on the beach after our early lunch, as nice as the surf sounds beyond the dune, so after Malcolm has paid up, we head back to the truck. I feel a heaviness in my steps, as if the idea of going back to work is a depressing one. And that's weird, because despite the long hours, I've begun to like my job.

Or maybe it's just that right now Malcolm is still holding my hand, and back in Ocala, he won't be able to.

Despite his warning about not knowing the route, he finds his way to Mackenzie Phelps's farm with ease. A slim woman in breeches walks out of a pretty center-aisle barn as we pull up. She shades her eyes with one hand, waves with the other. I'm surprised to feel a little stir of jealousy as her gaze lands on Malcolm and brightens with pleasure—this woman is *pregnant,* for heaven's sake; it's unlikely she's going to throw herself on Malcolm and kiss his face off. But jealousy seems to be a normal reaction for me when other women are around him, and I guess it's not going to get easier.

"Hey, stranger," she calls as we hop down from the truck. "I see you brought the new girl."

I flush. "Hi, I'm Evie," I say, before Malcolm can introduce us. "I'm the working student this spring."

Maybe by making this a seasonal job, I can feel less like a loser who is working an entry-level gig around these two professionals who are only a few years older than me. Like this is just a stop for me on a long and exciting road.

I mean, hopefully that's the case, anyway.

"Evie," Mackenzie says, taking my hand. "Mackenzie Phelps. Good to know someone so strong and capable is keeping an eye on Malcolm."

"That's me," I joke, to hide my confusion—do I come off as some kind of strong, sturdy little pony? "Strong and capable Evie, like everyone calls me."

Mackenzie's smiling, but she's already turning back to Malcolm. "And you, mister. Looking wonderful, I must say. Oh, those *boots*. Are you joking? Are those the ones from that Italian cobbler we met in Wellington?"

"They sure are." Malcolm turns his foot at all angles to show off the gorgeous boots. "Worth every penny."

"A *lot* of pennies," Mackenzie replies, still admiring them.

I can't believe it. He wore those boots to impress her.

"You always did like a nice pair of boots," she goes on. She lifts her gaze back to his and pushes a strand of hair back from her face.

Malcolm smiles and says nothing. I know I'm not imagining the buzz between them.

These two have been together.

I can't take it anymore. "So, we're here for a horse," I blurt. "Inside the barn, or—"

Mackenzie gives me a startled look. "Yes, the horse," she says eventually, eyes studying my face. "He's ready to go. Come into the barn."

I hang back and let Malcolm walk after her. He gives me a sidelong look, as if to ask if everything is okay. I nod shortly. It's fine, I think.

Fine that you clearly have a history with this woman, and she doesn't want you to forget it. Just *fine*.

A girl (considerably younger than me, big surprise) is putting shipping boots onto a tall warmblood gelding who is dozing in the cross-ties. She smiles up at us. "He's ready to go, Mackenzie," she says quietly.

"Thanks, Chris. Take him out to graze for a sec, will you? We'll just get his paperwork together." Mackenzie beckons to Malcolm, and together they walk into her office. It's at the end of the aisle, with windows on two sides, and the interior is as clean and tidy as if a housekeeper has just whisked her way through. I'm left in the aisle, watching as Chris unsnaps the cross-ties.

She gives me a shy smile. "You can walk out with us, if you want. Or if you need the bathroom, it's just over—"

"Thanks," I say. "I'll be out in a sec."

In the tasteful powder room next to the tack room, with fox-hunting wallpaper and a Costco-sized bottle of hand soap teetering on the edge of the sink, I blink back tears that are half-angry, half-humiliated. I know I didn't imagine the proprietary way Mackenzie looked at Malcolm, or gestured for him to follow her. She has a history with him. And she's probably not the only one in the community who does. Malcolm's a handsome man—please, he's *gorgeous*—and he's charismatic, too. All that bombast and temper he shows around the barn turns into something tantalizing and suave when he's out in public, as if women can sense the volcano beneath the surface and the potential for danger dressed in a dressage coat is too delicious to pass up.

"Is that what you want?" I whisper to my reflection.

But it doesn't matter what I want.

Much like my eventing career with Breezy ended when he was diagnosed with anhidrosis, this decision is out of my hands.

I've already fallen, hard, without an air-vest or even my hard hat for protection.

"You were great back there," Malcolm says.

We're back on the road, driving west through the pine trees. The sun is glaring overhead, threatening to sink just low enough to blind us on our drive home. I glance at him, confused. "Great?"

"Ice-cool," he clarifies. "No one would have thought we were just out to lunch together. I really admire that about you, Evie, because every time I looked at you, I was afraid it would show on my face."

"Afraid *what* would show on your face?" I know, but I want him to say it.

"I wanted to jump you," he says, his voice turning husky. "Put my hands in your hair and turn your face up to mine and just—"

"Oh, right," I interrupt breezily. "You wanted to make out with me." I'm quiet for a moment, imagining the scene. "Well, that would have made Mackenzie's eyes pop out of her head."

"Maybe," Malcolm agrees, chuckling. "She's had a few workplace romances, herself. Met her husband while we were both working for Daisy Goodwin, a hundred years ago."

"Daisy Goodwin?" I recognize that name. I turn in the seat to face him. "When was this?"

"Six or seven years ago, when I had my first Advanced horse. I took him to Daisy so we could survive our first three-day-event with an expert in charge. Mackenzie was there, too. That was when she had her horse Figaro. You remember him, I'm sure. He was giving her trouble—" And then Malcolm is off on equestrian memory lane, recalling everyone associated with the year he took Pickwick Prodigy to Fair Hill Three-Day Event and came in sixth, an excellent showing for a first-timer. I remembered, because I was still in Maryland back then, still thinking I'd get Breezy around that course someday, too.

When he's done reminiscing about how Mackenzie met her husband, I ask the only question that matters. "So you and Mackenzie, you never—uh—"

"What, hooked up? Dated?" Malcolm shakes his head. "Mackenzie thought I was gay the entire time I was there. She never gave me a second look."

I burst into shocked laughter. "Oh my god."

How could I have been so wrong?

"What? You don't think I'd make an excellent gay horseman? You did see my boots, didn't you?"

"No, you idiot. I mean, you'd make a fantastic gay horseman. The horse world should be so lucky. But I thought—I was *sure*— Mackenzie was giving me all kinds of territorial looks. Like she wanted me to know she could still have you if she wanted you. She was definitely giving me that vibe. Even if you never dated, she was ready to defend her right to you, trust me."

Malcolm glances over at me, looking slightly aghast. "Jesus, Evie, is that how women think?"

"Do you want me to be honest here?"

"God, I'm afraid to know."

"That's how women think, Malcolm. It's all about power and ownership. And it's way, way worse in horses because we're all so competitive."

"That's so frightening. I'm afraid of you now. I hope you're happy."

"We're scary, Malcolm," I sigh, tipping my head against the window. "We're a very scary group. It's better you know the truth."

Chapter Twenty-Nine

POSEY TEXTS IN the afternoon, just to check in, she says, as she hasn't heard from me in ages and is afraid Malcolm Horsham has turned into a vampire and offed me in the dark of night. *No,* I text back, *it's way more complicated than that.*

Posey replies that she'll be over at seven thirty with pizza and beer.

See you then, I reply, and add about sixteen smiley faces. A friend is coming over! That's exactly what I need. It's been isolating here. Maybe that's the reason I fell under Malcolm's spell so quickly. There was no one else to talk to, and I started thinking he seemed nice, but it was really just the crazed silence talking. Posey will help me get everything in perspective.

We finish the horses late in the evening, which is entirely Malcolm's fault for taking me to lunch when we should have just gotten the horse and come straight back to the farm. He *knew* we had riding lessons in the afternoon, as Alison reminds him repeatedly throughout the rest of the day, as we fall farther and farther behind schedule. The positive side of the afternoon is that I get to ride Bucky again, this time feeling a little less like a doll tied to a draft horse's back, because there's simply no way Malcolm can fit the horse onto his shortened schedule.

Even Wesley ends up riding one of the horses, although it's just a tack walk and Alison tells her that if she touches the horse's mouth with the reins even one time, she will personally drag Wesley off the horse. Wesley rides the horse on the buckle around the covered arena, a petrified expression on her face, and in everyone's opinion, the girl is better for the experience. Threats are exactly what this poor little rich girl has been missing in her life.

"Don't worry," I tell her cheerfully as she untacks the horse, still glancing around as if to make sure Alison isn't going to descend on her and read her the riot act for some unseen mistake. "Alison threatens me every day and I'm turning out great. You'll get used to it. Maybe you'll even *like* it."

Wesley's face is somewhat green as she replies, "Yay, can't wait to find out."

I store up the afternoon's stories to tell Posey, thinking that if I can fill our dinner with enough idle chatter about the barn, I won't feel compelled to spill everything about the morning with Malcolm. Or last night with Malcolm. Or any of it, really. But I know it's going to be the first thing she asks about. She said at the event that she thought the two of us had something going on. I'd told her she was crazy. But as usual, Posey knew better.

She has a great eye for this stuff, even if it took her forever to admit she was in love with Adam Salazar.

Malcolm lingers in the barn after Alison and Wesley leave, while I fiddle with Breezy's mane, hanging out in his stall like a teenager who doesn't want to go home. I have a little less than an hour to clean up before Posey comes over, and those limited minutes are leaning on me, trying to convince me to go back down to the office and see what Malcolm's doing.

Then he's standing outside the stall, his fingers grasping the bars as if I'm in prison and he's come to break me out. "Are you going to turn that horse out tonight, or what?" he asks, a smile playing around his lips.

247

"I mean, I should," I say demurely, fighting back a rising tide of excitement. He's here—he came looking for me—he wants to spend more time with me! It's simultaneously the best moment of my life and the most embarrassing—is this really what I've come to, going all goo-goo about a guy?

Romantic entanglements have never been my thing, but my goodness, this one certainly has me by the throat.

"Why don't I walk out with you?" Malcolm suggests. "Just to be sure you know the way?"

"And don't get kidnapped or sucked into a third dimension," I rejoin gravely.

"Correct."

"That's fine, I guess." I bite back a grin as I pull out Breezy's halter —the fancy one that Alison provided the day he arrived, not the old blue one I used back at home—and slip it over his head. The horse nudges me hard as I clip the halter snap. A reminder, maybe, that *he's* been my man for years and years, and I shouldn't let anyone else get between us.

Oh, Breezy. I run my fingers through his forelock. Does he know the only one in this barn that could possibly compare to him is Bucky, and that horse is in no hurry to buddy up with me and replace Breezy?

"Blue?" Malcolm asks as he walks at my side, Breezy ambling with us towards the paddocks.

"A little," I admit.

"My fault?"

"No, no. Just horse stuff. Breezy getting older and falling apart on me. The usual."

"They have a tendency to do that." Malcolm puts his hands into his pockets as we step outside; the night is cool, with a sharp north wind. "Is this the coldest winter we've ever had, or what?"

"I don't know about ever, but I've only lived here a couple of years." Breezy lifts his head and sniffs the wind. His pace quickens as he anticipates friends, grass, a night of wandering his paddock. "Do you want to talk about the weather?"

"No," Malcolm says. "I want to take you back to my house and feed you."

"How romantic."

"It is the way I want to do it."

I shake my head, but I'm smiling. "I have dinner plans, lover-boy."

"Great. *Now,* who is going to eat all that whipped cream?"

Breezy walks into his paddock and turns, ready for me to slip off his halter. Such a good boy. "It'll keep," I tell Malcolm as I set my horse free for the night. "I'm assuming it's in a can."

"Who do you have dinner plans with?"

"Jealous?" I drop Breezy's halter on the hook, purposely leaving it crooked. I want to see if Malcolm will straighten it.

He does. Too funny.

"Anyway," I go on, "I'm having dinner with Posey Malone. Who thought, at the event last weekend, that we would be cute together."

He glances at me. "She said that?"

"Something like that."

"Why would she say that?"

"To annoy me," I lie, because there's something about his face I don't like. Something wary. "Because you'd just yelled at me and I was mad. I was thinking maybe I should quit. Take my talents elsewhere. But Posey and Kayla thought I should stay, and they were right, so —"

"Kayla, who is Kayla?"

I look at him for a moment, wondering why he's suddenly so uptight. A gust of wind makes me shiver, and I start for the barn again, not waiting for him. "Kayla's my *friend,*" I retort. "They came to see me at the event, for support and whatnot. Why are you being so weird?"

Malcolm jogs to catch up with me. "I'm not being weird—"

"You are."

"Fine. I'm being weird because if it was obvious to your friends over a week ago that we might be—I don't know, *attracted* to each other—then it might be obvious to everyone now that we're—" He's looking for the words, so I finish for him as neatly as I can.

"Acting on that attraction?"

"Precisely."

"You think we're being obvious, is what you're saying."

"I didn't think so, before, but..."

We reach the barn and I step inside, just to get out of the teeth of that cold north wind. "I really have to get upstairs and cleaned up," I tell him.

Malcolm nods. "Listen, don't tell her anything."

"She's my best friend. She's not going to blab all over town that we're seeing each other outside of work. And anyway, what about it? A couple of dinners, lunch today. It's not like we're jetting off to the Bahamas for a romantic weekend." I force a laugh, but I know it sounds hollow.

There's no way Ocala can find out we're involved. Not while I'm working for him. There's literally no juicier tidbit of gossip than when the working student starts spending the night up at the trainer's house. It's everyone's favorite. Trust me. I know.

Malcolm reaches for my hands and clasps them tightly. His skin is warm despite the cold, and I take a step closer to him. The heat of his presence is more than just temperature and science; there's a whole other chemistry to the way the air around us flares and bursts into flame. He feels it, too. I can see it in the set of his jaw, the glint in his eyes. "Evie," he says softly, and for a breathless moment, I think he's going to tell me the whole thing's over.

"Evie, we have got to keep our heads down," he says instead.

"Okay," I agree, nearly fainting with relief. I'm not ready for this to be over. *This*—a few stolen kisses, a quiet dinner, lunch at the beach —it's not anything, not yet. But it could be.

If we can keep it quiet.

"I don't like sneaking around," Malcolm is saying. "But as long as you're working for me, I don't want a breath of gossip getting out about us. So while we're in the barn, while we're around anyone else, we keep it cool, okay?"

I nod. "Of course."

"And you're okay with that," he says. "Right?"

I don't have to think it over. "It is what it is, Malcolm," I say instead. "As long as you're okay, I'm okay."

He tugs me close for a kiss, and by the end I'm hungry enough to wish I'd canceled plans with Posey and just gone straight back to his house for that whipped cream and whatever else he had in mind for dinner. But that's not part of playing it cool. So I wave goodnight and watch him walk up the driveway alone, and then I go into my apartment, feed Romeo, and take a hot, hot shower.

I'm bundled up in flannel and fleece leggings when Posey finally makes it over, practically blowing in the door. "Whew, it's turning windy out there!" she exclaims, staggering to the kitchen counter with her burden of pizza and beer. "Is the oven on? I think this puppy needs a little reheat session."

"Yup, ready to go." The oven is also heating my apartment, which, it turns out, is very drafty. I can actually see the sheer curtains above the kitchen sink moving in the wind. "We can start on the beer while the pizza gets hot again."

"It's funny," Posey says, sliding the box into the oven. "To live so far from pizza places that when you get a fresh pie, you still have to reheat it at home."

"Okay, city girl." Always good to head off Posey before she heads down New York City memory lane. Sometimes she forgets that she came back to Ocala because she wasn't happy in the city. It's easy to be nostalgic for a place where there is pizza on every corner, but what about the horse access? Severely lacking, from what I've heard. "Come get under this fleece blanket and Romeo will warm you up," I suggest, and Posey's happy to drop the topic and get snuggly with my cat.

"So, tell me about Malcolm," she says, once Romeo is purring and kneading her stomach.

"No," I say. "No Malcolm talk."

"What? But that's why I'm here."

"I thought you were here because we are close friends who haven't seen much of each other in several weeks."

"I mean, *that,* yes, but also the Malcolm part. Because, he's the reason I haven't seen you. See! It tracks." Posey sips her beer, looking pleased with herself.

"There's nothing to say about Malcolm. He's a good trainer. I am learning a lot. Oh! I'm riding Bucky now. So that's exciting. Um..."

Posey's fingers turn in rhythmic circles around Romeo's ears. "Tell. Me. About. Malcolm."

"Okay, fine. We are kissing a lot when no one is around. Are you happy?"

Posey's mouth forms a perfect O.

"Mm-hmm. That's what I thought." I shake my head at her. "You're all talk until the gossip gets hot. Then you can't handle the kitchen."

"I don't know what kind of metaphor you're going for here," Posey says, recovering herself enough to talk back, "but no. That didn't work."

"It's complicated."

"The metaphor, or your love life?"

"Don't call it that." I cringe. "He's a guy, I'm a girl, there has been some attraction, we are kissing it out."

"Nothing else?"

"Nothing else." I try not to think about the whipped cream.

"Nothing else...*yet*."

I don't answer.

Posey laughs so hard that Romeo stares up at her, offended.

"It's not funny," I insist. "Why are you laughing?"

"Because you acted like he was Satan's assistant and now you're all smoochy...it's funny."

"It's *not* funny," I tell her. "He's my boss."

"Oh, that happens all the time." Posey waves her hand. "Every marriage in Ocala started with a boss and a groom, or a boss and a working student. Look at Alex and Alexander, for crying out loud. She was his *gallop girl*. Your old job, remember? And it just makes sense. I mean, when else are you going to meet someone, but at work? Plus, it's not like barns have a ton of staff. So you take limited time, you take a limited dating pool...it's gonna happen."

I stare at Posey for a minute. She's right. Why do I forget that Posey is very logical and nearly always right? I should keep this girl around more often. Especially if she's going to bring pizza. "You know what," I tell her, hopping up from the sofa to get the food out, "I never thought of it that way, but you're right. I mean, you're with Adam, and you guys basically met at work, right?"

"When we were teenagers, yes."

"But you wouldn't have met him again if you hadn't worked together last year, right?"

"That's true."

"So your point makes sense, that's all. You want a big piece?" The pizza is cut unevenly.

"A piece the size of my head," Posey confirms.

"Coming right up." I take a big slice, too. With this conversation actually happening, I feel like I need it.

Settled back on the sofa, I address the problem Posey seems to be ignoring head-on. "Malcolm doesn't want all of Ocala talking about us, so he asked me to keep things quiet. And I agree with him."

Posey makes a face. "Do you *really?*"

"I mean...you don't think I should?"

"I just think it's always sucky when a guy keeps a girl his little secret. Adam tried that, remember? Because of his awful parents?"

"Oh, right. Well, maybe you're not the most impartial observer, then."

Posey rolls her eyes at me and concentrates on her pizza. But I can't let it go.

"He's not keeping me secret," I insist. "He's keeping us out of the gossip mill. And there's all the consent stuff with the sport to think of, too. He could get in trouble with the governing bodies."

"If you made a complaint," Posey points out. "So, is he afraid you're going to have a reason to complain about him?"

I slump back on the sofa. I have to say, all this talk of legalities and gossip is taking the fun out of my clandestine workplace romance. "No," I say finally. "I think we're doing this the only way we can, Posey."

"Well, it's your journey," she says. "Speaking of journeys, I'm heading to the wilds of the kitchen for another slice. You want one, I assume?"

I sigh and hand her my empty plate. "Another big one, please."

Chapter Thirty

THE NEXT DAY feels different. Malcolm has Wesley and Alison tack his horses in the morning, and has me tack and ride the three I'm riding for the day—including Bucky, I'm pleased to note. I ride Bucky under his tutelage, feeling my connection with the horse growing with every circle and transition. We even achieve some simple lateral work and a balanced counter-canter, something I've always found challenging. Bucky's no schoolmaster, but he understands this work well enough to move smoothly along the rail on the wrong lead, helping me sit in the saddle without feeling like I need to slump to the inside and fix his balance.

"That was good," Malcolm says when we're finished.

Nothing else. No smile, no eye contact. He keeps riding Artsy around the arena as I dismount and walk Bucky inside alone.

We eat lunch in relative quiet, Wesley and I sitting on the sofa while Alison flicks through her phone and Malcolm looks at his email and asks her occasional questions about his upcoming schedule.

In the afternoon, he has Wesley tacking for him, while Alison sets me to a lot of grooming and cleaning tasks that need to be taken care of between shows.

"Why am I not tacking this afternoon?" I ask, looking at the revised schedule she's given me. I'm perplexed; it feels like Malcolm has been avoiding me all day.

"It's better if Wesley gets the practice," Alison says. "She needs to speed up or she won't be able to keep up with us at events. And Malcolm said he wants someone he trusts working on manes and fetlocks. I'm not giving Wesley free rein with the clippers yet."

"That's fair," I say. But something still feels off.

Students start showing up around two o'clock, and the second half of the day is louder than usual as clients and the handful of winter boarders move back and forth in the aisle and take over the arenas. Alison told me it would be busy here through April, then get quiet again for the summer months. I'm surprised at how much I miss the quiet of the first few weeks. Or maybe it's just that I feel left out, walking down the aisle with a footstool, a set of clippers, and an extension cord. The stalls all have a ring for tying up horses inside, so I can do their trims without dragging them down to the grooming stalls—which are busy now, anyway.

The day is warm and sunny, and soon I hear the *thunk* of poles being moved around in the jumping arena. I glance through the window of a horse's stall and see Wesley dragging the heavy wooden poles around while Malcolm barks commands. Even from this distance, I can see she looks freaked out and stressed. Malcolm's temper is in full effect; I'm surprised he isn't keeping it under wraps, since Wesley is technically still one of his clients. But I guess once she signed on as a working student, she lost the right to his fake calm.

And what about me? I clip Diamond's halter to the tie hanging on the side wall, giving him room to continue munching on his hay while I work. I carefully run the clippers along the long hairs sprouting from his mane, trimming him up so that the mane doesn't look blunt-cut, but naturally short. But my mind is hardly on my work, and when I accidentally take a half-inch chunk out right in the middle, I sigh at the devastation I've caused.

Diamond looks at me with one big eye, still chewing his hay.

"I have to shorten your entire mane now," I tell him. "You are going to be bald."

He sighs.

"Agreed, buddy, but this is what I get for trying to work while all I can think about is—" I stop myself before I say his name out loud. There's a phrase Sallyann likes to use, right before she shares something new and juicy over the feed store counter. *The stalls have ears.*

By the time I've gotten Diamond's mane under control—a little too short, but that will only hurt me, the person who has to braid him this weekend—and carried my footstool back into the aisle, Malcolm has returned and is shotgunning water before his next lesson. I'm at the stall closest to the office and I can't help but smile in his direction.

He gives me a blank look before stepping back into the office.

Ouch. The lack of expression on his face hits me like a fist in the stomach. Is he playing it cool?

Or just wrecking me systematically?

My brain says it's the first option; my weak, stupid heart is certain it's the second one.

My hands are shaking as I open the stall door. Oceanus waits inside. The big horse, literally and figuratively, who after Artsy is Malcolm's best shot at five-star competition this year. If I accidentally clip a notch into *his* mane, I'm going to hear about it. But I have to calm down before I can even make an attempt. An idea comes to me —I poke my head out of the stall door and call, "Malcolm? Can I ask you a question about Oceanus, please?"

He shows up immediately. "Is everything okay?" His eyes rove over his horse, anxious as hell.

"It's fine, I just wanted to get your opinion on his mane—" I usher him into the stall and close the door behind him. Oceanus walks over to greet Malcolm, his ears pricked. It's the reaction I want from Bucky when I walk into his stall, playing out right in front of me. I have to swallow my jealousy and get back on topic, though. I only have a minute to get an answer. Pitching my voice low to avoid being overheard by the riders in the aisle, I ask, "Malcolm, why did you put Wesley in my place today?"

He looks at me quickly, one hand still on Oceanus's questing nose. "Did you think—wait, I'm not punishing you. Is that what you thought?"

Well, now I feel silly. "I just didn't know what to think," I reply lamely.

"It's to keep us apart during the day," he says. "I got to thinking about your friends last night...I thought it would be best if we didn't have too much face-time while everyone's around. The barn is so full right now, you know?"

"Right," I say. "Of course." I have to swallow a suspicious lump in my throat. "So, we aren't going to work side by side anymore?"

"Just while we're so busy, I think it would be best..." He touches my arm; we're blocked from view by Oceanus, but I look over my shoulder, anyway. Already as afraid of being caught as he is. "Hey, I didn't want to do it, but with all these students...and Wesley is underage...it would look bad, Evie. Really bad."

"No, I know." I manage a weak smile. "Bet you're really sorry you hired Wesley now, aren't you?"

Malcolm grins. "You called it. I just didn't know *this* was why I'd regret it. So, are we okay? I'm sorry if my decision hurt you. I just don't want the outside world to think you and I are...something we shouldn't be."

I don't know what we are. But I definitely don't think it's something we shouldn't be. "We're okay," I tell him. "But we'd be better if we made some plans for that whipped cream."

Malcolm's grin turns wolfish. "Oh, Evie. Have I ever got a sweet tooth!"

I guffaw, but it's really to cover how much I like him. And how sweet my tooth is, too.

"Are you guys finished in there?"

My laughter is cut short. I look at Malcolm in panic. He widens his eyes at me—*shhh*—and then looks over Oceanus's curving neck. "I was just showing her where we like Oceanus's mane trimmed to," he calls. "You know, his neck is just a little shorter than I'd like, so if we—"

"I didn't ask for your life story," Alison grumbles. "Mel is ready to mount up. You coming?"

"Send her out and I'll be there in a second," Malcolm promises. He looks back at me, and his gaze turns hungry again. "This is going to be torture, isn't it?"

I don't laugh this time. I have the uncomfortable feeling that he's right.

The clippers get to buzzing again once he's gone, and I try to focus on the job at hand. Oceanus flicks his ears back, listening to the motor. "You don't mind getting clipped," I remind the horse. "You're a big, tough, event horse. You're not afraid of anything. You're not even afraid of—"

Oceanus snorts and leaps backwards, startling me. I feel myself falling and put out a hand to steady myself on his neck—unfortunately, it's the hand holding the clippers. I realize my mistake and drop the buzzing clippers just before I fall onto him. "Oof," I mutter as he sidesteps and snorts. "Sorry about that, buddy. Thank goodness I didn't hit you with the...with the..."

I look at the short patch of mane beneath my hand. Why is it only an inch long?

Why is there a hunk of mane missing from Oceanus's neck?

The clippers shut off when they hit the ground, but not before. And there, on the shavings next to the clippers, is the missing hunk of black mane.

My throat fills—I think it's with my beating heart, trying to physically leap from my body and run away from the scene of the crime. "Oh no," I murmur, kneeling by the shorn locks. "Oh no."

And then I say a *lot* of very choice curse words, some in Spanish, some in Greek, some in Aramaic for all I know—you learn a lot of foreign swear words, working in a racing barn—but none of them can put the mane back onto Oceanus's slightly too-short neck.

I scoop up the black hairs and for a moment I think of sticking them in my pocket, but it won't do me any good to hang on to them. I drop them into the manure pail outside the door and take a fresh look at the damage.

I can braid around it, but there's going to be a gap there. And when his braids are out, for cross-country, the hole is going to be plain to see.

How's *that* for a calling card, Evie?

In the end, I choose to shorten Oceanus's mane just a little more than I normally would. It doesn't completely cover up the gap, but it makes it a bit less noticeable. When he's moving at full speed, with his mane fluttering in the breeze, it might not show at all.

That's the dream, anyway.

But I know Malcolm won't be happy, and I'm cringing when he comes back into the barn, preparing myself for the return of Mean Malcolm.

He makes like he's ignoring me as he walks into the barn alongside his student, but I don't let him continue the charade for long. "Uh, Malcolm," I say, as soon as I'm sure he's finished talking to Mel. "I have to show you something."

A little flicker of mischief crosses his face, but fades when he sees I'm being deadly serious. He follows me dutifully, keeping a more-than-healthy distance between us. When I turn at Oceanus's stall, I glance back and see his face go pale.

"It's nothing serious," I say quickly. "Please don't worry."

"Oh my god." Malcolm lets out a breath. "You had me terrified for a moment there."

"No, it's purely cosmetic and it will grow back, I just—" I slide the door open and Oceanus pokes his head out. My handiwork is on display.

"That mane's very short, Evie," he says immediately. "Why would you go so short—*ah.*"

"Yeah," I say miserably, waiting for the barrage.

Wesley walks up, interested in the show. "What are we looking at? Gosh, his mane is short, huh? Wait—why is there a hole?"

Malcolm has a hand to his chin. He looks like he's trying to decide if he should chop me up in bits before he drives my dead body out to the forest, or just leave me by the side of the road. He rubs his hand all the way around the back of his neck and then over his chin. His short beard makes a scratchy sound beneath his fingernails.

Wesley glances at me. "Did you do that?"

And then Alison appears, holding the reins of a horse I haven't yet managed to disfigure. She's the one to explode. "Are you *kidding?* Evie, what the *hell?* He looks like a nightmare! Who is going to braid his mane when it's that short? And what about the huge, gaping hole? What were you *thinking?*"

Malcolm holds up a hand, stopping her tirade. We all stare at him.

This isn't right, I think.

I hazard a glance at Alison and Wesley and know they're thinking it, too.

Where's the bitch-out I surely have coming my way?

"I fell," I say, to break the silence. "I fell off the stool and the clippers must have caught his mane when I dropped them."

"That was clumsy of you," Alison informs me. "You didn't tell me you couldn't even stand on a step stool."

"It wasn't on the job application," I snark back.

She stares at me, shocked that I'd talk back to her in that kind of tone. I'm a little shocked, too. But it's all because of the silence of the trainer. The one who should be exploding at me right now.

"I'm not happy about this," Malcolm says finally, with a voice like two glaciers grinding together. "But it was an accident, and you cleaned it up the best you could. And it can still be braided. It will just mean a little extra work. Thank you for showing me instead of pretending he rubbed it off in the paddock or something."

Oh, jeez. I could have done that!

"Sure," I say weakly, wishing I'd gone for the paddock option.

"Okay," Malcolm says, and he turns on his heel and walks back to the office. I hear the fridge door open and close.

Alison and Wesley are both staring at me.

"What?"

Alison lifts her eyebrows and shakes her head slightly. "You should have gotten in *way* more hot water than that, miss," she says.

Wesley folds her arms over her chest and says, "I got yelled at this morning for putting the wheelbarrow too close to the arena door."

"Well, that's dangerous," I say, attempting to defend him, but it's no good. They saw that something is different between Malcolm and me.

I wonder if our attempts at subterfuge are simply not going to be good enough for these two sharp-eyed sleuths. And then what?

I watch Alison walk her horse back to the grooming stalls to give him his bath, while Wesley scurries off to help the next student get into the ring. I still have one more horse to trim for the dressage show, so I scoop up my step stool and clippers. It's mindless work, when I'm not falling down and creating a disaster, which means I'll have a solid twenty minutes during which my hands are busy and my brain is free to roam, going over all the nightmare scenarios in which Malcolm decides this thing we have is to risky and lets me go for good.

Chapter Thirty-One

BY EVENING TURN-out, I'm fairly convinced all is lost. Alison is watching me like a hawk. Wesley is taking a page out of Alison's book and peering suspiciously at me every time our paths cross...although I'm not sure she knows what Alison is looking for. Finally, tired of all the eyes on me (and feeling a bubble of nerves in my stomach with Malcolm so close and so far all day long) I duck into Bucky's stall with a handful of treats and some notion that I'll finally make this horse love me.

Of course, it's way too late in the day for that. Patti and Ed are leading horses out to the paddocks and Bucky is already looking out the window with excitement, waiting for his turn. When I come into the stall, he turns a quick circle and then shoves his nose against my chest, not even noticing the handful of horse cookies in my grasp.

Outside, his excited expression tells me. *Outside, outside, outside!*

"Whoa, buddy," I gasp, pushing him off me. "I brought you treats. See?"

He snuffles at my open hand and gobbles up the cookies like the big monster he is.

"Yes, I'm trying to buy your love," I try to explain, but he just turns another excited circle, the shavings rustling beneath his hooves. I sigh and give it up. I might as well throw on his halter and turn him out. Slipping back through the open stall door, I reach for the halter —and encounter Alison, hands on hips, blue eyes narrowed. At me.

I look up and down the barn aisle and realize that we're alone, at least for a moment or two. So she's chosen this second to confront me? Super. "Uh, did I do something wrong?" I ask, choosing the route of studied ignorance.

"There's something you need to know," Alison says, her voice pitched low. She glances up and down the aisle, a mirror image of my gesture a moment before. "About the last working student."

Suddenly, I know what she's going to say. I feel like a gaping round sinkhole is opening between us, but it's spreading towards *my* feet, and in a few seconds, I'm going to tumble headlong into it.

"She didn't quit," Alison says. "I had her fired."

The hole stops spreading. It's still there, but it's not getting any bigger and so far, I'm not falling into it. "Why would you do that?"

"She was obsessed with Malcolm."

The edge of the sinkhole begins creeping beneath my toes. I'm going to have to ask Malcolm about her, aren't I? After all the time I've spent being jealous of the other women who have worked with him, and all the time I've spent telling myself I'm foolish for being jealous, Alison is proving the worst part of me was correct. And now I'm going to have to get it out in the open. *Tonight,* I resolve. I have to talk to him tonight.

"Not that anything was going on between them," Alison continues, "but I couldn't have her mooning over him at horse shows and events. People were going to notice. There was going to be talk. Malcolm's good name is all he has. He's not rich, he's not a trust fund baby, and he can't just buy himself out of bad publicity."

The sinkhole has steadied again, but I'm confused about something else. "What do you mean, *all he has?* Look at this place! I'd say he's doing pretty well."

Alison tilts her head. "Are you kidding? I thought you'd been in this sport a while, kid. Of course Malcolm doesn't own any of this." She shakes her head and laughs convincingly as Patti, Ed, Wesley, and Malcolm all appear at once in the aisle, talking and joking. "You're pretty cute," she chortles, and I realize her laughter is convincing because it's real. "Malcolm, owning this place. Get real."

"Hey, ladies!" Malcolm's voice washes over me like a cool wave on a hot day. I turn my face towards him, aware that his charm can drown me as easily as his anger.

I'm really done for, I think wonderingly, right before the group joins us and I have to pretend that everything is fine.

As everyone splinters off to halter another horse for turn-out, I turn to take Bucky's halter off its peg. Suddenly I hear Malcolm's husky whisper in my ear: *"Don't forget dinner tonight."*

I glance up at him; he's so close, my skin prickles. I think my cheeks are turning red.

Malcolm sees it and a slow, sultry smile creases his lips. "Dessert first, Evie," he whispers, and then walks off, his stride swinging, as if he hasn't just melted all my bones and left me wobbling here outside my horse's stall.

I'm resolved not to dress up for him, but a roasting-hot shower can't be denied. Romeo watches me with a certain amount of feline dismay as I pull on a pair of skinny jeans and a black sweater. *You're going out?* his expression clearly says. *Already?*

"Sorry, baby," I tell my cat, kissing him on the head. He shakes his head in disgust. "Be back—soon."

I look both ways before I head down the stairs, making sure everyone's cars are really gone. Especially Alison's—I can't risk her seeing me walking up to Malcolm's house. On a whim, I pull out my phone and text him. *All alone?*

He texts back immediately. *And starving.*

I giggle nervously at that.

He opens the door as I hurry up the walkway, shivering a little in the brisk night air. *Was he watching for me from the window?* I float the last few steps, at least I'm pretty sure I do—there's no way my feet are touching the ground.

Malcolm greets me with a hungry kiss that raises an involuntary growl from the back of my throat. The sound clearly delights him; he rocks back on his heels and looks me over. "Today was torture," he informs me.

"You're telling me." *Did he walk around like there was a hive of bees in his belly, too?*

"Working with you is going to be tougher than I thought." He takes my hand and takes me towards the dining room.

"I hope you're not having any second thoughts," I say, trying to keep my voice light.

"About you, Evie?" Malcolm pauses at the hallway. I see a light in a doorway. "Not about you. But about dinner...definitely." He tugs my hand, and I realize we're making a detour on the way to the dining room.

"But I'm hungry," I laugh, tripping after him.

"Don't worry," he says. "Dessert is this way."

When we eventually get to dinner, we fall upon it like starving animals. The nice thing about pasta, I always think, is that you can eat it hot *or* cold. Doesn't matter to me one bit.

Once we've slowed down a little, we start talking horses. It's natural and easy, discussing the people and animals of our sport and our community. A little easier than hanging out with racehorse people, because while I love galloping Thoroughbreds, I don't pay any attention to the actual races at all, and I'm hazy on most

Thoroughbred breeding besides knowing Storm Cats are temperamental and Tapits are tall. Malcolm knows some of the trainers I rode with as a teenager and in my early twenties up in Maryland, and I've worked with some of the coaches that he's had here in Florida, too. We laugh over shared stories and silly inside jokes as if we've known each other for years.

It's good to be back amongst my own people, I think, more than once.

By ten o'clock, though, I'm yawning and Malcolm's looking a little heavy-eyed, too. "I should get back," I say reluctantly. "Romeo will be asleep and his feelings will be hurt if he can't put his paws on top of my head most of the night."

"I can't believe I'm jealous of a cat," Malcolm drawls.

"I can't believe any of this," I admit.

"Any of...this?" He smiles at me, waiting for a clarification.

"That my whole life just turned on a dime," I explain. "I know I've told you how completely stuck I was. I wasn't competing. I wasn't training. I wasn't doing anything but getting up, going to work, and going home to bed. And then I decided to try for that horse, and drove to Sarasota...and now, here I am."

I don't want it to sound like seeing Malcolm is the big prize, but naturally, he takes it that way. "Here you are," he echoes, rubbing his thumb over my palm in a way that always makes me shiver.

Oh well, I think. Let him believe that everything else—the horse, the lessons, the feeling that I'm back in my own tribe—is secondary to this clandestine love affair of ours.

It might even be true.

"Let me walk you back to the apartment," Malcolm says when we've finally decided it's too late to fool around anymore and still make it to work in the morning. "It's dark out there and I don't want any crazies running off with you."

"Oh yes," I say, slipping on my shoes. "The famed Ocala crazies."

"You know this town is full of them," he insists.

"From most of the gossip I hear, *we* are the crazies."

"We're not crazy," Malcolm says comfortably. "We're just horse-people."

"One and the same." I slip my hand into his and we head out into the night.

It's pretty out; the wind has died down and though it's still cool, it's manageable, even for this Florida girl. A slim crescent moon winks through the trees arching over the driveway, following us as we walk towards the barn. With my hand in Malcolm's warm grasp and the night birds twittering in the bushes, I feel a sense of contentment I haven't known in years.

Maybe not ever.

At the base of the stairs, he gives me a kiss goodnight that raises the hairs on the back of my neck. I have to give him a little push for that. "No more tonight, sir," I say with mock severity, and he bows in apology.

After he's walked away and I've locked the door, I look around the apartment. Romeo is asleep on my bed, tail curled right up to his nose, refusing to wake up and say hello to me. I'm being punished.

That's fair, I suppose.

It's only after I fall into bed and the little cat has relented, pushing his front paws into my hair, that I realize I never asked Malcolm about the last working student.

Chapter Thirty-Two

THE BUSY DAYS of Florida's spring eventing season begin to run together in rapid succession. Horses in, horses out. Lessons and riding and tacking up and hosing off. The dressage show we ride in to help out Hardy comes and goes so quickly it's like a blip; the next horse trials, two weeks later, is a struggle-bus weekend of rain and cold temperatures that has my teeth chattering. After that the weather turns warm and I have to body-clip horses one after another, my whole world reduced to fur on my skin, up my nose, in my mouth. And through it all, the riding. Bucky, Diamond, Frolic—my daily sessions in the saddle growing more intense every day.

That's not the only thing that grows more intense.

The air thickens and swirls around us when Malcolm and I share the same space. We get better at ignoring one another, but worse at hiding it, I think.

When I ride, I'm keenly aware of Malcolm's gaze, following me around the arena as I work to connect with Bucky's big gaits, the only time all day he really looks at me. All of my rides are lessons now, all of my rides are under his watch, his eyes searing my skin, his crisp commands challenging my body to stop wilting and instead sit up straight, push into the stirrups, lift from the sternum, rise from the saddle.

"Tits out," he often adds, and we laugh, a moment of levity in a highly charged day. With every ride my ambition rises, reminding me that the career I wanted isn't out of reach yet—in fact, it's now closer than ever. The heady blend of fierce motivation and hidden attraction brings up my pulse, my temperature, my anxiety. When I'm alone, I can barely eat for all the butterflies in my stomach, fluttering wildly with the constant tension and demand for perfection. When I'm with Malcolm, I eat like a horse, starving, falling upon everything in sight.

Alison added my extra riding lessons to the schedule without comment, rearranging our days and passing on more work to Wesley. Now and then, though, she gives me a quiet look which says everything: *Don't think I don't see this.*

I know that now I'm under her microscope now, and still, I don't get up the courage to ask Malcolm about the last working student, the one Alison supposedly had fired.

Supposedly—a word I add to make myself feel better. If Alison doesn't want me here, Alison will make sure I hit the road before my contract is up.

But that's okay, because I know what I'm doing around horses, even if I've made several stupid mistakes since I got here. And if I make myself indispensable, she won't send me away—even if she thinks my presence might be endangering Malcolm's good name. Hey, I've worked in this business a while now, and if there's one truism every horse-person can agree on, no matter what discipline or training philosophy they follow, it's this: *good help is hard to find.*

One Friday night in late February, with a weekend show waiting for us, finds me living up to my commitment to be the best groom the world has ever seen—or at least, the best *Alison* has ever seen. I'm in the barn sewing up braids like a rockstar at seven p.m., after the final lessons are finished and the horses who aren't showing tomorrow have gone out. Alison is on her way out too, but she pauses outside Mastermind's stall to watch me for a few minutes. He's not the new horse in the barn anymore, but a regular part of my days, and I like him. He has good stable manners, and he quietly chews his hay while I work on his second-to-last braid.

"Those look good," Alison offers after a moment's silence.

"Thanks," I say around a mouthful of rubber bands.

"This was a decent week. Wesley's getting tougher. I caught her admiring her biceps in the tack room mirror."

I snort a laugh, nearly dropping the braid. "Poor girl," I say, spitting out the last of the rubber bands. "She must be dead tired doing all this work and school."

"She'll be grateful for school after this season," Alison agrees. "She'll probably study a lot harder now and get a real job instead of trying to be a trainer."

"Her mother will send us a check every Christmas, thanking us for scaring her daughter straight."

"I know my mom would," Alison reflects. "Yours?"

"Probably," I admit. "If only because she's already gearing up to say, 'You're almost thirty and your life has no direction,' in another year's time."

"Twenty-seven's almost thirty, right? I remember that year." Alison shakes her head like twenty-seven is a long way back in the rear-view mirror, although I'm sure it was no more than a couple of years ago. "Well, maybe she'll feel better if you get a position as a barn manager somewhere after this. I'll give you a reference."

I shrug as carelessly as I can. I don't want to think about leaving, or where I'm going next. "Right now, I'm focusing on surviving my six months with you guys."

"But what comes after that?"

273

The last braid is always tricky. I squint at the coarse mane hairs above his withers, while Mastermind twitches his neck muscles in protest. "I don't have a plan," I admit, once it's clear Alison isn't going anywhere without an answer. "I just hope I'm connecting with Bucky and we're ready for some real competition once fall rolls around."

"And where will you take him?" Alison persists. "You'll want to board him someplace like this, with arenas and jumps, or you won't be able to keep up. Once you hit Prelim, you're going to need regular access to cross-country schooling, or at least a full jump course. And to keep the dressage tests accurate, you really need the right size arena, good footing..."

That isn't the half of it. I know Alison's right, though, because when I was competing Breezy at Preliminary I was using the fancy farm Kayla was barn-sitting to provide all those luxury amenities. But that deal is long over. Kayla's moved on with her life, and I'm going to have to, too.

A barn manager position at a nice eventing barn that offered board for Bucky would be the best bet. But leaving here? Leaving Malcolm?

"I guess if you got the right job you could board here," Alison muses.

"I would never have the money to board here, Alison. Let's be real." I finally pin down the final braid and get it wrapped in place. "I don't even know what board is, because I'm literally afraid to ask. Anyway, I have my own farm and a trailer. I can haul out for schooling and lessons."

But I don't know how I'll pay for those, either. My savings are being used up to pay my bills while I'm working here. I can go back to work for Posey when my contract ends, but that's all day, six days a week. When will I have time to trailer out for lessons and cross-country schooling?

The last braid falls limp in my fingers as I realize that I've been living in a fool's paradise. Even with Bucky, the horse of a lifetime, I won't have the money to make my eventing dreams come true. I'm only making it happen now because I'm working off his lessons and board, but that can't last forever. I'm not a kid. I have responsibilities, bills, bad credit—all the usual adult miseries that make horses into luxuries instead of necessities.

"Oh my god," I say blankly. "I can't afford Bucky."

Alison purses her lips. "I'm sure there's a way to manage things," she says eventually, sliding open the door so I can carry out my step stool. She hands me the braid-tamer I had hanging over Mastermind's blanket bar. "Just put good vibes into the atmosphere," she suggests. "And the right position will be there when you need it."

I glance at her suspiciously. "Good vibes does not sound very Alison."

"I may be a realist," Alison says with a little shrug, "but that doesn't mean I can't believe in good vibes. Sometimes it feels like the only way we get through the day in this business is with vibes and luck."

"That's true."

"And getting favors from the right people."

"Sure."

"And not pissing off the wrong ones."

I pause, the braid-tamer halfway over Mastermind's neck. "Alison," I begin.

"Yeah?" She sounds like she knows exactly what I'm going to ask her. Like she led me down this path on purpose. It wouldn't surprise me. Vibes and good luck, indeed. Alison has never relied on the universe for anything. "What was her name?" I ask finally.

"Tara Gilroy," Alison answers promptly. "Know of her?"

I shake my head.

Not yet, I think.

"That's good," Alison says. "If I were you, I'd steer clear. She's not going to like anyone who took her place."

The day starts at six a.m., two hours earlier than usual. After two months away from my racehorse schedule, every predawn alarm is like a slap to the face. Even Romeo looks annoyed when I climb out of bed and stumble out to the kitchen to start the coffee and get his food in a dish. He stays wrapped up in my duvet, purring encouragingly, as I tug on leggings and a sweater for the early set-up at the farm where we're showing today. I'll put on my show clothes later, in the trailer dressing room.

Malcolm's already in the barn, double-checking the piles of tack I set out the night before, while Patti and Ed feed the horses breakfast. It's early for them, too, but they most certainly don't mind. Bucky calls for his food as I walk past, and for a moment I pretend it's because he's excited to see me.

"Why didn't we pack the trailer last night?" Malcolm asks me as I walk up.

I recall the night before, when I suggested I stay late to pack the trailer and Malcolm suggested we eat pasta and go to bed early. "Do you really want me to answer that question?"

He looks up the aisle and sees Alison on her way in, a tray of coffees in her hand. "I do not."

I smother a grin and shake my head at him.

Alison is not impressed with the unpacked trailer. She hands me my coffee with an expression which clearly states I am being spoiled and do not deserve it. "Were you sick last night?"

"Migraine," I say blandly, accepting the coffee. "Had to take the big meds to get any sleep. Thanks for the caffeine."

"Migraines are terrible," Malcolm offers. Alison gives him a hard look, but says nothing.

God, we're so close to being found out, I think. I take a step away from Malcolm, certain there's a loud snapping and crackling whenever we're within touching distance. This much electricity *can't* go unnoticed.

"Well, grab a wheelbarrow and get it loaded," she snaps.

I let her temper go without feeling too bothered by it. Last night, as I walked back to my apartment, I took out my phone and did a search on the name Tara Gilroy. And I found out a few things about the former working student I've been so jealous of for the past month.

One: Tara Gilroy is an infantile twenty-two years old.

Two: Tara Gilroy is built like a pixie with good biceps, and she likes to wear sleeveless shirts to make sure everyone knows it.

Three: Tara Gilroy now rides in California with a hotshot young guy who won the Young Riders championships just three years ago. Much more age-appropriate, in my opinion, than lusting over Malcolm, who is over thirty.

Not that I have any proof she's now seeing her new trainer on the side, but if she was really lusting over Malcolm to the point where Alison was afraid of gossip, then it didn't seem unreasonable to think she was going to carry on the same way with her new boss.

And that's fine. Let her do that.

In California, far away from Malcolm and me.

Because the last thing I need is this suntanned pixie showing up somewhere both Malcolm and I are riding, and putting on some kind of show for the masses. Just the idea gives me a little shiver of horror. But I mean—twenty-two years old! She's only five years younger than me, but the distance from here to there when we're talking public decorum can be pretty significant.

Anyway, I'm grateful to Alison for giving me the name. Now I can sleep a little better at night.

So I let her snipe and snark at me without talking back today.

Tomorrow maybe I'll stand up for myself, but today's all about Alison.

This dressage show, like the one we attended a few weeks ago, is relatively small—a schooling show for the students and younger horses. Malcolm likes to drop in a confidence-builder periodically throughout the spring season, which gets tougher and more testing as the days grow longer. Ocala is notorious for its high level of competition, so there are no easy A's at the recognized events. And even here, I spot a few upper-level trainers alongside Malcolm, experienced riders who are well able to put on a good test on a green horse.

I have dressage chops of my own; last summer, I was able to ride Breezy with a pretty good dressage coach and we did some shows at Legends Equestrian Center, riding in the posh air-conditioned indoor arenas. The climate control provided the only way to show Breezy with his anhidrosis, and I was grateful for the opportunity to put on some red lipstick and pretend to be a dressage queen, if that was what it took to get my horse in the arena again. He wouldn't be able to manage this outdoor show today; even though it's still technically February and winter, a warm blanket of air has settled over Florida. The forecast is for a lean, mean, eighty-two degrees.

With Wesley's help, I get the horses off the trailer and into stalls, then head back to the farm for the others. We're just doing day-stalls, or this work would have been done last night. Alison stays at the show-grounds to get the first horses tacked up and into the arena; Malcolm is stalking around in white breeches and polished dress boots with his usual show-day temper, making her so nervous she snaps at him to go find some friends by the warm-up and leave her alone.

Wesley bounds in the passenger seat of the truck and watches the scenery go by; we're only fifteen minutes from the farm, but we pass more than a dozen million-dollar farms along the way. "I want to live in Ocala year-round," she says dreamily.

I'm surprised by that. I thought we were exhausting her to the point of giving up her equestrian lifestyle. "Really? I thought you liked living up north in the summer."

"No, I like it here. All horses all the time. This is better." She sighs. "My mom doesn't know about it, though."

"Moms can be tough," I agree. "My mom is in Maryland. I think she wishes I'd come home and go to nursing school or something."

"Nursing...that sounds disgusting," says the girl who just learned how to muck stalls last week and squealed so much Alison told her to knock it off or go home and never come back.

"It really does," I agree, the woman who has reached halfway up her arm in a horse's backside to do a rectal exam when a vet was running late, and thought nothing of it. "Sounds nasty. Sick people and wounds and—"

"Ugh, stop!"

"Have you been more than a working student before, or is this your first time working in a barn?"

I laugh, slowing the rig to allow another horse trailer ahead to gain speed after they pull out of a palatial farm entrance. "I've been working on farms for almost ten years."

"But you're a working student now," Wesley says, confused. "Like me?"

I nod. "Same as you. That's something, right?"

"Yeah," she says. "Must be kind of disappointing. I mean—not to be rude. But you probably were, uh, hoping to have your own place by now, right?"

"I'm twenty-seven," I tell her. "I was hoping for a lot of things by now. And I do have my own little place. Nothing fancy, but it's mine."

"I want something fancy," Wesley admits, like it's a weakness she can't help.

"We all do. But most of us won't get it."

"Something like Malcolm's farm. Although I know it belongs to the Coles."

I glance at her. The truck swings a little with the motion, and I have to catch the wheel before I let a tire go off the road. Hedges flash by on either side. "What do you know about the Coles?" I ask, making it sound like I know quite a lot.

An old trick I learned to get good gossip.

"I know Dr. Cole is a neurologist in Miami," Wesley offers. "And I know Mrs. Cole knows Malcolm from way back somehow...and that she's from Jamaica. I met her at a polo match last year."

He's not a trust fund baby, Alison scoffed at me that night, and I never had the courage to follow up on that or anything else she said. "Right," I say, keeping my eyes trained on the road. The farm sign rushes up to us and I make the turn slowly, carefully. "How was the polo match?"

"Pretty exciting," Wesley says, accepting the change of subject without noticing I'd turned it. "Sometimes I think I'd like to try it. My mom says no way, though. Dangerous, and full of dangerous men."

"All men are dangerous," I remind the teenager. "And most of the women, too."

"What's that supposed to mean?"

I pull up in front of the barn so we can easily load the last four horses. "Just that the horse business is full of sharks, in every discipline. If you're going to stay in it, don't trust anyone too much."

"But I trust you," Wesley says, hopping out of the truck. "I trust Malcolm, and I trust Alison. Are you saying I shouldn't?"

I hesitate. That's really the last thing I want to tell this girl. I feel like *I* am trustworthy, like I'm not one of the rest. But what if we're all fooling ourselves? *Everyone's crazy but me.* That's not exactly a ringing endorsement.

"It's not that you shouldn't trust us," I say finally. "It's just that in the end, we all work towards our own best interests. And that might mean it's not what's best for you. Or you might want something that isn't best for Alison or Malcolm."

Wesley flicks her hair over her shoulder, an impatient little teenage gesture. "Obviously," she says, shaking her head at me. "But I'm not going to double-cross you just to get ahead, Evie, no matter what you think of me."

"Hey! When did this turn into me not trusting you?"

Wesley's smile is knowing. "I'm one of you guys now," she reminds me. "So, in a way, wasn't it always about me?"

"Good god," I snort. "Get a lead rope and put a horse on that trailer. I don't even care who."

She laughs and heads down the aisle, leaving me shaking my head after her.

That girl sure can talk in circles. I better keep an eye on her. She might get us all into trouble one of these days...and she might have fun doing it, too.

Chapter Thirty-Three

"PUT THIS ON." Alison is rushing up to me with an earpiece, the kind that clips over the earlobe. She has a little box in her hand. "And snap this on your belt."

I'm sitting on Bucky, stretching my ankles before I slip my feet into the stirrups. "What's this?" I ask, taking the earpiece and box from Alison. "Oh, a wireless set?"

"So he doesn't have to shout at you in the warm-up," Alison explains. "I got these for shows and this is the first time he's agreed to use them."

"Gotcha." Some trainers use wireless get-ups all the time, but Malcolm enjoys shouting so much, I can see why he hasn't been in a hurry to try the system out. Why give up a favorite pastime? I slide the earpiece on and make sure it's secure inside my helmet harness. I hate it immediately, hanging off my ear like a piece of children's dress-up jewelry. "This is going to be sweaty and gross," I complain.

"Yeah, like everything else on earth." Alison rolls her eyes. "This is Florida. Get used to it. And get over to the warm-up right now. He's waiting for you."

Two paddocks down from the stabling, a handful of riders are warming up their horses on the grass. Most of them have taken off their jackets, or maybe they didn't even bring one. I consider asking Malcolm to hold my jacket for me, but decide that would be too telling a favor to ask. He can't just walk around with his working student's jacket over his arm. It would be out of character enough for people to notice.

"Hey, Evie," he says, coming up beside me as I halt Bucky just inside the open pasture gate. The horse has his head up, watching the proceedings with pricked ears. Malcolm pats him on the neck and looks up at me. "You look beautiful."

I bite my lip, trying to conceal a big smile that's threatening to burst across my face. I put on a little makeup for this test, just a touch of mascara, a little lipstick—a good dressage queen knows that without it, a rider in black and white can look like a ghost on horseback. I'm not big on makeup, but even I know that a little goes a long way in making all my best features that much cuter.

Sultry and beautiful, even if I do say so myself.

"Now, let's get you riding," Malcolm says, stepping back, and from that point on, it's all business.

At least, I expect it to be.

But I underestimated what it would be like to have his voice murmuring in my ear, just for me, after spending every day so frustrated, working in his company while surrounded by others who aren't allowed to know where our relationship has gone. And the low, husky tone he uses as he speaks, trying to keep from being heard by the other trainers and grooms on the ground near him, makes things that much more—uh—*educational.*

He murmurs dressage terms which somehow sound suggestive in his silken whisper. "That's it, Evie, just close your inside fingers gently on the rein, good, and ask for the trot with the slightest lift of the pelvis—that's it, just your seat, your leg close, sink down in the saddle, now lift your shoulders, lift your chest, Evie—focus now—"

I hear the amusement in his voice and have to bite back a laugh before it even comes out of his mouth.

"Evie, *tits out.*"

He whispers it, and my forehead is creasing with the effort not to laugh. I hazard a glance at him as we trot up the long side of the grassy warm-up and see he's grinning. That nearly does me in. But it's okay to smile at each other, I think, and I let myself cast a grin at him as Bucky trots by.

He smiles back.

I'm sweating all over now, thanks in part to this sultry February heat wave but also thanks to his voice and his smile, his eyes on me as I trot this horse around the paddock, avoiding other horses and riders intent on their own warm-ups. I'm intensely aware of all my parts, which actually helps my riding...and there's a certain poetic justice to that, since I am his working student, after all.

He's making me a better rider in every way, I think, a little smirk on my face, right before he whispers for me to sit deep in the saddle, still my body, and think *halt,* and I do so, with a shiver of awareness running up my spine.

"Give him a pat on the neck and a little walk before we canter," Malcolm advises. "You're riding beautifully, Evie."

"Thank you," I whisper, forgetting I don't have a mic to reply to him. A girl trotting past gives me an odd look.

What, I think, a girl can't talk to herself?

Or to the secret boyfriend in her ear?

There is barely time to speak in person all day, but three times I clip on that earpiece and go to the warm-up, and three times, Malcolm's voice is for me and me alone. I savor every word he says to me, even when he's being more than a little judgy—at one point, I want to ask him if it *really* matters so much that my chin has a tendency to point down at the canter. But it would be a pointless question, because to Malcolm, everything matters. He's a perfectionist. That's why I'm the only person here still sweating my way around the dressage arena in a black coat.

Well, that's not true. So is Alison, and so is he.

By Frolic, the third of my rides and the last horse on the farm's show-roster, I'm feeling just a little wrung out. There has been a lot of work back at the stabling, getting our horses out while also managing my own rides, and the constant tension brought on by Malcolm's warm-ups has only added to the physical devastation that dressage on a hot day can wreak on a person. I'm a little unsteady in the canter on Frolic, and Malcolm finally tells me to quit our warm-up a few minutes early and just walk him in the shade.

"You look frazzled," he tells me through the earpiece.

"Because of you," I whisper. I've been talking back to him more and more with each ride, feeling a certain freedom in my ability to murmur replies that no one can hear, especially not him. "You make me frazzled."

"You know, I see your lips moving."

I press my lips together and shake my head. Of course he can.

"I wish I could read them, but you're a little too far away."

Can he read lips, is that what he's saying? I clap one gloved hand over my mouth. Malcolm, a good hundred meters away, standing in the shade of an oak tree, must be smirking now.

"It's been making me a little crazy," he whispers, "knowing you're talking back to me, not knowing what you're saying."

"You think *you're* the one going crazy?" I murmur, dropping my hand back to the reins. Frolic is charging towards the tree line at a marching walk, his ears pricked and locked on Malcolm. He must think Malcolm has carrots in his pocket.

"Evie, you have no idea what you do to me," Malcolm says, his voice so faint I can barely hear him. I know he's taking no risks now, but he can't resist talking to me, and I can't resist listening. I breathe shallowly, desperate not to make a single sound that might drown him out. "You in your dressage queen makeup today...you're always beautiful, but today, you took my breath away."

I'm not breathing at all now. We're closer. Sixty meters, the length of a small dressage arena. He stands beneath the tree and waits for us.

"You make me break all my own rules," he murmurs, his words a breath of wind. "I'd let it all fall down for you, Evie."

My mouth falls open. A rider on a fractious chestnut horse canters past, hooves thundering, and I'm afraid I'll miss something, but Malcolm waits. Forty meters. The width of two circles. His hands are in his pockets, his heart is on his sleeve, but only I can see it.

"Evie," he whispers, "Evie."

Twenty meters, and I draw Frolic to a halt. We look at each for a moment, and then I know I have to drop my gaze.

This little world is watching us.

"It's because you're together too much," Posey says. "The same thing happened to me and Adam. Everything moves way too quickly because you're literally together all your waking hours. If you were just dating and had normal jobs, this wouldn't be happening for months yet."

"But it *is* happening," I remind her. "And I'm out of ice cream and I don't know what to do."

"You could check *his* freezer," Posey says snidely.

"Thank you. That's very helpful."

Posey smiles at me. She's actually just a face on my phone right now, propped up against my coffeemaker so we can chat while I ransack my tiny kitchen for junk food. The problem, of course, is that I don't have much money and I haven't been able to waste any on empty calories. If I want whole-wheat bread and natural peanut butter, I'm golden. But after today's whispered revelations, all I want is sugar, fat, and cream.

The real staples.

"Evie," Posey says, yawning theatrically, "it is nine of the clock and yon racetrack is calling me awfully early in the morning. Please state your business so I can give you helpful advice and go to bed."

"He all but told me he's falling in love with me," I remind her. I settle for a yogurt and peel back the lid moodily.

"So fall in love with him back," Posey says. "You two are a great match. Eventing lovers."

"We can't date in public, remember?"

"Forbidden love is twice as hot," Posey reminds me.

"But we work together and someone is going to find out, and that someone is going to be Alison, and she'll make him fire me. She made him fire the last girl."

"Wait—the last girl?" Suddenly, Posey is paying attention. "You didn't tell me about the last girl. What did you find out?"

"She's nothing," I say around a mouthful of yogurt. "Alison said she had the hots for him. I looked her up. She's in California with a guy her own age now."

"She's younger?"

"Of course she's younger. My job is entry level. I'm old for it."

"And he definitely wasn't into her?"

"Not according to Alison. And she's way too young. And—" I stop suddenly, spoon in the yogurt. "Posey, you don't think he *was*, do you?"

"No!"

"Posey, why would you say that?" I moan. Yogurt won't do the trick anymore. I push it aside. "Now I'm afraid he was!"

"He wasn't," Posey says firmly. "Trust Alison on this one."

"Maybe it doesn't even matter if he was."

"Well, it would matter."

"Why?"

"I would be afraid he played this game with her, too."

"Game?" I repeat. A pit forms in my stomach.

"The whispering into the headset. The perfect lines about yearning for you. People all around, him revving you up while no one knows but him." Posey shrugs. "I'm not saying it was just a game, obviously, but it would be a very good one...if it was."

I'm devastated, I realize. Devastated. That might even be too trivial a word for what I'm feeling right now.

"No," I say at last. "He didn't have a headset before. That's new."

A silence stretches between us. I know it's a very trivial defense, and so does she.

"Evie, I'm sorry," Posey says. "Forget I said anything, forget—"

"Okay," I reply weakly. "I'll let you go, alright?"

"No, Evie, wait—"

"Goodnight," I say, and after I end the call, I sit down on the kitchen floor, and I don't get up for a long time. Romeo curls up on the bed and watches me through the open bedroom door, and the look on his face says *I told you so.*

Chapter Thirty-Four

SOMEHOW, I HOLD all the scary feelings in until Monday. I press back the worry that Posey introduced into my life, and let the workday on Sunday pass by in a rush of cleaning tack and showing Wesley how to clean out a horse trailer and getting through the horses who didn't go to the show. Alison sets out a game-plan for the coming week, since we're moving horses to the horse park on Wednesday for a big horse trials running Thursday through Sunday. I spend the evening with Malcolm and neither of us makes it weird by talking about the things he said into the headset the day before. It's actually a good day.

But on Monday morning, I set off to get a few things straight.

My first stop on Monday is always my farm, which is lonely and dark without me. The cloudy day means the interior of my little trailer is even gloomier than usual. I flip on all the lights to make sure the electricity hasn't done anything bizarre over the past week, flick on the gas stove, and run the water in the taps for a few minutes. The refrigerator is humming away and there aren't any mice in the traps. "Hang in there," I tell the house as I lock up. "I'll be back soon. Well, not too soon. I hope."

I pause.

"Nothing personal, house."

You can't be too careful.

With the farm secure for another week, I head down the road past Malone-Salazar Farm, glancing only a little wistfully at the manicured driveway leading back to the training barn, and into Ocala. The feed store with the best gossip is on the west side, where Sallyann rules the counter with a tattooed fist.

She's propping up the counter as I walk in, her lank yellow hair falling over her shoulders. "Evie!" she crows, in a voice rough with cigarette smoke. "Girl, where have you *been?*"

"Working," I drawl. "Don't tell me you don't know."

"I heard something about you and Malcolm Horsham, but I know that ain't right." She leans on her elbows, grinning. "You want to tell me?"

"It's true." I lean my hip against the counter and look at my fingernails, nonchalant as can be. "I'm his latest working student."

"Girl!" Sallyann brays. "That is the craziest news I heard all month."

"You're telling me."

"So, how are things going?"

I'm prepared for this question. I sketch out a little world that's a very vanilla version of my life these days. No mention of romance, obviously. Instead, I talk about horses, riding lessons, keeping up with Alison's tough schedule.

"Alison's a tough cookie, is what I understand," Sallyann agrees. "You know she came up here from Wellington. She worked for Helen Hooton."

"The big-time dressage rider?" I raise my eyebrows. "I didn't know that."

"Oh, yeah. Had a falling-out with her. The way I heard it, she moved to Ocala to start over."

"*Really.*" That's super interesting. I didn't come in expecting to get some details on Alison, but now I find I'm gathering more than I anticipated. "What kind of a falling out?"

"The romantic kind," Sallyann says, waggling her eyebrows suggestively.

"Wait—Alison and *Helen?*"

"Yup."

"I had no idea." That's putting it mildly. "And she was Helen's working student, right? Before she was Malcolm's?"

"Correct. But I never heard of any funny business with Malcolm and a working student. Probably because he's such a cold-blooded stiff, hah!"

"That must be it," I agree, forcing a laugh of my own. Suddenly, I don't want to gossip anymore. I think that this whole situation may have cured me of my little addiction. But I came here for one last piece of information. "Sallyann, I do have someone I need to ask about...Tara Gilroy. Did you know her?"

Sallyann's smile is all I need to answer *that* question. Luckily, she elaborates without my having to beg her. "Tara Gilroy, your predecessor? Sure, I knew her. Everyone comes through the feed store, right? She's in Cali now, though. Out of your hair."

"I didn't say she was in my *hair*—"

"Seems like it though," Sallyann observes. "You're blushing."

Oh, sh—I put my hands to my face. "Sunburn," I attempt, but Sallyann snorts.

"Well, Tara had a definite agenda, if you ask *me,*" Sallyann continues, letting me off the hook. "She didn't just want an education, she wanted a farm. And she must have thought Horsham owned his place."

We're tearing right through my index cards now. "Yeah, everyone kind of does, though. I just found out he doesn't."

Suddenly, Sallyann turns to the cooler behind the counter. She pulls out a can of Diet Coke and puts it in front of me. Then she reaches into her voluminous purse and pulls out a miniature of Jack Daniels. "Real quick," she says. "Throw that together and have a nice swig."

"I can't drink that here," I protest. "It's the middle of the day and I'm driving."

"Oh, it's a tiny bottle," Sallyann says. "Hear me out. I got something to say and you're not going to like it without some medicine to help it go down."

"What?" I'm wary, but something about her face makes me follow her bizarre instructions. The Jack and Diet goes down smoothly. I smack my lips to show her I've obeyed, as a warm feeling unfurls in my midsection. I can't say I don't like it. "Delicious. Now say what you've got to tell me."

"That farm of Malcolm's," Sallyann says, her face so serious I feel a prickle of fear despite the whiskey. "It belongs to a Dr. and Missus Cole, from down around Wellington."

"I know that," I say, but she waves a hand at me.

"Malcolm runs it, but they really bought it for their daughter. Malcolm Horsham's fiancé, Haley Cole."

Suddenly, the room starts spinning. I clutch at the counter for balance. Sallyann nods sadly at the Diet Coke, but it's not more Jack Daniels I need right now. It's *details*. "What else do you know about Haley Cole?" I demand, still gripping the counter like I might all off the earth without it.

"I don't know nothing about her," Sallyann says. "Just that someone from down in Welly came up here, and we got to talking and she said, 'Oh the Coles? They bought that place waiting for Malcolm to marry the daughter, as an engagement present,' and that's all that was ever said."

This doesn't make sense. Malcolm—engaged?

Absolutely not.

But why else would some doctor and his wife buy a farm like that?

"I have to find out who she is," I mutter.

"Not really horse-people," Sallyann says. "Lillian Cole, that's the lady's name—she likes polo players, from what I hear. Someone must have gotten her mixed up, and she thought eventing was like polo."

Lillian. I've heard that name. But I can't place it right now. I'm too busy trying not to throw up the Jack and Diet. I run a hand over my face and realize it's trembling.

Sallyann is shaking her head with regret. "I can't believe you went and got a crush on Malcolm Horsham. Of all the people in the world. Don't he yell and scream and holler like everyone says?"

"Of course he does," I say, turning away from her. "He's awful."

I pull the Jeep into a neighboring parking lot, just so I'm out of Sallyann's view, so that I can sit there and do some Google searches for Haley Cole of Wellington, Florida. But it's an annoyingly common name, and the Internet has gotten tougher when it comes to tracking people down. People aren't as open as they used to be; there was a time when you could learn a person's whole life story right off their Facebook page without even trying. It's not like that anymore.

Then there's the whole issue that I don't know which South Florida city she's actually from. Wellington doesn't bring up any hits. Her father's name shows up alongside half a dozen hospitals from Boca Raton to Miami, but the home address eludes me.

I try Lillian Cole next and find that she's the owner of several polo horses and LC Investments, which I recognize as the owner of record for Oceanus and Artsy Ballad.

Both of Malcolm's top horses. So this is the Lillian who calls him asking questions about his business, who encourages other riders to try his top horses, who generally makes him crazy? She owns everything. My mouth runs dry at the scope of it.

Finally, I do something I swore I wouldn't do—I log into LinkedIn, which is potentially dangerous because it shows users who checked their profiles, and find Haley Cole of Weston, Florida almost instantly. Her job title is Director of Operations for a fancy resort in West Palm Beach; her expression is bright and challenging at the same time, a wide smile, tanned skin, dark hair tucked neatly into a bun. She looks professional and put-together...nothing like a horse girl.

Sighing, I toss my phone aside and rub my face. He can't be engaged. He *can't* be. Certainly not to her.

Ugh, and Sallyann's face when she told me...she knew I had feelings for him. I wore my emotions like a flag in there. So stupid of me to go in there and let her see my feelings. I'm not immune to the gossip game. She has every right to pass this on to the next bored equestrian who walks into her feed store. *Did you hear about Evie Ballenger, used to ride at Malone-Salazar? She's in love with Malcolm Horsham. And he's engaged. Oh yeah, big love triangle shaping up there!*

God. What a mess I've made of everything. I should have just stayed working for Posey. Stayed at my own little farm. Stuck with Breezy and not worried about getting my aunt to give me this horse. Minded my business and stayed at home and been happy with things as they were.

Now my heart is all twisted up in my chest and the blabbiest woman in Ocala knows my inner hurts.

Well, I know one thing for sure.

Evie Ballenger is done with gossip.

Chapter Thirty-Five

"YOU'VE BEEN QUIET this week."

I look up at Alison. She's just dismounted and is holding out the reins to Wesley, but it's me she's talking to.

"Just trying to keep everything on track with this event coming," I say, trying not to sound evasive.

"Hmm, well." Alison shrugs. It's an unusual movement for her. Alison *never* shrugs things off. "I'm sure things will go just fine. You have your list, and you're ready to get everything down to the horse park, right?"

"Yes." I hold up my phone for confirmation. "List is ready, tack room is almost packed."

"Perfect. Why not go ahead and start loading the trailer? Get started a little early. Wesley can get on the last horse on your list."

I hear a squeak from the grooming stall. Wesley is only allowed to hack horses when we're desperate for help getting through the schedule. But I'm sure she's capable of putting a horse in a frame for an easy flatwork school. If she can ride that demon horse of hers, she can get on one of our quietest horses and ride him around the covered arena under supervision.

One of *Malcolm's* quietest horses, I mean. I correct myself mentally, hoping I don't slip up and say "our" out loud. Alison would probably take it as a show of barn loyalty, but...

That's not what it would be.

I'm feeling possessive. That's the hard truth. Ever since I found out about Malcolm's supposed engagement, I've been desperate to lay my claim to him. Because if I can't, then that makes it possible that everything else—everything Sallyann said—is *true*. And if it's true, and if he's been lying to me this entire time, well...

Then I just don't know what I'll do.

It's not that I'm in love with Malcolm Horsham, because I'm not. That would be absurd. I've only known the man a little more than two months; I've only been kissing his face off for one of them. But I think we have something special. We have a connection. It can't be made-up. This can't be fake. If it were, the air wouldn't snap and crackle between us every time we get too close.

"Are you going?" Alison is giving me an odd look and I realize I've been standing around after a direct order—that's not the Fine Day Farm way.

"Right now," I say, and hustle for the tack room.

"Evie!" Kayla squeals, running across the grassy lawn between the two stables. "You're *here!*"

I drop the buckets I was carrying to the barn and hold out my arms, catching her in a giant bear hug. "I have missed you so, so, so much," I mutter against her shoulder. Suddenly I'm wondering how many mistakes I wouldn't have made if Kayla had been around to stop me, instead of living in a barn in Alachua with her boyfriend.

"I missed *you*," Kayla growls. "Look at you, though!" She steps back and regards me. "You look fantastic!"

"Do I?" I glance down at myself. I'm wearing the eventing uniform of sun-shirt and breeches and beat-up sneakers. "I think I look the same."

"You look different," Kayla assures me. "Happier. Skinnier."

"I definitely wasn't going for skinnier." Happier is nice, though. Am I happier?

I think I am, despite all my nerves.

"Well, you won the skinny lottery." Kayla puts a hand behind her head and bumps out one hip in a modeling pose. "Whereas couple's life agrees with me a little too well. I've put on ten pounds since I moved in with Basil."

"That's the lack of galloping, not the cohabitation," I tell her. "How many horses are you getting on every day?"

She snorts. "Three or four."

"Pathetic."

"Are you doing so much better?"

I have to laugh. "No, we're even. But they're really hard rides, every day. Malcolm's a taskmaster, let me tell you."

Kayla squeals with laughter, drawing attention from the other eventers setting up their stabling. "Did I ask about your love life?"

I feel my extremities go hot, then cold. My fear must show on my face, because Kayla stops laughing immediately. "I won't tell anyone," she says loyally.

"How do you know? Did Posey tell you?"

"I know because I know you," Kayla says. She squeezes my hand. "For me, it's all over your face. I'm not saying anyone else can tell, although..."

"What?"

"You probably shouldn't look at him too much when there are other people around. Something tells me that your expression will give you away every time."

"That's great, Kayla. I just won't make eye contact with my boss the entire weekend."

"Hey," Kayla shrugs. "I didn't tell you to jump into the sack with your boss. That's all you, Evie."

I'm too annoyed to even bother reminding her that she did, in fact, tell me to do it.

Kayla is grooming for Briar Hill Farm this weekend, which means she's helping out Pete Morrison and his wife, Jules Thornton-Morrison, with their string of horses. Jules spends half her time at the neighboring set-up—her lesson barn, Alachua Eventing Co-op, where about a dozen kids are running around like tiny Alisons, getting their barn into ship-shape before the horses come down in the morning.

The whole scene is full of life and laughter, with Jules's sweet old beagle, Marcus, weaving in and out of legs and begging for food every time he comes upon a kid with a bag of chips or an orange. He's the only dog I've ever seen who eats Mandarin orange slices. Jules says Marcus never met a snack he didn't like.

My own stabling area, which faces the Briar Hill-Alachua joint venture across the mown lawn between barns, feels much quieter by comparison. I mean, it's just me, so there's that. But once I've finished setting up the stabling, even the tack room with its saddles carefully tucked into their lined bags and the stalls with their fluffy white shavings in the center are just lacking the enthusiastic brightness which all that life is bringing to the stable across the way. It just feels a little sterile.

Like the Morrisons have set up an eventing candy store, and I've set up an eventing laboratory.

Oh, now I'm just *looking* for things to complain about!

"I have to cancel dinner with you."

I look up at Malcolm in surprise, then at the tack room door. "Alison's in there," I mouth.

"She has in earbuds," he says. "She's going over her dressage test one more time."

Still, there is Wesley, there are students, there are the stall-cleaners...I consider listing all the threats in this barn, but choose not to. He's already explaining himself, the reason why he's canceling on me when I was looking forward to dinner with him after a long day of pretending we aren't dating.

"Her name's Vedda Jones, she's from Idaho or Utah or something."

"And you're meeting her because...?"

"I just said, because she wants to buy into Mastermind's syndicate. A huge chunk, actually. We'd be fully covered and I can keep him in our barn if she buys into it. She's got all kinds of cash."

"Well, then, by all means wine and dine her," I sigh. "I could use a quiet night in, anyway."

"Worn out?" Malcolm grins familiarly.

"Yes," I say shortly. "I just set up the show-grounds for the next four days, remember?"

His smile fades. "You're mad at me."

"Of course not. You're free to go off and convince the nice hick lady to give you money. And I'm free to take a bath, eat a cup of noodles, and fall asleep before nine o'clock for once. We all win."

"If you're sure you're not mad..."

I put on my most convincing smile. "There's no reason for me to be mad, Malcolm. Is there?"

I leave him to puzzle on that while I pretend to hear Wesley calling for my help down in the grooming stalls.

He gets home late.

I lied to him; I didn't go to sleep before nine. I ate my cup of noodles and then I sat on the couch, stroking Romeo's ears to keep him from going to bed without me. I sat and I waited to see when he'd get back to the farm.

When his car drives past the barn, I can see he's not alone.

There's a silver car behind his truck, the body gleaming in the moonlight as it slides up the driveway. I watch the two cars disappear over the hilltop, the trees closing their branches behind them to ensure their privacy, and then look at the time. Nearly eleven o'clock.

What is he doing to get this woman's money?

What did he do to get Lillian Cole's money?

What is this life worth to someone with ambition, drive, and talent—but not the wealth to go it alone?

And where on earth can someone like me fit in to a life like that?

Chapter Thirty-Six

LESS TALKING, MORE work.

I say it to myself periodically, a reminder to keep my gaze down and my smile fixed.

Less talking, more work.

The event is flowing like...like lava down a mountainside. Not a perfect simile, because a good event is a good thing, and lava is, well, generally considered bad for people and other living things. But I can't think of any good comparisons right now. I'm too tired, too distracted, too freaked out by the constant, preening presence of Vedda Jones. In the holy trinity of women I do not know who freak me out, Vedda has suddenly taken the top position, nudging Tara Gilroy and Haley Cole into the runners-up. Still in contention, but not so immediate.

In her fringed jacket and cowboy boots, she isn't the typical eventer. But Malcolm doesn't want to win her over for her style. He wants her for her money. And if the story Sallyann told me is true and Malcolm Horsham isn't necessarily broke, but definitely isn't independently wealthy the way most people (myself included) have always thought, then he *needs* her money.

I am scared of what that might make him do. And worse, I don't know how I could blame him for going beyond the bounds of professionalism to secure Vedda's signature on a check. Hold up a secret relationship of a month against the potential to acquire a big new buy-in for a horse he wants to compete, and how does the relationship stand a chance?

Add in that this weekend, Malcolm and I are staying as far apart as a boss and his employee can, and the separation anxiety is real. I feel like I've lost a limb. The feeling itself frightens me.

My dressage test on Bucky is the bright spot of Friday. We go around the arena like we've known each other all our lives, and when I turn him to leave the arena after our final salute, I see Malcolm smiling near the in-gate, clapping his hands. Our score comes in under thirty percent, a highly respectable twenty-eight point eight, and all day long people I know from the last season I evented are waving and calling, "Nice score, Evie!"

We end up third once all the rides are in, within three-tenths of a point of first place, so all we need is a perfect cross-country round and stadium jumping round...and for one of the top two finishers to make a mistake.

It could happen.

When I get back to the farm after the first day of the event, exhausted through and through, I sink into bed and stare at the ceiling for hours. Romeo purrs beside me until even his powers of insomnia are spent, and then it is just me and the snoring cat, until the wee hours.

On Saturday morning, Alison notices the dark circles under my eyes and prescribes caffeine. In coffee form, in chocolate, in soda: "I don't care how you consume it, just wake yourself up!"

"I'm awake," I protest. "And this is my third cup of coffee. There is a hole in my stomach lining with today's date on it."

"I don't care if it eats through your entire digestive system," Alison hisses, which feels like an exaggeration neither of us needs right now. "Just stay on it today!"

It's cross-country day. There is no room for slip-up. "I'm not going to mess up," I assure Alison. "I don't need sleep to be a good groom."

"Thank god," she snorts, and flounces off to start tacking the first horse.

Oceanus is high as a kite and ready for action this morning. The gap in his mane is almost hidden by my careful trimming and a few weeks of growth, and his neck ripples with muscle as Alison and I get him ready for cross-country. The extra equipment that goes onto an advanced cross-country horse is thick and mighty, with solid brass hardware on doubled leather straps. There is no room for error out there, not when the fences are *this* large, when the speeds are *this* high, when the consequences for a stumble or a hung leg can be *this* dire.

It can be life or death on the cross-country course. Riders don't like to bring it up; fans don't want to talk about it. Every sport has its statistics, for sure, but in eventing the accidents are so *public*.

The course out there today is touted as one of the safest in the country. More frangible pins—those are connectors that allow seemingly solid jumps to collapse if a horse knocks into one hard enough, preventing a fall or a flip—than on any other course yet. Spared no expense, John Hammond style. If I squint, I think, maybe I'll see a herd of dinosaurs.

Or is it a flock?

Oh my god, I need more coffee.

Alison leaves me to boot up Oceanus while she stalks off to make sure Malcolm is fully prepared for his course. I strap on his galloping boots and bell boots. As I'm finishing the last hind boot, a voice startles me.

"Which horse is this?"

Vedda Jones, in her fringed glory, stands above me.

Natalie Keller Reinert

I straighten up and put a protective hand on Oceanus's hip. He's a tall horse, towering above my tiny frame, and it's funny to think I could somehow be his knight in shining armor. But I don't know Vedda and I don't like that she's just shown up in the stabling area, unannounced and unchaperoned. She's not an owner *yet*.

"Oceanus," I reply shortly.

"Not Mastermind? I'm supposed to be looking at Mastermind."

"He goes later today." I flick through my mental schedule. "At two twenty-seven."

Vedda guffaws. The sound is explosive, sending Oceanus sideways. I reach for the reins and steady him before he can back up and feel the tie on his halter. "That's pretty precise," Vedda declares, evidently finding our nice, tidy eventing schedule to be funny.

"Precision *matters*," I say, like it's some kind of mantra, and then I hear Alison calling for me. "Time to go."

Vedda trails after me as I lead Oceanus to Alison and Malcolm, standing at the end of the barn. Malcolm's eyes flicker over me before lingering on the horse. I can understand that; I could never be jealous of his big horse. But when he smiles at Vedda and acts as if she belongs there, I do feel a stirring of ripe, hot jealousy.

She doesn't even go here, I think rebelliously.

Alison gives Malcolm a leg up; he springs into the saddle like a cat and gathers the reins as Oceanus shifts anxiously, ready to go. All this equipment and the constant chatter on the loudspeakers can mean only one thing to this horse.

Cross-country day.

Malcolm starts to ride off, then circles Oceanus back. He looks at me and for a moment, I feel the air flare and heat between us. Then the horse turns again, breaking our eye contact. "You can come see us at the water complex if you're quick," he calls to me. "We should be there about four minutes after we leave the box."

304

I nod, not trust my voice to say thanks. He rides off, Alison half-trotting at the horse's side. She has the grooming bucket in her hand; she'll be the one to wipe off his boots and send them off. As it should be.

Then she stops and turns back. "You go with him," she says hurriedly. "I just remembered something I have to do."

"But—it's *Oceanus.*" We'd already agreed the Advanced horses were her responsibility. I stare at her in dismay, but Alison has already thrust the bucket into my hands.

"Don't screw up!" she calls, running towards the barn. I see her hand creep into her pocket, pulling her phone free.

"Well," Vedda drawls, "looks like you're in charge now."

I look at the bucket in my hand in disbelief. Then I do the only thing I can do: I take off after Malcolm and Oceanus, running as fast as I can across the grass.

I'm in charge now.

Malcolm has a rigid set of rules for the cross-country warm-up; Alison knows them inside and out, but he has to call commands to me. His voice is harsh as he shouts where he wants me, by this jump, no that one, bring the water, take the whip, give it back, check the girth. I can feel the stares of other grooms, and I know they all pity me. The latest working student crazy enough to work for Malcolm Horsham.

Oh, but they have no idea.

Oceanus is sweaty but still breathing evenly by the time we have to head to the start box. Malcolm raps out a command as he halts the horse, and I know to kneel and check the horse's cross-country boots. I put my finger on every strap, every buckle, and tuck in every keeper as firmly as I can. These boots are going nowhere. Next I run my fingers over the breastplate, check the noseband, feel the cheekpieces of the bridle. I am leaving nothing to chance.

"You be safe out there," I let myself say, looking up at him.

His eyes are fierce; I feel like he's going to war, and maybe I'm the squire dressing him for battle, or maybe I'm the maiden draping my favor over his lance.

For just a moment, his gaze softens and I want to clutch his boot, melt against his strength, be the maiden and the squire and the princess in the tower. But I'm none of those things. I'm the groom, the working student, the lowest of the low in the barn, and he's the boss, and everyone here can never know it has gone farther than that.

His lips curve in the smallest of smiles, a private one meant just for me. "This will be you one day," he promises. "We'll get you here, okay? All the way to Advanced."

It's like a declaration of love, a promise of war. I straighten the curve in my spine and put my shoulders back. *Tits out.* "You think so?"

"I know so. You're going places, Evie. Now—" His smile widens ever so briefly. "Get out there and find a spot by the water. I'll see you out there."

"Malcolm, you're on deck!" a volunteer calls, checklist in hand.

"On my way," he calls back. He nods at me, and then gathers the reins, all business again. I stand back, and let my soldier ride off to war.

The water complex isn't overly close to the starting box, and I have a gallop of my own to get there in time to watch Malcolm ride Oceanus through its obstacles. I'm panting by the time I reach the hazard, and a few other observers smile and nod at me as I find a spot on the hill above it, one hand on my side to ease the stitch there.

The water hazard is a pool of knee-deep water in a grassy hollow; oak trees hang back on all four sides as if to give plenty of room to this artificial pond. The Advanced level course means a jump up and over a log, a few strides of canter down the slope, a jump into the water, a canter through the water to a small boat-shaped jump, and then a canter to the other bank to jump out and gallop away from the hollow.

It's a clean, uncomplicated obstacle as far as Advanced complexes go, designed to give a comfortable ride to knowledgeable riders with rate-able horses, but it could get a little bumpy for riders who come in too hot and miss their distances, or who don't have enough impulsion to get their horse cleanly over the boat.

I can't imagine Malcolm having any trouble. Not with Oceanus, who is so closely aligned with him, they might as well share one brain while on course.

The rider before Malcolm comes cantering down the slope and there's a little flutter of anticipation amongst the audience. His canter is sticky, hanging back a little with each stride, as if he doesn't trust the sloping ground. She'll have to pick him up and get him ahead of her leg, or there will be hell to pay getting over that canoe.

"Hah!" she urges her horse as his ears focus on the first jump, then flick back as he realizes there's water ahead.

"Hah!" she says again, as he jumps the log but sucks back on the downward slope.

"Hah!" she announces as he splashes into the water and hangs for a moment, undecided.

She gives him a little pop with her crop, just enough to let the horse know she's deadly serious about jumping the boat, and he accepts her decision, plunging through the water and taking the boat with a herculean effort. Luckily, he's strong enough to push through the water resistance. A few seconds later, they've splashed out of the water and are galloping up the slope, the rider patting the horse on the neck.

"His first time at this level," someone says, and there's a murmur of approval. She did all the right things to help her horse understand his job and do it safely.

We can hear a distant loudspeaker if everyone is quiet, and there's a mutual agreement to be silent as it crackles to life: "That's Alicia Bett through the water clean on Marablue, and now we have Malcolm Horsham on Oceanus coming through the forest walk, and he'll be at the water next."

"Malcolm's a genius on this horse," someone murmurs, and another voice says, "I think it's the best horse he's ever had."

"Better than Artsy Ballad?"

"At least that good."

"He deserves some good luck," the first person says. "After that mess with the Coles almost running him out of business."

I feel faint.

"Whatever happened with that?"

"Oh, my god. The daughter, Haley Cole, she was all in on Malcolm. Then he got caught with his barn manager, is what I heard."

I slide down to the ground and wrap my arms around my knees. *Got caught with his barn manager.* That can't be right.

"So Haley freaks out and runs to Mommy. Lillian Cole tries to take the horses back, but Malcolm's got a contract. He's not an idiot."

"Wow," someone murmurs, loving the gossip.

That used to be me.

"He fights back and says they'll take Fine Day Farm when he's ready to give it back to them, not a moment before, and then Lillian backs off because the daughter runs off with that jumper guy, Jan

Something or Other. And she's in Belgium now, at that guy's farm. She's not coming back."

"Holy cow."

"I know."

"And he's still got the farm?"

"Oh, the Coles are totally embarrassed. And it's an investment for them, anyway. Ocala real estate is crazy. So, Lillian Cole still owns this horse and Artsy, but the daughter's out of the picture."

"They're probably waiting for him to find a good offer somewhere else and then they'll sell it...hey, is that him now?"

"Here we go!"

I don't know how I see any of it. Malcolm and Oceanus flash through the trees and take the first log in stride, but my head is swimming, my ears roaring, and I see it all as if we're at the bottom of the sea. There's a little gasp as he jumps into the water, but I don't know why. And then as Oceanus rises to jump the boat, I see it.

A loose galloping boot.

The right front boot is hanging from his cannon bone; they're moving fast as they leave the water, but despite the speed, I think I see the top strap is flapping. The boot is sliding down.

They are only halfway through the course.

"Oh my god, did you see that?"

"The boot—"

"Could that end up injuring the horse?"

"Hot tendons are soft as butter, I heard."

"The groom is dead meat, I can tell you that much."

I realize that I have five minutes to get to the finish line, and I take off running.

I'll faint *after* I've been executed for ruining Oceanus.

Chapter Thirty-Seven

THE BOOT IS still hanging by one strap as Oceanus thunders past the finish line timers, and Malcolm leaps out of the saddle while the horse is still trotting. He runs alongside him for a minute, then brings the horse down to a walk. I dive down and unbuckle the last strap while he halts Oceanus for a split-second, then he walks him off again, watching his movement carefully.

I stand there with the battered boot, staring at Oceanus.

He's sound.

Of course he's sound; there's no way Malcolm would have kept going if he'd felt a bobble or a bad step. The horse was so intent on doing the job he loved, he never noticed the loose boot sliding down his leg, and luckily for us all, the bell boot's curved top caught the galloping boot and kept it from slipping down to the hoof. It looked so much worse than it actually was.

But it could have been disastrous.

And it was my fault.

I stuff the boot into my grooming bucket, conscious of the stares and whispers, and run after Malcolm. He ignores me.

"Malcolm, I'll take the horse," I say.

He ignores me.

"Malcolm, you both need a drink of water."

He ignores me.

"Malcolm, everyone is staring at us."

He turns his head and gives me his fiercest glare. "Isn't that what you want?"

"What?" Now I'm baffled. Be mad at me, by all means, Malcolm, but make sense while you're doing it! "I don't understand."

"You've been upset with me for weeks, ever since I told you to keep things quiet. Oh, don't deny it!" He's spitting out the words, but somehow he keeps his diatribe to a low hiss, preventing the fascinated onlookers from hearing him. And it's not for lack of trying. Everyone wants to know what the monstrous Malcolm Horsham is going to say to his working student after a fuck-up *this* phenomenal. "Don't act like you don't want the world to know. To be seen with me. You think that will guarantee a spot with me after your contract ends, don't you? Move into the big house? That's what all this has been, right?"

"Malcolm, what the *fuck* are you talking about?" I'm so bewildered I can barely manage my footing; I trip over a clump of grass as I stumble after him. We're already halfway back to the barn, moving fast as Oceanus rolls onward, fueled by adrenaline.

"But I didn't give you what you wanted, so you sabotaged my ride —well, that's really special, Evie, *really* quite a move. How does this help your case, huh? Why would I want to be with you now?"

"*Idiot,*" I snap, anger taking over my confusion. "Ask yourself that same question and then consider why you would come after me with such a *stupid* accusation."

And I don't say it quietly. Heads turn.

"Don't talk back to me in that tone," Malcolm warns, still barely above a murmur.

"I'll talk to you however I want," I inform him. My own adrenaline is pumping now; I have no trouble matching his long strides, although with my short stature, that means taking two for every one of his. "I'm a free woman in the United States of America and you just decided you can make gross accusations against me, so I'm going to bitch you out right now, loudly, in public!"

"No, you're not," he says.

"Yes, I am!"

"No," Malcolm insists. "You're not. Because if you do, I'll fire you and I'll keep Bucky for myself, too. The contract allows for me to show him for a year, and we both know it. So ask yourself what you want more—Bucky, and this job, or the chance to bitch me out."

He has me.

"I do want Bucky," I allow, lowering my voice. "But I don't know about this job. Not now."

"Well, tough luck," Malcolm growls. "Because you're not going anywhere."

I stop short, staring at him—why wouldn't he fire me, when he clearly thinks I'm out to get him? But Malcolm doesn't stop or explain himself. He just walks Oceanus straight back to the barn, where Alison has reappeared and is waiting with buckets of water for drinking and bathing.

"He's tough to work for, right?" Suddenly there's a comforting voice in my ear; I turn and see a vaguely familiar girl wearing the eventing uniform of sun-shirt and breeches. "My trainer is looking for someone, if you're quitting. Barn three, Rainbow Eventing."

"Thanks," I croak, shaking my head. "But I think I'm set for work."

"Well, if you change your mind. I know she'd never treat you the way Malcolm treats his staff."

"Hey," I say, intrigued. "Have you ever heard of a Haley Cole?"

The girl thinks for a moment. "Um, I think she's the one who's engaged to Jan Peeters, the Belgian show jumper."

"Engaged?"

"Yeah, I follow a bunch of jumpers on Insta. Pretty sure that's where I saw it..." The girl looks around. "Sorry, I gotta run. Good luck, okay? Rainbow Eventing, don't forget."

"Thanks," I say, waving. Then I trudge back to my own barn. Rainbow Eventing, that's cute. But if there's a pot of gold over there, it's not for me.

My life is too tangled up with Malcolm to just walk away now.

Alison watches me carefully as I tack the next horse, and she runs her fingers over the galloping boots after I finish. "I still can't believe that happened," she mutters, glancing beneath the horse at Malcolm, who is deep in conversation with Vedda while he drinks bottle after bottle of water. He's still wearing his cross-country vest, but he's already changed into his new number.

"It was a freak thing," I repeat, as I have been ever since she started hovering over me. "I checked those boots. I triple-checked them."

"Tape them, then," she orders. "There's tape in the tack trunk, right?"

"Yes." I put it there myself.

"Go and get it. Hurry."

I want to ask her why the women at the water complex said she was caught with Malcolm, why they think she threw off the Cole engagement and nearly lost Malcolm his biggest investors. But that can't be true; Malcolm never would have forgiven her unless he loved her...and if he loved her, none of this would have happened with me.

And Tara Gilroy...did she tell me about Tara as a red herring? To throw me off her trail?

Or because Tara was really angry that she'd been fired for no reason, just the suspicion of flirtation, and Alison was genuinely warning me to steer clear of her in case there was a grudge against Fine Day Farm?

So many questions, buzzing in my head, I feel half-crazy. No, all-crazy.

Alison gives me a little shove. "Go on, Evie! We don't have time for you to zone out, okay? You messed up, it's over. Let's get the next horse out."

I didn't mess up, I want to say, but it's pointless.

I walk past Vedda and Malcolm to the tack stall, noticing the way he draws back slightly as I pass him. As if he doesn't want to brush against me, and I know why.

If he does, he'll have to admit to himself that he's not as angry with me as he thinks.

His voice falters slightly, then continues in its usual strong tone as I rummage through the tack trunk for the black plastic tape. "The thing about eventing," he says, "is that anyone can play at the very top. There isn't any high society blue-blood nonsense standing in your way. My family's from Jamaica, which isn't one of your traditional horsey places, but it hasn't stopped me from making it to Advanced or getting great sponsors."

Amazing sponsors, I think. *Ones that want to sell you their daughters.*

What is it about Malcolm that attracts parents like moths to a flame? The way my aunt wanted to push my cousin at him, the way the Coles bought a whole farm for him.

Are they really waiting for him to decide to move on from Ocala?

Well, they're crazy if they think *that* is happening. Who would leave Ocala now? It's become the epicenter of the entire horse world.

"Well, I like that it's something you can do from anywhere," Vedda drawls. "Even in Texas, you know. I was looking at a real big ranch in Texas."

I find the tape, but I stay hunched over the tack trunk, waiting.

"I heard Bluebonnet Equestrian Center was for sale," Malcolm says. There's a careful cadence to his speech. As if he's been building to this minute.

No, I think, clutching the tape in my hands.

"That's the one," Vedda agrees. "I always did like Texas. A lot of space. Not a lot of government poking their nose in my business. In California, now, you need permission to take a shit."

Malcolm laughs. Again, it's careful. Vedda surely can't tell, but that wasn't his real laugh. "I've heard that," he says. "Bluebonnet has a full cross-country course, apparently. Competition-quality, although of course they haven't run an event there in years. It was before I'd have been advanced enough to travel that far. The eventing community's growing there, too..."

His voice trails off suggestively.

"It's expensive," Vedda says. "But of course, anything that big is gonna cost a pretty penny."

"You'd never get that much land in Florida or California for less than, oh, five million."

"That's what I've been thinking."

For the second time this morning, my head is swimming. Maybe it's all the coffee, I think.

Or maybe it's that the whole world seems to be conspiring in ways I hadn't realized until this very moment.

Alison starts shouting my name, interrupting the tete-a-tete outside the tack stall. "She's in here," Malcolm says roughly. "Evie? What are you doing in there?"

"Found the tape," I reply, straightening up. "Ignore me. I was never here."

I feel his eyes on me as I walk back to the horse. But what difference does it make, I think, if he's going to seduce Vedda into buying him a massive farm in Texas?

Because that's what is going on, right? She's the replacement for the Cole money. She's his escape from the clutches of Lillian Cole, who must be impossible to work for after the engagement with her daughter fell through. They want him gone. They want him to break his contract. And Vedda will be the key.

Or else I'm going crazy and making it all up.

There's no one I can ask, no one I can trust with these suspicions. Once I would have gone to Sallyann to get her take on the juiciest gossip this side of the state line, but now I'm afraid of what her inquiring mind manages to find out. Once I might have gone to Posey or Kayla and pleaded for their take on the matter, but now I'm embarrassed that I've let things get so deep with Malcolm.

This problem is just mine.

Lucky me.

Chapter Thirty-Eight

THE CLOCKS CHANGE on Saturday night, making Sunday morning that much more brutal. Usually I'm a huge fan of spring forward, because it means that sunset is later—a godsend for horsey folks who don't want to finish with riding and chores by six o'clock just because that's when dusk turns to darkness. But when I've barely slept in a week and it's stadium jumping day, with horses in the top of each division and a boss who seems determined to live up to every awful behavior he's ever been accused of, the lost hour just seems like a cruel joke.

To make matters worse, Wesley's mom calls and says her daughter is sick. I suspect her illness is more about the abysmal dressage score and appalling cross-country ride she put in the day before, guaranteeing her that no amount of bad luck for everyone else in the stadium jumping ring can get her in the top ten. She probably woke up, thought, 'Why bother?' and told her mom she had the stomach bug.

I kind of wish I could do the same thing.

Still, I'm at the horse park by seven a.m., feeding our hungry horses and refilling water buckets before Malcolm or Alison shows up.

Alison comes in at seven thirty, texting rapidly on her phone. She has to be talking to another horse-person, or someone in Europe—

it's way too early on a Sunday to be texting this much with a normal person on the Eastern Time Zone. She barely looks up from her phone, just asks if the horses are fed and disappears into the tack stall. I can hear the little whistle of a new text coming through. She's been so weird lately, but so has everyone. So have I.

Malcolm is the next to arrive. He looks tired, his expression grim as he glances over all the horses. I watch him while I fill water buckets, suddenly exhausted with the subterfuge. Can't we just go back to being friends, if nothing else? I turn off the water and duck into Oceanus's stall, the last place I saw him.

He's on his knees next to the big horse, taking off his ice wraps. He glances at me and for a moment, his expression is soft, unguarded. I feel a lurch in my heart—that's the Malcolm I knew before this week, before things got weird. "Hey," he says, and for once there's no harsh growl in his tone. "Oceanus is looking good."

"He came out of the cross-country great," I remind him. "You've got this horse in peak condition." I drop to my knees on the other side and start pulling back the heavy Velcro fasteners on the other ice boot. "Malcolm—"

"Yeah?"

We look at each other, the horse standing between us, shifting his weight subtly as he pulls at his hay-net. I feel shy, tongue-tied. Then I remember the way he looked at me yesterday, before he took this horse out for his cross-country round. Like he cared about me. Like we were more than this. And I know exactly how I feel, and it sucks.

"I don't want to work for you if we can't be ourselves," I say at last. "And we can't be ourselves, because...of Ocala. And things."

The things being his past, like that old fiancé he hasn't told me about, the one I have yet to investigate on Instagram, because I am afraid she is tall and willowy and everything I am not, and that he wishes she would come home from Belgium and marry him and let him stay in Ocala forever.

Like Alison, the only person on earth until very recently who isn't afraid to shout back at him.

Like all of Ocala, the equestrian community that feasts on its heroes and thrives on gossip, true or false, believing that he's had an affair with his barn manager.

Like his five-star lifestyle and his Novice-level bank account, making him catnip to people like my aunt, and the Coles, and to Vedda, who are happy to pay for talented and handsome arm-candy for their daughters...or themselves.

"So you're saying it's over, Evie?"

His voice is too low to read.

"I'm sure." *I'm not sure.* "I don't want to pretend, Malcolm. It's exhausting. And it's just going to make us hate each other."

He nods slowly. "But you're not leaving the farm, are you? What about Bucky?"

"You shouldn't have used Bucky against me."

"I know. I'm sorry. I was—I was angry."

"You were an asshole."

"That too," Malcolm agrees. "Really awful. I'm so sorry."

"You were the person they all say you are."

"I'm starting to see it," he says, rubbing at his face. He leaves a streak of dirt on his sweaty cheek. "But, Evie—"

"Self-awareness is a beautiful thing." The last fastener pulls free and I slide the ice boot away, running a hand down Oceanus's cool, tight leg. No bumps, no swelling, no heat. "I'm going to take him out for grass and a walk," I decide, even though it's not my call. "I'll be back in half an hour."

"Evie," Malcolm says, "I don't want you to quit."

"I know."

"But you and me—it's just—"

"I know," I say, and this time I feel a hot burning behind my eyelids and in my throat, because we have to move on from this moment as employee and employer, nothing more.

And it *hurts.*

"I can't stay," I tell him, and he stays in the stall as I halter Oceanus and lead him out into the hot Florida morning.

I pack up my things slowly, so slowly that Romeo settles into my suitcase while I'm dithering about what clothes to take out of the dresser, and I have to be the bad guy and move him. He blinks at me reproachfully from a cozy spot on my pillows, as if I'm to blame for everything.

"It's not me, it's him," I tell my cat, but wouldn't you know, I think the little feline jerk doesn't believe me.

I didn't know I was quitting until I did it, and now I'm stuck with the decision. I know I'm losing everything, starting at square one. But it's the way things have to be. I shouldn't have fallen for Malcolm. I shouldn't have acted on it. I picked a boy over a horse, and now I don't get to have either.

Breezy, at least, will be okay about going home early. He will go back to twenty-four-seven turnout. No more stalls during the day for him. But he'll miss his friends; I'll talk to Posey about getting one of her off-track Thoroughbreds, starting over again with a project horse. That way Breezy will have a pasture buddy, and I'll have something that might be ready to compete at Novice level in the fall.

It's not what I wanted, it's not what I thought I'd gotten, but it's what I can have.

Be content with that, I tell myself, over and over again.

Malcolm is off the farm when I leave. It's better that way. Monday is the perfect day to quit a horse job; there is no one in the barn to watch you go.

I tell myself that, over and over again.

On Monday night I sit on my own porch, trying to get used to the late sunset, to the sounds and smells of my own farm. The pine smell that hangs around a stable doesn't exist here, because Breezy doesn't come inside often enough to warrant buying shavings. I smell wood smoke from the neighbors, who are burning branches; I smell the mustiness of my trailer, windows and doors flung open to let in a nonexistent breeze. I hear traffic on the county highway a short distance away, and the distant moan of a train whistle. Barking dogs carry on from a neighbor's yard. Breezy grazes on the new grass popping up in his paddock, occasionally looking around wistfully, wondering where his herd has gone.

My heart aches for him and for me.

A strange car pulls into the driveway and Romeo sits up straight next to me, his whiskers trembling at attention. Posey climbs out.

"Where did you get that car?" I call.

"My mom's," Posey says. "I took it to get an oil change."

She sits next to me on the porch. "I can't believe you really left."

"I had to."

"You guys couldn't fake it?"

"Honestly, Posey, I didn't know *what* he was faking."

She looks at me, and says nothing. Waiting.

"I heard some things about him. Other girls. Investors. It was weird. There was a lot."

Posey winces. "You and your gossip."

"That's over now."

"Too late."

"Yeah, maybe."

She gives my thigh a little squeeze—solidarity. "What did you hear?"

"That the farm belongs to the parents of his ex-fiancé."

"His *what?*"

"Who is apparently now the fiancé of Jan Peeters." Posey shakes her head. "A show jumper. I looked them up. They seem pretty happy together in Belgium."

"Wait, Belgium? Slow down."

"The parents want to sell the farm, and he knows it, so he's sniffing around a new woman with money. She's thinking of buying him a farm in Texas."

Posey is shaking her head. "I can't keep up with this," she complains. "Who is the new woman?"

"Vedda Jones. Wait, you know her?" I add, surprised when Posey's eyebrows go up.

"Yeah, I know her. She owns three broodmares at the farm. And she can't afford a farm in Texas."

"How do you know?"

Posey laughs. "Because she's in collections with us for non-payment of board. Sweetie, Vedda's absolutely just leading him on."

"Oh, god." That doesn't help me at all. But it's none of my business now. "Well, good luck to him."

"You're not going to tell him? I can show you the paperwork, if you want proof."

"No. He lied to me." By omission, but still. "He should have told me."

"About what? About the ex-fiancé in Belgium? Guys get sensitive about that kind of thing. I'm not surprised he kept it on the down-low. And this Vedda person...did he straight up *say* he's making a play for her, or is it more like, he's letting her dangle money without saying no? I know that's still gross, but this is an expensive game. I can see why he'd let her grab his knee or whatever she's doing. As long as it didn't go any farther than that, I think I'd let it fly. If he's facing getting kicked out of that nice farm, he has to think on his feet."

Posey rattles on about all the ways in which Malcolm could still be an actual nice guy until I'm seriously wondering whose side she is on in all this. When she runs out of breath—or excuses—I list my last reason for leaving.

"He shouted at me in front of everyone at the event."

Posey purses her lips and nods. After a moment, she says, "Okay."

"Okay?"

"Okay, yeah, if the temper thing is real, then I can see that being a deal-breaker. You can't live with some kind of maniac who shouts at you all the time."

"He doesn't shout all the time," I admit. "At least, not at me."

She glances sidelong at me, an eyebrow lifted.

"And," I continue, with an air of confession, "he was really upset about the galloping boot slipping."

"Uh-huh."

"I think he would have shouted at anyone; I was just *there*."

"Mm-hmm. Evie?"

"Yeah?"

"Are you having second thoughts about all this?"

"No," I say, stroking Romeo's coat. "Absolutely not."

"Because it sounds like you are."

"No. I decided to quit, and I'm sticking to that. It wasn't going to work out."

"Okay," Posey says. "But just in case you're feeling sad about it, I brought ice cream. It's in a cooler in the back seat."

"Good grief, why didn't you say that *first*?"

Chapter Thirty-Nine

THE ICE CREAM helps, and so does a promise of some serious horse-shopping over the next few days. Posey has a few horses back the farm she thinks I might like as eventing prospects, and she says if none of them work, we can go over to our friend Amanda's place and see what she's got on the back burner. One thing Ocala is never lacking in: Thoroughbreds looking for a new job.

"It won't be an upper-level contender *yet*, but you never know what you might have in five years," she reminds me as she leaves.

I know it takes time, but I also spent years with Breezy, hoping he'd take me up the levels, only to lose his health in the end—right when we were stepping up. I know as well as anyone else that horses are a gamble, and Bucky was a better bet than most.

Bucky was a better bet than I'll ever have again.

I send my aunt an email telling her that I resigned from the working student position, but Bucky is still at Malcolm's farm in training as per their contract. And although it's painful, I admit to her that competing Bucky is now beyond my means.

I can't keep him in that kind of training with my income, I type, biting down on my lower lip as I write it. *And I can't afford the level of upkeep a horse of his caliber is used to or requires.*

Maybe if I hadn't spent the past three months making almost no money and using my savings to pay my mortgage, I could have managed to keep Bucky. But that was the decision I made, with the information I had at the time. No going back now.

If you want to leave him in training and competition with Malcolm for the extended contract, I think it will be a successful partnership. I hit send before I can change my mind. She writes back the next day, thanking me for my honesty. *Not what I envisioned for the horse,* she writes, *but everything happens for a reason.*

I scoff at the platitude, feeling more embittered by fate than I ever thought possible. *Sure,* I think, *but for what reason?*

The last person I expect to call me is Alison. She's furious at me for quitting on them, even more so than I expected. So the first two times my phone lights up with her number, I ignore the calls. I don't need to be yelled at more, thanks. I'm doing just fine beating *myself* up.

But the third time in five minutes makes me nervous. I hit the mute button on the TV and the green button on my phone. Alison's already raging at me before I can lift the phone to my ear. *"...took you so long, there's no time for this!"*

"Uh, Alison? Did you interrupt an argument to call me?"

A huff comes down the line that could blow me over. "Idiot. Do you have any idea what's going on here? Malcolm is going out of his mind. Whatever you said to your aunt—"

"I didn't say anything to my aunt. What's going on with Malcolm?"

"You said *something,* because she's selling the horse."

I shake my head quickly. "No, I didn't tell her to sell him. I said I couldn't keep him and told her to leave the horse in training with Malcolm. Like he wanted all along."

"Owners don't do what their ungrateful nieces say," Alison says nastily. "Imagine that!"

"Can you just please tell me what's going on?"

"I've been *trying* to. Vedda is going to buy Bucky. Not a piece of him. *All* of him. And the Texas deal is off. I don't think it was ever on. She's a liar. I knew it the minute I saw that fringe coat and all that turquoise. Who did she think she was fooling? She's from Los Angeles, not the Mojave Desert."

"But won't Vedda leave Bucky in training with Malcolm?" The idea is sickening: Vedda Jones buying *my* horse. The one I'd just begun to connect with!

But even worse: the idea that Vedda will be hanging all over Malcolm at every event, while he competes Bucky in her name. Assuming that she actually has the money; Posey said doesn't pay her bills. What if she leaves Malcolm hanging, thousands of dollars in the hole for boarding and training and competition fees that will never be paid?

I close my eyes. This is not my problem. This can't be my problem. Malcolm and I are not a thing anymore. I have to let it go for my own sanity.

Alison is still lambasting me with her sharp tone. "She *says* she'll leave him in training, but Wesley has already seen her around the horse parks with at least three other trainers. Every one of them is single and available, so draw your own conclusions."

"At least she's not a home-wrecker," I say feebly, a pathetic attempt at a joke.

Alison snorts. I guess that's almost a laugh. "You need to get your ass back here, tell Malcolm you want your job back, and tell your aunt that it was all a silly lover's spat."

"Hey, hey!" I exclaim, alarmed. "Who said anything about lovers?"

"Please, you think I don't know what's going on between the two of you? And he's twice as horrible without you here. Even before this

Bucky drama started up. Listen—" Alison pauses, then begins again in a softer tone. "I know I warned you about flirting with him. I told you about Tara to keep you on the straight and narrow. But the truth is—"

She stops short.

"What's the truth, Alison?" I feel like I'm dying inside.

"The truth is, I fired Tara because I knew she'd make a big scene and take the heat off me."

That's it. I'm dead. Alison had an affair with Malcolm. Forget it. Forget everything. "I have to go," I mutter.

"No, no, no! It wasn't true, that was the thing. Malcolm and I have never, ever been involved. I swear it. But Haley Cole was pressuring him to get married, and he had this idiotic idea that if she thought we were sleeping together, Haley would just disappear. He told her we couldn't keep our hands off each other and she flipped out, threatened to tell a bunch of people. She never did, it turned out, because she was embarrassed. But by the time we realized she'd gone off with Jan, we'd already sent Tara packing to make it look like she was the problem."

"And that's why she would be mad if I ran into her with a Fine Day Farm shirt on."

"Exactly," Alison says. "Look, none of it was the right thing to do. We all made some mistakes. And people got hurt. But you don't need to be one of them, okay?"

I take a deep, cleansing breath. It feels good to know that Alison wasn't with Malcolm last year. That there's no way he's longing for his lost fiancé, Haley. That his last working student wasn't involved with him, and the idea Posey inadvertently planted in my head that night, that Malcolm was playing an elaborately sexy game with me, isn't true.

But that doesn't change a few key facts.

Mainly, that we have to keep a relationship a secret, and that led to scenes I simply can't live with. If no one knows we're together, they'll continue to feel free to whisper and gossip and openly flirt with him right in front of me, and there's nothing I can do about it.

I can't live that way.

"Come back. The farm needs you." Alison pauses. "Malcolm definitely needs you."

I shake my head, even though Alison can't see me. "He doesn't need me, Alison. I'm really sorry about everything else. But I'd just get in the way of his career. He can't get caught with a working student—"

"Half the trainers in this town are either sleeping with or married to a former working student," Alison shouts, reaching the end of her rope. It occurs to me that she's the one with the most fierce temper in town, not Malcolm. Something the rest of the world would know if she wasn't so busy firing his staff. "Are you *insane?* Are you really more worried about *gossip* than you are about his *feelings?* And what about your feelings? I know you're in love with him."

"No," I say quickly. "I'm not in love with him."

"Fine," Alison snorts. "Have it your way. But the horse is going to be out of here the minute Vedda has the papers signed, I'm sure of it. She's looking for someone she can manipulate. Someone who isn't already in love with someone else."

There's dead air after that. Alison has ended the call.

With *that?* She says Malcolm's in love with me and *hangs up?*

The girl is a sadist.

An effective sadist, because now my heart and mind are all riled up. I tip backwards on the sofa and promptly hit my head on the hard back of it. "Ow," I mutter. "I forgot how old and hard this sofa is."

My whole house, actually, is a lot older and harder than I remembered it.

Romeo looks up at me from his bed and mews gently. "Let me guess, you miss the barn apartment, too," I retort. "Breezy misses his herd, Romeo misses his soft sofa, and I miss..."

I stop myself before I can say it. But the word is there, floating in front of me, mocking.

Malcolm.

I go outside and pick up the manure fork, desperate for some physical labor. I have to get this shaking feeling out of my skin, the lump out of my throat. Breezy hasn't had time to make much of a mess in his paddock, but I push the wheelbarrow around anyway, scooping up manure. The job feels good to my bored muscles, but it isn't doing anything for my racing thoughts. If anything, it gives my brain *more* free time to consider the situation, and choose to panic.

Malcolm's going to lose Bucky to another trainer; my aunt is going to sell him to Vedda; *she's* going to take him to someone who isn't *in love with someone else.*

He's going to lose a top prospect to another trainer, because of me.

And me, what do I get out of any of this? A broken heart, no horse, and the end of my eventing dreams. Because obviously I won't be doing anything like this again. That was my last apprenticeship. I can't afford to make the same mistake twice. I'll have to go back to work at Posey's farm, and focus on producing a project horse who might have the talent to go all the way...but which I'll probably get through Novice or Training Level before I sell to an amateur rider in need of something safe and honest, then start all over again with another greenie. The endless cycle of the backyard trainer.

I can still stop it, a little voice whispers. Clearly not my Good Sense, voice. Because that's not really an option, is it? Going back?

No. Of course not.

* * *

Posey's horses aren't quite right for what I'm looking for. The first one seems long in the pasterns—"Exactly why he isn't racing material," Posey agrees—and the second one has a wide-eyed, wild look to him that just doesn't feel like *Evie* material. "Not vibing with this guy, sorry," I tell Posey, and she laughs.

"If only I could pick and choose horses based on vibes."

"Hey, I'm the one that has to train and event this horse, hopefully," I remind her. "Not like I'm dropping him off at the track for a jockey to deal with."

"No, I know. Just teasing." Posey walks the three-year-old colt back to his stall; he swishes his tail with every step, looking for trouble. "It was more about attitude with this one, anyway. I thought he'd have that killer instinct to demolish every scary jump on course."

"And poor little me," I suggest. "He reminds me of Wesley's horse. Just a little too aggressive to be fun."

"You need a friend out there," Posey says, closing the stall door. "Right? It isn't just competing for you. It's about partnership."

"Pretty much. That's what made Breezy's condition so tough to deal with."

"I know." Posey sighs and looks up and down the shed-row. It's mid afternoon; the doldrums for a training barn. Nothing going on but snoozing horses. "Horses are tough."

"Brutal," I agree, leaning against the wall. "Hard to imagine anything worse for the human heart, actually."

"Is your heart doing okay?" Posey asks gently.

"Not great," I say. "Not great."

Malcolm is constantly on my mind. And when it's not Malcolm, it's Bucky. It's the vision I had of myself on that horse's back, taking on the competitions that I've dreamed about since I was a little kid.

The whole future I'd thought might be in my grasp at last, trampled and left for dead.

Not great, as I said to Posey. It sums things up nicely.

"Listen, I know it's tough when things go south like that, but you'll get another horse who gives you a shot at the big-time," Posey begins.

I cut her off. "Not like this, Pose. Top barn, top trainer, daily coaching—there are only two ways to get that kind of training. You either pay a fortune for it, or you work your ass off for it. I tried one, and I can't do the other. I'm on my own now. It's going to be all amateur stuff from here on out. And I can't even afford coaching now that I've spent all my savings on my mortgage while I was working for him." I shake my head. "I really screwed up."

"What would you have done differently?"

I sigh. "I wouldn't have gotten involved with Malcolm, obviously."

"But what if that part wasn't a choice?"

"Then I guess I never had a chance in the first place," I say, wiping away a few rogue tears. "I guess it was all just destined to fall apart."

And then, even though we're both hot and sweaty, Posey wraps her arms around me. "Nothing's destined to fall apart," she whispers, while I sniffle and try to hold back more tears. "It wouldn't happen without a reason."

"I don't believe all that."

"Yes you do," Posey says. "I know you, Evie Ballenger. I know you believe in *all* of that. You've just never been in love before."

"Why do people keep saying I'm in love?"

"People?" Posey steps back and looks at me. "What people?"

"You, Alison..."

"Alison the *barn manager*? She knows?"

"Apparently. She said so on the phone yesterday."

"And what else did she say?"

"I told you, about Vedda wanting to buy Bucky, and stalking a bunch of other single trainers—"

"No," Posey says sharply. "What did she say to you about *Malcolm?*"

I bite my lip, remembering. "How do you know she said anything?"

"Did she ask you to come back?"

"Yes."

"Because..."

"Because Malcolm might lose Bucky."

"No," Posey retorts. "Because—"

"He's in love with me, she said." The words cost me. They cost me *everything.*

"Idiot," Posey says, affectionately. "You're in love with him, too. Don't you see it?"

"Oh, god," I realize. "I *am* an idiot."

"That's okay," Posey tells me. "Everything is fixable."

Chapter Forty

THE HIGHWAY SLIPS beneath my Jeep's wheels, taking me out of horse country. I hate to drive the wrong direction, but this is the kind of thing that has to be done in person.

The traffic grinds to a halt well before Tampa, and I have hours ahead of me to deal with stop-and-go driving, as the temperature rises and tourist tempers spill into the asphalt lanes of I-75. It's spring break season, and there's no easy way to get to Sarasota without dealing with the combined mess of commuting sprawl and beach-bound traffic of the west coast. The license plates are from Ontario, Michigan, Ohio—all places where people can drive straight down 75 to Florida. The west coast gets the Midwesterners, while the east coast gets the New Yorkers and New Jersey snowbirds who drive down I-95. It's the reason there are so many half-decent delis on the Atlantic side of the state, and a whole Amish community on the Gulf coast. Simple interstate math.

I don't actually care where any of them are from. I just wish they'd get out of my way. I don't know what kind of timeline I'm on, but if Alison's urgency on the phone yesterday is anything to go by, my aunt is hustling to get Bucky sold and out of her life forever. And since I couldn't see how an email or a phone call was going to fix the mess I'd made for this horse, for Malcolm, for all of us, I decided late last night I'd better get on the road.

She needs the whole story if I am going to change her mind.

I roll into Aunt Rachel's canal-lined neighborhood around seven o'clock in the evening. Leisure hour for the leisure class. Purebred dogs are being walked along the winding avenues; a family of sandhill cranes flies over, their rattling cries echoing across the pool decks and palm trees, as they leave their feeding grounds on the nearby golf course. The sun is slowly sinking beneath the Spanish tiles of the rooftops, a welter of yellow like a burst egg yolk spilling over the western sky.

Madison opens the front door, a smile on her face. "You made it! We're just sitting down to dinner on the patio."

"Oh, perfect." I can't wait to say my piece over a plate of pork chops and mashed potatoes. It would be a lot easier if this was just a quick in-and-out. *Hi Aunt Rachel, I screwed up and now everyone's lives are kind of wrecked. Can we go back to the way things were? Great! Thanks! Bye!*

That was my dream, anyway.

But so far, my dreams haven't exactly played out in real life.

The patio is really the screened pool deck, with the canal deep and dark just past the short expanse of lawn. Aunt Rachel is sitting at a round table; there's a big dish of something bright in the middle, and three places. One for me, how nice.

"I hope you like paella," Aunt Rachel says.

"I'm not sure I've ever had it," I admit, taking a seat. "Smells delicious, though. Did you make it?"

"Oh, lord no. It's from Sofrito." She says the restaurant name as if I'll immediately recognize it.

"How nice," I say.

"Mm-hmm. So, young lady, I was disappointed by that email. I hope you've come ready to explain yourself."

Madison is spooning paella onto our plates. She gives me a grin: *solidarity.* I think. I hope. "I did, actually," I say. "I've made a real mess of things across the board. I came to ask you for a second chance."

There, that wasn't so bad.

Rachel's eyes narrow at me. "A *second chance?* After I've already told Malcolm to sell the horse? Madison doesn't want him, you don't want him; I assumed he was a hot mess and that was the issue. Now I've got a buyer ready to take him off my hands, so why should we keep him?"

"Because none of this was the horse's fault," I say. I can't hold her gaze; I flick my eyes down to the rice and seafood on my plate. It really does smell good, but I know I can't stomach a bite of it. Not until the words are out. "It's my fault. I—I got involved with Malcolm."

Madison's fork clatters onto the floor. "Oops," she says sweetly. "I'll just go get another one."

Rachel ignores her daughter. "You got *involved* with him?"

I nod miserably. "I didn't mean to. I know that's not what this was about."

"I spent a fortune on that horse, hoping Madison would waltz back to Ocala and put in a bid for the wealthy young trainer and find some purpose in her life, and what does my niece do? She snags the fella and then *leaves.*"

Rachel's talking to the sky now. I assume she's having a conversation with her god about what a ridiculously fickle set of genes she's been cursed with.

Madison has disappeared into the house. "Does Madison know you bought the horse hoping she'd fall in love with Malcolm?"

"Oh, of course not," Rachel chides me. "Don't be silly. I know my daughter isn't really interested in men. But it would have been a good partnership. He needs investors; she needs a hobby. I just wanted to see her happy. Horses used to make her happy. Now they don't. I can't understand it. But now, you're no better."

"I'm asking you to let me start over," I say desperately. "Let me try again."

"With Malcolm? Or with the horse?"

"Both," I admit.

"So you want him back."

I nod.

"He'll take you back?" Rachel asks. "You've made things very messy with him. If I choose not to sell the horse, I mean. He loses this client, I assume."

"He's going to lose her, anyway." I swallow any explanation, everything I know about Vedda's finances and Alison's suspicions that she's looking for men she can toy with. After all, the last part might not be true. Alison might see things that aren't there. Maybe Malcolm and Vedda are destined for each other, and this gambit isn't worth the gas it took to drive here.

I won't know until I try to talk to him again.

Madison reappears with a fork. "Got one!" she announces cheerfully. She's trying to break the tension, and I love her for it—even if she's unsuccessful. "So, um, Mom," she continues, sitting down again, "I was thinking about how cool you were about the whole horse thing. You know, with me not really wanting to get back into it. And I'm just really glad you gave Evie the chance, because I know it's her whole life. I hope it's working out for you, Evie." She gives me an innocent smile.

"Thanks," I say weakly. "That's so nice of you, Mads."

"Well, you know, family has to stick together. And we don't have much of it, right?"

"No, just you guys, and Mom...up in Maryland."

"Exactly." Madison spears a shrimp with her fresh fork, looking satisfied. As if her work here is done, she takes a big bite and begins digging around in her paella for another mouthful. *Dinner is served,* her expression says.

Aunt Rachel looks at me and sighs. "I'll put things back the way they were," she says. "But just this once. Fall in love with the barn manager instead, and I'm selling him."

I slump, as if all my bones turn to jelly.

"Fall in love with the barn manager?" Madison repeats in a singsong voice. "Mom, you're so funny!"

Aunt Rachel looks at her daughter for a moment, then she picks up her fork and begins eating.

And after a moment, so do I.

With the lion bearded in her den and Bucky's fortune back in my hands, there's only one thing left to do—the very worst thing, actually.

Face Malcolm again.

I text Alison as I'm leaving Sarasota. It's past nine o'clock—too late, really, to be bothering her. But she answers me right away, and I have to wait for the next red light to read her reply.

Just go over there and fix things. I don't care how late it is!!

God, I think. How bad is this situation?

I put the pedal down and the Jeep's engine growls as it takes me back to Ocala.

Marion County after midnight is a dark and silent place. At least, it is until you look back barn lanes and see the broodmare barns lit up. It's breeding season, and foaling season, and one of those two things happens late at night. Not the one you're thinking—the foaling, actually.

As I drive past Malone-Salazar Farm, I peer through the hedges lining the black-board fencing, wondering if any broodmares have Posey or her mother up late tonight. But the barn is too well hidden to see, and anyway, my business is with mature horses, not babies.

Mature horses and the drama we create while we're training them to their full potential.

I drive past the barn and up the lane to Malcolm's house. It's dark, and for a moment, my courage fails me. Am I really going to wake him up over this? Maybe I should go home, get some sleep, and see how I feel in the morning.

No. I can't put this off another minute.

I get out of the Jeep, stumble up to the front door, and pound on it like a crazy person. Like a spurned lover. Like an idiot who gave up everything for nothing. I feel like maybe I'm all of those things, and hey, what's the worst that can happen now? There's no one here to see me.

Malcolm opens the door much quicker than he should have. I look at his un-mussed hair and realize he wasn't asleep, after all.

He stares at me, his expression unreadable. "What are you doing here?"

"I fixed things with my aunt," I say. It's not how I meant to start this, but it's the first thing that comes out.

"I don't—what?"

"I'm keeping Bucky," I explain. "Here, with you. Instead of selling him, I'm going to keep him and ride him, like I was before."

Malcolm shakes his head, and fear settles like a lead weight in my stomach. "I can't—Evie, I'm not ready to just be your coach. We can't just go back to how things were."

"I don't want the way things were," I say. "I want them to be better."

Is it my imagination, or does hope dawn in his face? "Better...
how? What do you envision for us, Evie?"

And now I have to say it. Everything I thought on the drive back
from Sarasota, the speech I'd recited to myself so many times, I'm
sure I'll never forget it.

"I want to work with you," I say. "And I don't care what Ocala says.
What *anyone* says. I want to spend all day with you, helping you run
this barn. I want to ride with you and eat lunch with you and walk
home to have dinner with you at night. Not every night," I add,
flustered. "But some of them. I want to go to events with you and
catch your horse after cross-country. And I want to take lessons with
you. But most of all, Malcolm, I want to be with you. Even if there
were no horses, I'd want that. I love you, Malcolm. Maybe it's a bad
idea, but I love you."

I wait then, all out of words, wondering if he'll believe me.
Wondering if he feels the same way.

"Evie, my god," he says slowly. He rubs at his chin, the dark stubble
of a day-old beard. I don't know what he's going to say. And then he
says, "It's not as easy as you think. People will talk. Are you okay with
that?"

"They're already talking. The thing is, they have no idea what
they're talking about."

Malcolm nods.

He hasn't said that he loves me. *That's okay,* I tell myself. *Baby
steps.*

"Evie, it's not a bad idea."

"What?"

Malcolm's eyes take on that jade-green sparkle that always makes
me breathless. "I love you, and it's *not* a bad idea."

And then he pushes the door all the way open, opening up his
arms to me.

I feel a tiny sound escape the back of my throat, like a sob, like a laugh, and then I fling myself into his open arms.

"It's not the horses that make this life so hard," I say against his chest, a million years later, or maybe just ten seconds. It's hard to know for sure. "It's the other people."

"Yes," he agrees. "Other people are hell. I'd like it to be just me and you, Evie."

"Can you imagine that?" I laugh a little. "What a dream."

Chapter Forty-One

"NOW THAT YOU'RE both here," Alison says, crossing her legs in a formal manner, "let's talk about the future."

Malcolm looks up from his sandwich. "We're trying to eat lunch here, Alison," he says mildly. "Can't we have a little break, please?"

"No. It's the end of March and there's one more month of pure insanity before everyone goes back north. So it's the perfect time to tell you."

I look at her in alarm. "Tell us what?"

She drops her gaze, then looks back at me, defiant. "I'm giving my notice."

"What?" I shriek, just as Malcolm drops his sandwich. It hits the desk and flops apart, shredded lettuce littering the paperwork and his tablet like green confetti.

"You can't be serious," Malcolm thunders. "Absolutely not."

"I'm dead serious," she retorts. "Don't think you can stop me."

Malcolm opens his mouth and then shuts it. He settles for looking furious.

I feel I have to take over. "Alison, why would you leave? We've just got everything sorted out."

I'm not a working student anymore; Malcolm and I thought that was a little dicey, the whole apprenticeship thing, trading work for room and board, et cetera. I'm officially Alison's assistant, and a friend of hers in the legal trade gave us a piece of H.R. boilerplate that says we acknowledge we are in a professional relationship that is separate from our personal relationship, blah-blah-blah, legalese, legalese. It doesn't stop Ocala from chattering about us, but it does keep Malcolm's clients from claiming that he's acting irrationally or inappropriately.

He even sent out an email letting everyone know about the staffing change.

But that was over a week ago, and since then we've settled into our working rhythm again, the same as it was before—only with less suspicion and subterfuge. Vedda Jones vanished after Rachel told her Bucky was off the market, and I'm taking him on our first outing as a team in late April. It's Open Novice and we'll probably look like amateurs next to the professionals who will dominate that division, but at least I'll be getting my first round of eventing miles on my big horse.

For half a moment, I thought everything was perfect.

If Alison leaves, though...

"I have an opportunity to run my own barn," Alison says proudly, "and I can't turn it down."

"You're joking."

"Thanks for sounding so confident in my abilities, Malcolm."

"No, I mean—" Malcolm shakes his head, confounded. "I just— *who?*"

"Who?"

"Who is bankrolling you?"

"No one," Alison replies, fluttering her eyelashes. "I'm bankrolling myself."

"I know what I pay you, and there is no way—"

"You don't know everything about me," Alison says cooly. "I happen to be an excellent investor."

I watch Malcolm, the former finance guy, blink at his barn manager while she explains the way she's come up with the money to rent a nice property about five minutes from Fine Day Farm. She's proud of herself, but I think she's holding back as she describes the place. I know the farm she's talking about, and it's a classy little facility. Alison feels bad, I think, because she's better with money than Malcolm has been, and she doesn't want him to realize it.

I love her more for showing this kind of empathy than she'll ever know. But I'm also going to miss her like crazy.

"I've been meeting with my wealth advisor a lot this spring," she continues, "and I had to make a few really quick decisions, but now I'm comfortable and ready to make this leap."

"The times you ran off or left work early," I recall. "I thought maybe you were seeing someone."

"Hah!" Alison slaps her own knee. "Trust me, I'm not a pushover like you, kiddo. I will never love anyone as much as I love myself, and that is why I work so hard to give myself a better life."

Malcolm snorts at that. "You're too much."

She twinkles back at him. "You taught me to trust no one."

"Is that what I was doing? Damn."

"*Now* who is going to work with me?" I sigh.

"You can hire Wesley full-time for the summer," Alison suggests. "Then you just have to get through May without a full-timer on staff. You can do it; I did it alone before you got here."

"But her mom goes back up north in the summer."

"She can stay in the barn apartment. She just turned seventeen; our little girlfriend can handle living on noodles and Gatorade for a few months. It'll be good for her."

"No, I'm not having Wesley as a roommate," I declare, shaking my head. I moved back to the barn apartment right away; Romeo and

Breezy are both happier here, and I'm making enough money now to keep covering my mortgage while I decide what to do with my place.

Alison gives me a long, unblinking stare. I realize what she's intimating with her silence and I glance nervously at Malcolm.

He gives me a little smile. "We can talk about it."

Alison's impending departure makes everything feel more urgent. I want to follow her around taking notes, but she shakes me off every time she feels me trailing her, telling me that I know plenty enough about running barns, and this one in particular. "You'll be a good barn manager," she insists, pushing me aside when I try to look over her shoulder at her scheduling process. "Just keep up with the schedule the way it works for you, and make sure Malcolm follows it, because otherwise you'll be out here until nine o'clock every night."

"No one said anything about making me barn manager," I argue, but Alison just laughs.

"Of course you're going to be barn manager. You're my assistant. You know the job. What do you think, he's going to call up Equistaff and ask for someone new to come run the place?"

I have to admit that would make absolutely no sense.

"So stop *worrying,*" Alison says, but of course, I can't stop worrying.

Why quit something I'm really good at?

The last horse trials of spring is at the horse park; I set up there with Wesley's help, my methods almost mechanical at this point. Jules and Kit, one of the Alachua instructors and a top rider in her own right, swing by with a box of donuts and congratulations for me.

"Congratulations?" I ask blankly, accepting the donuts.

"We heard you're the new barn manager, now that Alison is leaving," Kit explains. She looks anxious. "Are we wrong? Is that not what's happening?"

Jules looks like she couldn't care less. "Well, if you didn't get the job, these are sympathy donuts."

"No, I'm taking the job." Malcolm and I talked about it the night after Alison's announcement. Like Alison, he seemed to think it was a done deal from the moment she gave her notice. I was apparently the only one who didn't realize I was next in line for the gig. "I just didn't think anyone had shared the news yet."

"That's Ocala for you," Jules drawls. "Listen, we're going to walk the course before everyone else is out there tramping around. You want to come?"

"I'll wait for Malcolm," I say. "But thanks."

Jules waves, unconcerned, and Kit gives me a little smile before she chases after her boss.

"She's kind of rude," Wesley says, taking a donut. "Isn't she?"

I shrug. "She's Jules Thornton-Morrison. Kind of well-known for doing whatever she wants."

"I'd like to be like that," Wesley muses.

"I don't think this town is big enough for two of her."

We're working our way through the donuts when Malcolm arrives, looking harried. "You ready to walk the Novice course?" he calls, not bothering to come into the tack stall where we've sat down to snack. He brushes his hands down his breeches; the beige ones, with the missing button. Someday, I think, I may replace that button.

Until now, I like that it's an imperfection in his dapper attire.

Something unique about him, that I can keep close to my heart... to remind me, when we're arguing (and I'm sure we will, since Alison will be leaving and the brunt of his temper will inevitably fall on me) that my boyfriend isn't as perfect as he thinks.

* * *

Bucky is tugging at the bit, flinging his head up and down, his breath coming hard and fast.

"I knew I should have used a running martingale," I fret, turning the horse in a quick circle and riding him away from Malcolm.

"He doesn't need a martingale," Malcolm says brusquely. His voice is in my ear, but it's anything but sexy. We've mostly concentrated on keeping Bucky and me alive.

This cross-country warm-up is crowded with young, upset horses...and the riders on their backs are mostly unconcerned with how much room they're ceding to others trying to use the space. The Novice divisions are going onto the course with their times all mixed up, meaning Open Novice riders like myself, who have competed at higher levels, are riding alongside the Novice Rider competitors, who have never gone higher, and are possibly making their debut today. The oil-and-water of experience versus no experience is leading to some out-of-body moments of fear, near-collisions and shouting matches about who called what jump first.

Malcolm has kept me out of the worst of the fray, telling me to circle when he sees trouble ahead and sending me over the warm-up fences only when he can see no one else near them. But the high temperature of the warm-up has Bucky spiced up, and he's threatening to live up to his barn name.

"Just walk him," Malcolm commands tersely. "Walk around the outside of the warm-up."

"He needs circles," I mutter. But I'm too far away for Malcolm to hear me now.

"Outside of the arena!" Malcolm demands as I turn Bucky in another ten-meter circle. "Stretch him!"

"No," I say, finding it easy to be defiant when my words are just between me and my horse. "We're *circling,* aren't we, Bucky?"

Bucky bobs his head and threatens to buck.

"That's why you don't make tight circles," Malcolm says.

Ugh! I straighten the horse out and get him around the warm-up. As we loop past the mayhem a second time, Malcolm gestures towards the starting box. "Time to go," he says in my ear. "Are you ready?"

I look down at my sweaty, nervous horse. His ears are flicking back and forth, the veins are popping on his dark neck, and his nostrils are flaring with every breath. I'm sure I don't look much better.

I raise a hand to Malcolm to acknowledge that yes, this is as ready as we'll ever be.

He meets me at the starting box. There are two horses ahead of us, one just leaving the box, one circling behind it. The starter, a bearded guy with a walkie-talkie in one hand, gives Malcolm a wave. "I'll have your girl ready in a jiffy," he says.

"Thanks, Bobby," Malcolm says.

"The advantage of my boyfriend knowing everyone." Bucky quiets as Malcolm walks up to us and puts his hand on my boot. "I feel like people have been watching me out here."

"You're on a very nice horse."

"I think there's more to it than that."

Malcolm smiles. "Are you accusing me of something, my dear?"

"Just being very famous and handsome." I smirk. "I mean, your good looks are the key to your success, right? It's not your riding or anything."

"On deck," Bobby calls.

Malcolm waves to him. "You're going to do amazing out there," he says to me.

"How do you know?" I feel more steady with his hand on my leg, but that's about to end in three...two...

The starter sends out the horse before me. He turns and waves.

...one.

"Because you're my student," Malcolm says, squeezing my calf the way I squeezed his just a few months ago. "And I'm a very good trainer."

"And?" I give him one more shot to not make this all about him.

"And you're more than ready for this," he tells me. "Have a nice ride."

That's good enough.

Epilogue

SEPTEMBER

Bucky's strides are swift and sure, driving us up the hillside. The blue, blue sky rears up all around us, but I feel him the moment he sees the fence perched atop the slope's apex. It's a big wooden barrier, set at just the right angle so that as the horse and rider approach, it looks as if we'll be leaping into the wild blue yonder.

Actually, it's just level ground on the other side.

But Bucky doesn't know that. He has to trust me when I tell him nothing bad is waiting on the far side of the fence. "Come on, buddy," I urge him, pressing my hands into his hot neck like I'm back on the training track, galloping a young Thoroughbred. "Just up and over, like we do at home, like we do at every event."

The words come out in huffs of breath, because we're both tiring now. The white numbers on the black diamond-shaped sign alongside the fence say *20*. Three more fences after this one, all of them on a slow slope downwards towards the stabling area.

But Bucky doesn't know that.

I deepen my heels and give his sides a few rhythmic squeezes with my calves, telling him to lengthen his stride every time he pushes off with his hind legs. Ears pricked, head up, still watching that fence which threatens to send him off into oblivion, Bucky picks up the pace.

Three—two—one—*jump!*

He lands on the other side with a snort that could only signify relief, seeing the gentle downhill slope that we're about to gallop down, the rest of the cross-country course laid out around us and the stabling area glinting in the distance like an equine Shangri-La. Now he really stretches out, sensing the carrots waiting for him at the finish line, and I lean my thighs against the saddle and let him run his way, pushing into the bridle. There's time before Fence 21—a simple straw-bale stack—and Fence 22, a typical fruit-stand style jump, to balance him up and make sure he jumps cleanly. Then we're sweeping through the timers, a few kids are clapping, and my eyes find Malcolm, waiting a couple dozen feet away with buckets and the aforementioned carrots.

His face is alight with pride and joy.

The cross-country announcer's voice rolls across the show-grounds from two dozen speakers perched atop telephone poles, trees, and barns: "And Fern Grove Buckeye with owner/rider Evie Ballenger make it home clean and under time to maintain their first-place score, keeping them the unofficial winners of Open Training here at Oak Grove Horse Trials!"

I shake my head at Malcolm, grinning, as I bring Bucky down to a jog.

"What?" he mouths.

"I shouldn't be winning," I say as soon as we're in earshot. Bucky slows to a walk and Malcolm steps alongside us, unfastening his noseband. "I shouldn't win my first time out at this level. That's not how it works."

"Not how *what* works, Evie?"

"This. Any of this." I drop the reins and spread my arms out. My sweaty cross-country jersey clings to my muscles, the sage-green of Malcolm Horsham's Fine Day Farm. "I'm not this kind of lucky."

"You are now, my love," he laughs. "Now get off this good horse so we can get him watered and full of carrots."

The ride back to the farm that night is short; Oak Grove is just fifteen minutes away from home, making it a lovely one-day event for us. Malcolm slows as we pass a red truck heading in the opposite direction just before our farm lane, and we both wave at Alison, driving into town. "She's still bringing over dinner tonight, right?" Malcolm asks, flicking on the turn signal.

"That's the plan," I reply. "I bet she's going to get pizza and wings."

"Oh god, I hope so. The perfect post-event dinner, if you ask me."

The barn is clean and quiet; the horses who didn't go with us to Oak Grove are turned out, tails swishing against the late-evening flies. Patti and Ed left us a note on the white-board in the feed room: "Everyone good. Hope you guys had fun at your little show today!"

"They have no idea what we do with these horses, do we?" I ask, smiling at the note.

"Absolutely none," Malcolm agrees. "Where do you want this giant blue ribbon?"

I turn and admire the huge rosette Malcolm has brought in from the truck. It's the biggest ribbon I've ever won. Almost makes up for the two-hundred-dollar entry fee I paid in order to get a shot at it. "I'm going to make a brooch out of it," I laugh. "And wear it everywhere."

"Maybe we'll settle for hanging it on Bucky's stall," Malcolm suggests.

"It's kind of sad," I say, watching him fix the rosette to the blanket bar on Bucky's stall door. "No one is around to see it and find out how incredibly talented and successful I am."

"Fall's just around the corner," he reminds me. "The migration's about to begin. The first winter boarders arrive next month."

"That's sad, too," I laugh. "We had a nice summer together, didn't we?"

"And me, too," Wesley says, coming out of the office. "I was here, remember?"

"Wesley! What are you doing here?" Malcolm does a double-take. "I thought you'd be halfway back home by now. Hasn't school started?"

"Missed my flight," Wesley says cheerfully. "It turns out my mom thought I'd arrange my own airport service, isn't that funny? Moms are crazy."

"Is she going to be mad?" We hadn't heard much from Wesley's mother all summer; she'd seemed pretty pleased to have dumped her teenage daughter on us like some kind of summer camp of one. "Doesn't she expect you to come home?"

"Nah," Wesley says. "She said if I do my classwork online I can stay here. So...that's cool, right?"

I have to laugh. Horse girls. All alike. And Wesley has come a long, long way since the spoiled student who handed me her horse nine months ago and told me to walk him, no grass. "I'd love to have you stay. Malcolm?"

"Absolutely," Malcolm says, smiling. "You can start by putting ice boots on our horses while we go shower, okay?"

"On it, boss," Wesley agrees, hopping into her paddock boots and setting off for the tack room.

Malcolm takes my hand as we walk up the barn aisle, leaving Wesley to her work. "Today was a good day," he says. "I'm so proud of you, getting that horse around Training *and* winning, first time out!"

"I couldn't have done it without you," I say modestly.

"I'm not sure that's true," Malcolm says.

"Well, I'm not either," I admit. "But you certainly helped."

He laughs and squeezes my hand. "We're a good team, Evie Ballenger."

"The best," I agree. "And everything's sorted out with the Coles? The lease is good for a year and the syndicate sales are approved?"

"That's right," he says. "I talked to Lillian today. She signed. Alison was right; we should have negotiated a fair lease a long time ago, and we were foolish to leave the horses in her name. I wasn't comfortable having Lillian in charge of the place or the horses when push came to shove, and it turns out Lillian didn't care for it, either. She just didn't want to be the first to bring it up. Now everyone's happy."

"Everyone's happy," I echo, looking around the paddocks of Fine Day Farm. "Isn't that the truth?"

Acknowledgments

OH, I HAD so much fun writing this one!

Evie's story spun out of my head in record time; I wrote the first draft in just about two weeks, and the revision didn't take much longer. I knew exactly who my characters were, what they wanted out of life, and how Evie and Malcolm were going to fall for each other... slowly, then all at once!

I think workplace romances are the best, possibly because I am still in one, more than twenty years after we met. Even with anxious H.R. directors and unromantic paperwork, people will continue to fall in love at work, because, as Posey reminds Evie—that's where people meet each other!

Writing a working student/trainer romance comes with a side of thorny consent issues, but since Evie is twenty-seven, not twenty, she is equipped with the maturity to make decisions for herself, and Malcolm never pushes her for anything she doesn't feel safe with. That's love, in a nutshell.

I'm so looking forward to writing Book 4 in Ocala Horse Girls— thanks to all of you for making this series a hit!

As always, a special thanks to the Patreon members who read my first drafts, often one or two chapters a day for several weeks on end. Your comments, concerns, and cheers keep me going like nothing else ever could! I love you all so much, even when you tell me something didn't work and I'm mad at you for like, a day. My books are so much better thanks to your feedback.

You can join us at patreon.com/nataliekreinert or at Ream Stories, a new subscription site, at bit.ly/NKR-Ream-Stories.

My Patrons and Ream subscribers include: Renee Knowles, Alyssa, Shauna, Lisa Leonard Heck, Dianna, SailorEpona, Lindsay Moore, Erika Thomas, Shelby Graft, Nicole Russo, Karen Wolfsheimer, Pamela Allen-LeBlanc, Raina Kujawa, Kellie Halteman, Jennifer Williams, Natalie Clark, Megan McDonald, Adrienne Brant, Sally Testa, Becca B., April Lutz, Julia Koeger, Heidi Schmid, Mel Sperti, Susan Lambiris, Cathy Luo, Elena Rabinow, Laura, Dörte Voigt, Empathy, Gretchen Fieser, JoAnn Flejszar, Nancy Neid, Elizabeth Espinosa, Libby Henderson, Maureen VanDerStad, Sherron Meinert, Leslie Yazurlo, Nicola Beisel, Mel Policicchio, Kylie Standish, Harry Burgh, Nicole, Kathlynn Angie-Buss, Peggy Dvorsky, Christine Komis, Annika Kostrabula, Thoma Jolette Parker, Karen Carrubba, Emma Gooden, Katie Lewis, Silvana Ricapito, Sarine Laurin, Di Hannel, Jennifer, Claus Giloi, Heather Walker, Cyndy Searfoss, Kaylee Amons, Mary Vargas, Kathie Lacasse, Rachael Rosenthal, Orpu, Diana Aitch, Liz Greene, Zoe Bills, Cheryl Bavister, Sarah Seavey, Megan Devine, Tricia Jordan, Brinn Dimmler, Lindsay Moore, Caitlin Harrison, Rhonda Lane, C. Sperry, Heather Voltz, and Kim Keller.

What an incredible list! Thank you all so very much.

The Hollywood Horse

WHAT ABOUT ALISON?

If you loved Malcolm's snarky barn manager and want to know where her life is headed, watch for Book 4 of Ocala Horse Girls, *The Hollywood Horse,* coming later in 2023.

Running her own farm is Alison's dream, but starting a new business is never easy. When Hollywood comes calling with a rogue actor who needs reining in before his new movie—and some riding lessons—Alison can't say no. Even though she'd really, really like to! The thing is, she already has a history with this guy...and she's *not* one of his biggest fans.

Preorder *The Hollywood Horse* ebook from my website at nataliekreinert.shop, and don't forget about my everyday promo codes while you're there! You'll be the first to receive the new book when it's published. You can also sign up for my newsletter and get twice-monthly updates on the latest books and offers, plus a free ebook, at https://subscribepage.io/getbold

About the Author

A FULL-TIME writer, I work from my farm in North Florida, where I live with my family and two horses. In the past, I've worked professionally in many aspects of the equestrian world, including grooming for top event riders, training off-track Thoroughbreds, galloping racehorses, patrolling Central Park on horseback, working on breeding farms, and more! I use all of this experience to inform the equestrian scenes in my novels. They say that truth is stranger than fiction, and those of us in the horse business will certainly agree!

Visit my website at nataliekreinert.com to keep up with the latest news and read occasional blog posts and book reviews. For previews, installments of upcoming fiction, and exclusive stories, visit my Patreon page at patreon.com/nataliekreinert or Ream Stories at bit.ly/NKR-Ream-Stories and learn how you can become one of my team members. Visit my store at nataliekreinert.shop for the best value on print and ebook editions.

For more, find me on social media:

Facebook: facebook.com/nataliekellerreinert

Group: facebook.com/groups/societyofweirdhorsegirls

Bookbub: bookbub.com/profile/natalie-keller-reinert

Instagram: instagram.com/nataliekreinert

Join my email list and receive an ebook at https://subscribepage.io/getbold

Email: natalie@nataliekreinert.com

Podcast: adultingwithhorsespodcast.com